To Accompany Webster's *Auto Mechanics*

AUTO SHOP ACTIVITY GUIDE

Second Edition

Jay Webster
California State University, Long Beach

Glencoe Publishing Company
Encino, California

ACKNOWLEDGMENTS

The author wishes to acknowledge the cooperation of the following companies in providing material and illustrations used in this *Auto Shop Activity Guide*.

Lancia   Chrysler Corporation   The Women's Garage   Proto   Snap On Tools Corporation
General Motors Corporation   Hein-Werner Corporation   Lincoln, Division of McNeil Corporation
Owatonna Tool Company   Kleer-Flow Company   Beloit Tool of California, Inc.   L.S. Starrett Company
Go-Power   Pontiac Motor Division   Ford Motor Company   Perfect Circle   Dodge/Chrysler Corporation   Union Carbide Corporation   Chevrolet Motor Division   Delco-Remy Division
Zoom Perfection American Company   Buick Motor Division   Plymouth/Chrysler Corporation
Hydramatic Division   Cadillac Motor Car Division   American Motors Corporation   Monroe Auto Equipment Company   Moog Automotive, Inc.   Raybestos   Bendix Corporation   Temps Products
American Honda Motor Company, Inc.

Copyright © 1986 by Glencoe Publishing Company, a division of
Macmillan, Inc. All rights reserved. No part of this book
may be reproduced or transmitted in any form or by any
means, electronic or mechanical, including photocopying,
recording, or by any information storage and retrieval
system, without permission in writing from the Publisher.

Printed in the United States of America

Glencoe Publishing Company
17337 Ventura Boulevard
Encino, California 91316

ISBN 0-02-829920-5 ASAG
ISBN 0-02-829930-2 ASAG Key

2 3 4 5 6 7 8 9   91 90 89 88 87 86

CONTENTS

CHAPTER		PAGE NOS.	SHEET NO.	DATE COMPLETED	GRADE
1	The Automobile	1–4	Assn. Sht. 1	_____	_____
2	Working in the Automotive Service Industry	5–7	Assn. Sht. 2	_____	_____
3	Working Safely	9–12	Assn. Sht. 3	_____	_____
4	Using Hand Tools	13–16	Assn. Sht. 4	_____	_____
5	Using Power Tools and Equipment	17–20	Assn. Sht. 5	_____	_____
6	Using Metal working Tools	21–23	Assn. Sht. 6	_____	_____
7	Using Measuring Systems and Tools	25–28	Assn. Sht. 7	_____	_____
8	Using Fasteners	29–30	Assn. Sht. 8	_____	_____
9	Using Service Manuals	31–33	Assn. Sht. 9	_____	_____
10	Fundamentals of Engine Operation	35–37	Assn. Sht. 10	_____	_____
11	Types of Automotive Engines	39–41	Assn. Sht. 11	_____	_____
12	Piston Engine Components: Crankcase, Cylinders, Crankshaft and Bearings	43–45	Assn. Sht. 12	_____	_____
13	Piston Engine Components: Pistons, Rings, Pins, and Connecting Rods	47–49	Assn. Sht. 13	_____	_____
14	Piston Engine Components: Cylinder Head and Valve Train	51–55	Assn. Sht. 14	_____	_____
15	Piston Engine Service	57–59	Job Sht. 1	_____	_____
		61–63	Job Sht. 2	_____	_____
16	Engine Size and Performance Measurement	65–68	Assn. Sht. 15	_____	_____
17	The Lubrication System	69–70	Assn. Sht. 16	_____	_____
18	Lubrication System Service	71–72	Job Sht. 3	_____	_____
		73–76	Job Sht. 4	_____	_____
19	The Cooling System	77–78	Assn. Sht. 17	_____	_____
20	Cooling System Service	79–80	Job Sht. 5	_____	_____
		81–82	Job Sht. 6	_____	_____
21	The Fuel System	83–86	Assn. Sht. 18	_____	_____
22	Fuel System Service	87–88	Job Sht. 7	_____	_____
		89–90	Job Sht. 8	_____	_____
23	Electrical Systems and Fundamentals	91–93	Assn. Sht. 19	_____	_____
24	Storage Battery	95–96	Assn. Sht. 20	_____	_____
25	Storage Battery Service	97–98	Job Sht. 9	_____	_____
		99–100	Job Sht. 10	_____	_____
26	The Starting System	101–104	Assn. Sht. 21	_____	_____
27	Starting System Service	105–106	Job Sht. 11	_____	_____
		107–109	Job Sht. 12	_____	_____
28	The Charging System	111–112	Assn. Sht. 22	_____	_____
29	Charging System Service	113–115	Job Sht. 13	_____	_____
		117–118	Job Sht. 14	_____	_____
30	The Ignition System	119–122	Assn. Sht. 23	_____	_____
		123–124	Assn. Sht. 24	_____	_____
		125–127	Assn. Sht. 25	_____	_____
31	Ignition System Service	129–131	Job Sht. 15	_____	_____
		133–134	Job Sht. 16	_____	_____
		135–136	Job Sht. 17	_____	_____
		137–138	Job Sht. 18	_____	_____
		139–140	Job Sht. 19	_____	_____
		141–142	Job Sht. 20	_____	_____
32	Manually Operated Clutch	143–144	Assn. Sht. 26	_____	_____
		145–147	Assn. Sht. 27	_____	_____
33	Clutch Service	149–150	Job Sht. 21	_____	_____
		151–153	Job Sht. 22	_____	_____

CHAPTER	PAGE NOS.	SHEET NO.	DATE COMPLETED	GRADE
34 Manually Operated Transaxle and Transmission	155–156	Assn. Sht. 28	_____	_____
	157–158	Assn. Sht. 29	_____	_____
35 Manual Transmission and Transaxle Service	159–160	Job Sht. 23	_____	_____
	161–164	Job Sht. 24	_____	_____
36 The Automatic Transmission and Transaxle	165–168	Assn. Sht. 30	_____	_____
	169–172	Assn. Sht. 31	_____	_____
37 Automatic Transmission and Transaxle Service	173–174	Job Sht. 25	_____	_____
	175–176	Job Sht. 26	_____	_____
	177–178	Job Sht. 27	_____	_____
	179–182	Job Sht. 28	_____	_____
38 Drive Line Arrangements	183–185	Assn. Sht. 32	_____	_____
39 Drive Line Service	187–188	Job Sht. 29	_____	_____
	189–190	Job Sht. 30	_____	_____
40 Differential Assembly	191–192	Assn. Sht. 33	_____	_____
	193–195	Assn. Sht. 34	_____	_____
41 Differential Assembly Service	197–198	Job Sht. 31	_____	_____
	199–200	Job Sht. 32	_____	_____
	201–203	Job Sht. 33	_____	_____
	205–207	Job Sht. 34	_____	_____
42 The Suspension System	209–212	Assn. Sht. 35	_____	_____
	213–214	Assn. Sht. 36	_____	_____
43 Suspension System Service	215–217	Job Sht. 35	_____	_____
	219–220	Job Sht. 36	_____	_____
	221–222	Job Sht. 37	_____	_____
	223–225	Job Sht. 38	_____	_____
44 Steering and Wheel Alignment	227–228	Assn. Sht. 37	_____	_____
	229–230	Assn. Sht. 38	_____	_____
45 Steering and Wheel Alignment Service	231–232	Job Sht. 39	_____	_____
	233–234	Job Sht. 40	_____	_____
	235–236	Job Sht. 41	_____	_____
	237–238	Job Sht. 42	_____	_____
46 The Brake System	239–240	Assn. Sht. 39	_____	_____
	241–242	Assn. Sht. 40	_____	_____
47 Brake System Service	243–244	Job Sht. 43	_____	_____
	245–246	Job Sht. 44	_____	_____
	247–248	Job Sht. 45	_____	_____
	249–251	Job Sht. 46	_____	_____
48 Tires and Wheels	253–254	Assn. Sht. 41	_____	_____
	255–257	Job Sht. 47	_____	_____
49 Tire and Wheel Service	259–260	Job Sht. 48	_____	_____
50 Heating and Air Conditioning System	261–263	Assn. Sht. 42	_____	_____
51 Emission Control Systems	265–266	Assn. Sht. 43	_____	_____
	267–268	Assn. Sht. 44	_____	_____
	269–271	Assn. Sht. 45	_____	_____
52 Emission System Service	273–274	Assn. Sht. 46	_____	_____
	275–276	Assn. Sht. 47	_____	_____
53 Electronic Fuel Injection Systems	277	Assn. Sht. 48	_____	_____
	279	Assn. Sht. 49	_____	_____
	281	Assn. Sht. 50	_____	_____
	283–284	Assn. Sht. 51	_____	_____
54 Computerized Engine Control Systems	285	Assn. Sht. 52	_____	_____
	287	Assn. Sht. 53	_____	_____
	289–290	Assn. Sht. 54	_____	_____
55 The Future of the Automobile	291–292	Assn. Sht. 55	_____	_____
	293	Assn. Sht. 56	_____	_____
English–Metric Conversion Chart	294			

NAME _____ SECTION _____ DATE _____ SCORE _____

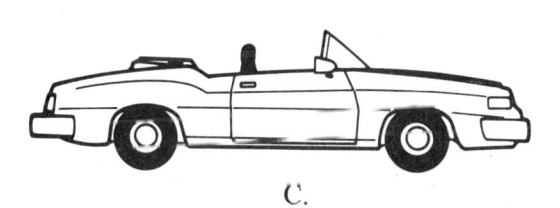

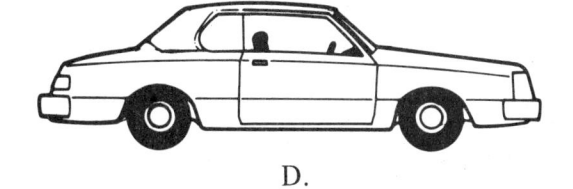

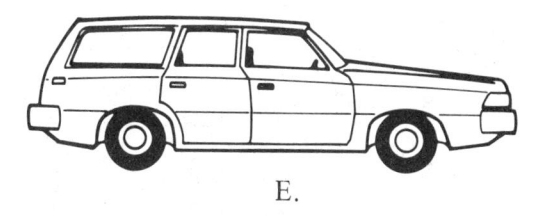

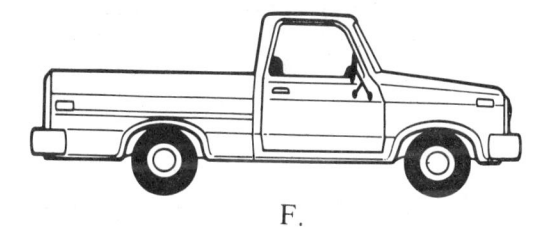

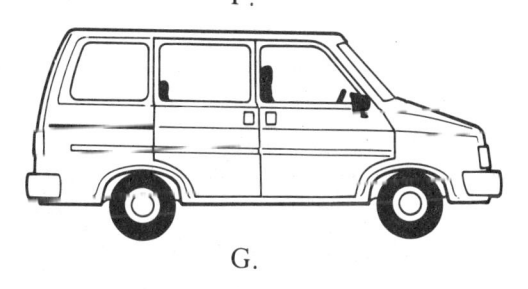

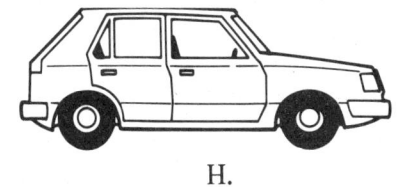

Chapter 1 THE AUTOMOBILE
ASSIGNMENT SHEET 1

Classes of Automobiles

Before you begin: Read Chapter 1 in *Auto Mechanics*. Match each body style with its name. Place the letter of the body style next to the name.

_____ 1. Van

_____ 2. Two-door sedan

_____ 3. Four-door sedan

_____ 4. Truck

_____ 5. Convertible

_____ 6. Station wagon

_____ 7. Hardtop

_____ 8. Hatchback

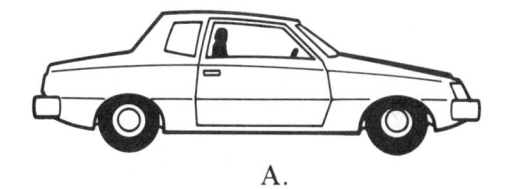

A.

B.

C.

D.

E.

F.

G.

H.

1

Components of the Automobile

In the space below each figure, name the major automotive component shown and write a brief description of its purpose.

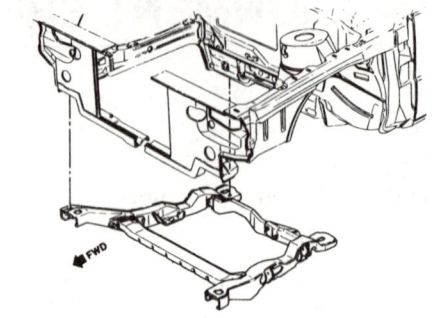

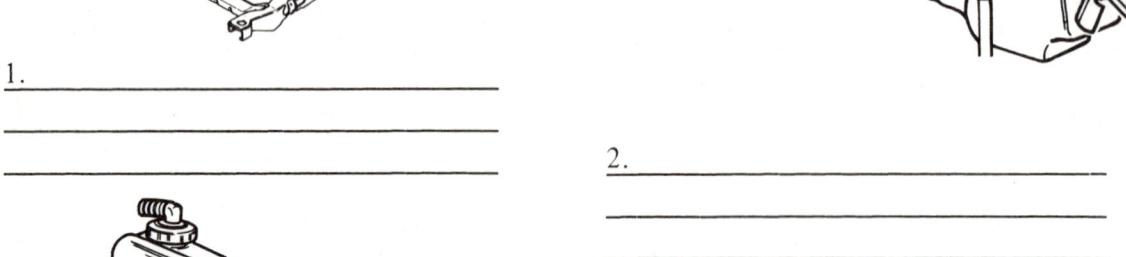

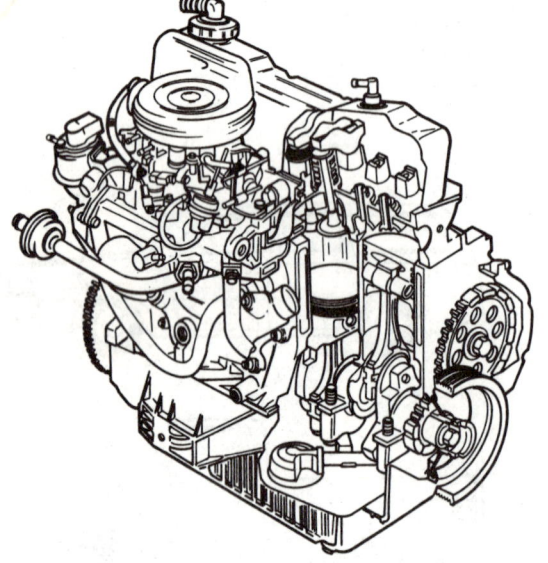

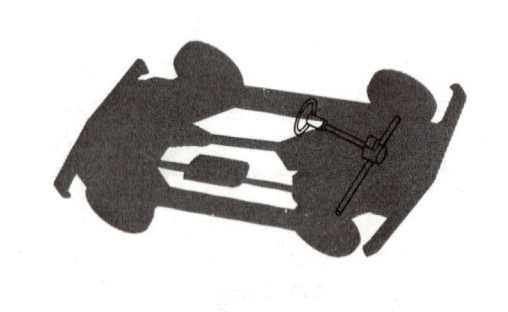

1. _____
_____
_____

2. _____
_____
_____

3. _____
_____
_____

4. _____
_____
_____

5. _____
_____
_____

6. _____
_____
_____

NAME _____ SECTION _____ DATE _____ SCORE _____

Review of New Terms

For each definition in Column 2, select the term in Column 1 that best matches its meaning. Write the identifying *letter* of the term in the Answer column.

Column 1

A. Body
B. Chassis
C. Cooling system
D. Electrical system
E. Engine
F. Four-wheel drive
G. Framework
H. Front-wheel drive
I. Fuel system
J. Ignition system
K. Lubrication system
L. Power train
M. Rear-wheel drive
N. Tread
O. Wheelbase
P. Transaxle
Q. Rotary engine

Column 2

1. An engine system that provides the high voltage spark necessary to ignite the air-fuel mixture in the engine.
2. One of the four major components of the automobile. It converts the explosive power of fuel and air into rotating power to drive the automobile. Also called a powerplant or motor.
3. The length of an automobile measured from the center of the front wheel to the center of the rear wheel.
4. One of the four major components of the automobile. It delivers power developed by the engine to the driving wheels.
5. That part of the automobile, usually formed from sheet metal, used to house and protect the driver and passengers.
6. An engine system that maintains the proper engine temperature.
7. A drive system in which the front wheels of the automobile are driven by the engine.
8. An engine in which the power is developed by a rotating rotor instead of pistons.
9. The major components — such as framework, engine, and power train — under the automobile body.
10. A drive system in which all of the wheels of the automobile are driven by the engine.
11. An engine system that circulates oil between moving engine parts to prevent wear, reduce friction, clean, and seal.
12. An engine system that provides the engine with the proper mixture of air and fuel to be burned.

Answer

1. _____
2. _____
3. _____
4. _____
5. _____
6. _____
7. _____
8. _____
9. _____
10. _____
11. _____
12. _____

(Continued on next page)

3

Column 2   *Answer*

13. An engine system that provides electrical current for starting and powering all accessories. 13. _____

14. The width of an automobile measured between the front or rear wheels. 14. _____

15. A metal platform under the automobile to which the other automobile components are attached. 15. _____

16. A drive system in which the rear wheels of the automobile are driven by the engine. 16. _____

17. The combination of a transmission and differential in to one unit. 17. _____

NAME _____ SECTION _____ DATE _____ SCORE _____

Chapter 2 WORKING IN THE AUTOMOTIVE SERVICE INDUSTRY
ASSIGNMENT SHEET 2

Where Automotive Service Workers Work

Before you begin: Read Chapter 2 in *Auto Mechanics*. Record the name of each of the service operations shown below and write a brief description of what is done at each type of service operation.

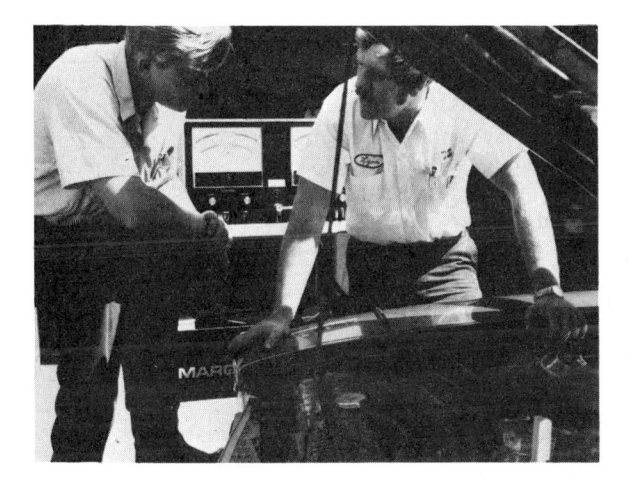

1. _____

2. _____

3. _____

4. _____

5

Filling Out A Job Application

When you want a job in the auto industry you must fill out a job application form. Fill out the practice form below. Remember to be as neat as possible.

APPLICATION FOR EMPLOYMENT

NAME _____ DATE: _____
        (Last)   (First)   (Middle)

SOCIAL SECURITY NO.: _____

ADDRESS _____
       (Street)   (City)   (State)   (Zip)

Telephone No.: _____ How long have you lived at above address? _____

Position applied for: _____ Would you work full-time? _____ Part-time? _____

If part-time, how many days and hours? _____

List of friends or relatives working for us: _____

Date available for work: _____ 19 _____ Rate of pay expected: $ _____ per week

Do you have any physical defects? _____ If yes, describe: _____

Have you had a major illness in the past 5 years? _____ If yes, describe: _____

Have you ever been convicted of a crime? _____ If yes, describe: _____

Education:

Last school attended: _____ Dates attended: _____ Graduated? _____

Previous schools: _____ Dates attended: _____

_____ Dates attended: _____

_____ Dates attended: _____

Qualifications you feel you possess for this job: _____

Work Experience: List the jobs you have held in the last ten years, beginning with the most recent:

Company   Dates   Supervisor   Duties   Pay   Reason for Leaving

_____

_____

_____

Personal References:

Name _____   Name _____

Address _____   Address _____

Telephone _____   Telephone _____

Position _____   Position _____

Name _____   Name _____

Address _____   Address _____

Telephone _____   Telephone _____

Position _____   Position _____

NAME _____ SECTION _____ DATE _____ SCORE _____

Review of New Terms

For each definition in Column 2, select the term on Column 1 that best matches its meaning. Write the identifying *letter* of the term in the Answer column.

Column 1

A. Diagnostic center
B. Fleet garage
C. Line mechanic
D. Parts supplier
E. Specialist mechanic
F. Dealership
G. Detailer
H. Independent garage
I. Lubrication specialist
J. Service station

Column 2

1. A business organized to stock and sell replacement parts for automobiles.
2. A mechanic who specializes in the repair of one component, such as brakes or transmissions.
3. A place that is equipped with testing equipment to analyze the automobile and determine the condition of all systems.
4. A service worker who may service any part of the automobile.
5. A place that maintains a group of company-owned vehicles.
6. A place where new automobiles are sold. Most dealerships also have a service operation.
7. A service worker who cleans an automobile to prepare it for sale or delivery to a customer.
8. An independently owned service business that may service any type of automobile.
9. A service worker who specializes in the lubrication of automotive components.
10. A service business which is organized primarily to sell gasoline and oil but which ordinarily has a repair operation as well.

Answer

1. _____
2. _____
3. _____
4. _____
5. _____
6. _____
7. _____
8. _____
9. _____
10. _____

NAME _____ SECTION _____ DATE _____ SCORE _____

Chapter 3 WORKING SAFELY
ASSIGNMENT SHEET 3

Safety

Before you begin: Read Chapter 3 in *Auto Mechanics.* Answer each question below by writing *Yes* or *No* in the space provided

Personal Safety Rules

_____ 1. Do you always get help in lifting heavy objects and pushing cars?

_____ 2. Do you always wear safety shoes when working?

_____ 3. Do you know where a well-stocked first-aid kit is available?

_____ 4. Do you always avoid wearing long ties, rings, or watches with metal bands?

_____ 5. Do you wear gloves to avoid cuts when replacing headlights or light bulbs?

_____ 6. Do you always lock the ignition and remove the key when working on the engine?

_____ 7. Do you always avoid checking overheated radiators until the coolant has ceased boiling?

_____ 8. Do you protect your hands and face from any rush of steam and hot water by using a heavy cloth over the radiator cap?

Fire Prevention Safety

_____ 9. Are all pieces of electrical equipment located far away from flammable vapor areas?

_____ 10. Are you sure all fire extinguishers are fully charged and in good working condition?

_____ 11. Is your shop equipped with the proper extinguisher for fires from lacquers, thinners, gasoline, or grease?

_____ 12. Do you know the location and proper use of each fire extinguisher in your shop area?

_____ 13. Do you have a blanket or a large canvas handy to roll a person in to smother flames?

Around the Shop

_____ 14. Do you always observe no-smoking regulations?

_____ 15. Do you avoid running an automobile in gear with one wheel jacked-up?

_____ 16. Do you keep floors, aisles, storage areas, and service bays free from litter?

_____ 17. Do you know where the emergency cut-off switch for the gasoline pump is located so that the flow of gasoline can be stopped instantly?

_____ 18. Do you keep flammable liquids in approved containers away from all ignition sources?

_____ 19. Do you clean parts only in a well-ventilated area and use a non-flammable solvent?

_____ 20. Do you make sure all electrical devices are well grounded?

_____ 21. Do you keep creepers in an upright position or under a work bench when not in use?

Working on Vehicles

_____ 22. Do you know the danger of attempting to start an engine by pouring gasoline into the carburetor while the engine is being turned over?

_____ 23. Do you use a fuse puller for cartridge-type fuses?

_____ 24. Are all your electrical power tools properly grounded?

(Continued on next page)

_____ 25. Do you always disconnect the battery ground cable before working on a wrecked or badly damaged car?

_____ 26. Do you make sure all parts removed from a car are placed out of the way?

_____ 27. Do you make sure you never have a jack handle sticking out from under a car?

_____ 28. Do you always wear goggles and/or a face shield for all operations such as chipping, grinding, sanding, drilling, welding, battery service, or working with liquid chemicals?

_____ 29. Do you make sure chemical and solvent containers are properly sealed and labeled?

_____ 30. Do you always use exhaust eliminating outlets for all work on running engines?

_____ 31. Do you always lift heavy objects using chain hoists or other mechanical types of handling equipment?

_____ 32. Do you sound the horn before passing through entrance or exit doors?

Using Equipment and Tools

_____ 33. Do you make sure specialized shop tools are in good condition?

_____ 34. Do you keep your hand tools clean?

_____ 35. Do you replace or repair broken extension cords and plug-in attachments before using?

_____ 36. Do you know the danger of standing on a wet floor when using electric tools?

_____ 37. Are you sure all electric tools are correctly grounded with a third wire?

_____ 39. Do you make sure to never allow sharp objects to protrude from hip pockets?

_____ 40. Do you make sure there are protective guards on grinders and all other equipment with moving parts?

_____ 41. Do you always use an approved respirator when grinding or sanding?

Using Lifts, Hoists, and Jacks

_____ 42. Do you always lift vehicles until the wheels clear the floor, then recheck for proper positioning?

_____ 43. Do you make sure there are no children or pets in the car before raising it?

_____ 44. Do you make sure to never overload the lift by hoisting a large truck on a passenger car lift?

_____ 45. Do you warn customers not to walk under the lift when it is being raised?

_____ 46. Do you make sure the lift safety leg or hoist safety pin is in position when it is fully raised?

_____ 47. Do you always support the car or truck with support stands of the proper capacity after using a hydraulic jack?

_____ 48. Do you always block the wheels to prevent the vehicle from rolling when using a drive-on lift?

Working on Batteries and Tires

_____ 49. Are all air lines equipped with line pressure reducing devices to prevent tires from being inflated at line pressure?

_____ 50. Do you always double check lock rings on truck tires to make sure they are secure before inflating tires?

_____ 51. Do you keep rubber cement and flammable solvents used for patching tubes in safety cans properly closed when not in use?

_____ 52. Do you always stand to one side when inflating tires to avoid being injured by blowouts or split rims?

_____ 53. Do you always use a battery carrier strap when removing batteries?

(Continued on next page)

NAME _____ SECTION _____ DATE _____ SCORE _____

_____ 54. Do you always disconnect the battery ground cable first when removing batteries and connect it last?

_____ 55. Do you refrain from smoking around batteries at all times?

Using Welding Equipment

_____ 56. Are all of the compressed gas cylinders or acetylene welding units stored with protective caps over the valves?

_____ 57. Are all the oxygen-acetylene tanks securely held in a cart or against a wall to prevent them from falling?

_____ 58. Do you always wear a helmet or goggles when welding?

_____ 59. Do you keep a fire extinguisher nearby at all times when welding?

_____ 60. Do you know the danger involved in lubricating fittings or parts of welding or torch cutting equipment?

General Safety Rules

_____ 61. Do you keep all floors in the service area clean?

_____ 62. Do you always observe the rule of not using gasoline to clean anything?

_____ 63. Do you always stand to the side of a vehicle when guiding it into a service bay?

_____ 64. Do you observe the rule of never draining gasoline in the lubrication pit?

_____ 65. Do you always replace the safety chain around the pit when it is not in use?

Review of New Terms

For each definition in column 2, select the term in Column 1 that best matches its meaning. Write the identifying *letter* of the term in the Answer column.

Column 1

A. Compressed air
B. Electric arc welding equipment
C. Fire prevention
D. Hand tools
E. Hydraulic hoist
F. Hydraulic jack
G. Oxygen-acetylene welding equipment
H. Power tools
I. Storage battery

Column 2

1. Tools that use electricity, compressed air, or hydraulic fluid.
2. Stopping fires from happening by observing safe practices.
3. A hydraulic device used to jack up an automobile.
4. A device that uses chemicals to store energy.
5. Air under pressure, used to fill tires, to power tools, and to spray paint.
6. An automobile lifting device that uses hydraulic power.
7. Welding equipment that combines two gases into mixture that burns hot enough to melt metal.
8. Equipment that uses an electrical arc to fuse metal together.
9. Tools that are guided and operated by hand.

Answer

1. _____
2. _____
3. _____
4. _____
5. _____
6. _____
7. _____
8. _____
9. _____

NAME _____ SECTION _____ DATE _____ SCORE _____

Chapter 4 USING HAND TOOLS
ASSIGNMENT SHEET 4

Identifying Hand Tools

Before you begin: Read Chapter 4 in *Auto Mechanics*. Write the names of the hand tools in the spaces provided below.

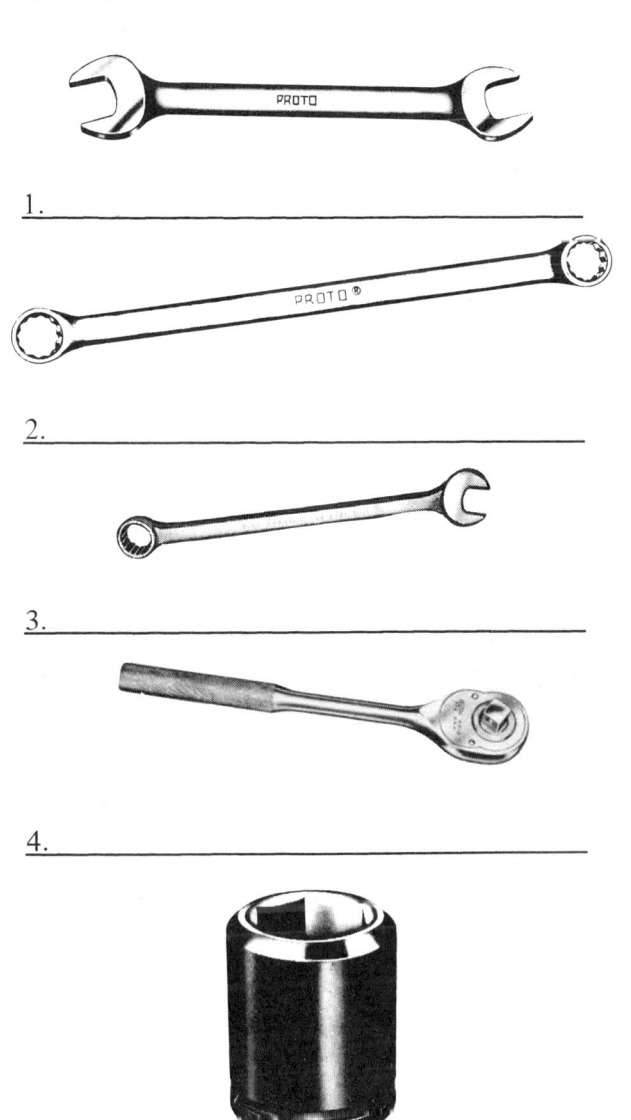

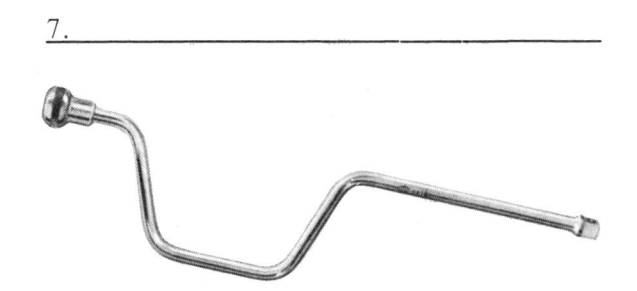

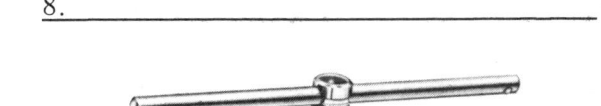

1. _____

2. _____

3. _____

4. _____

5. _____

6. _____

7. _____

8. _____

9. _____

10. _____

(Continued on next page)

13

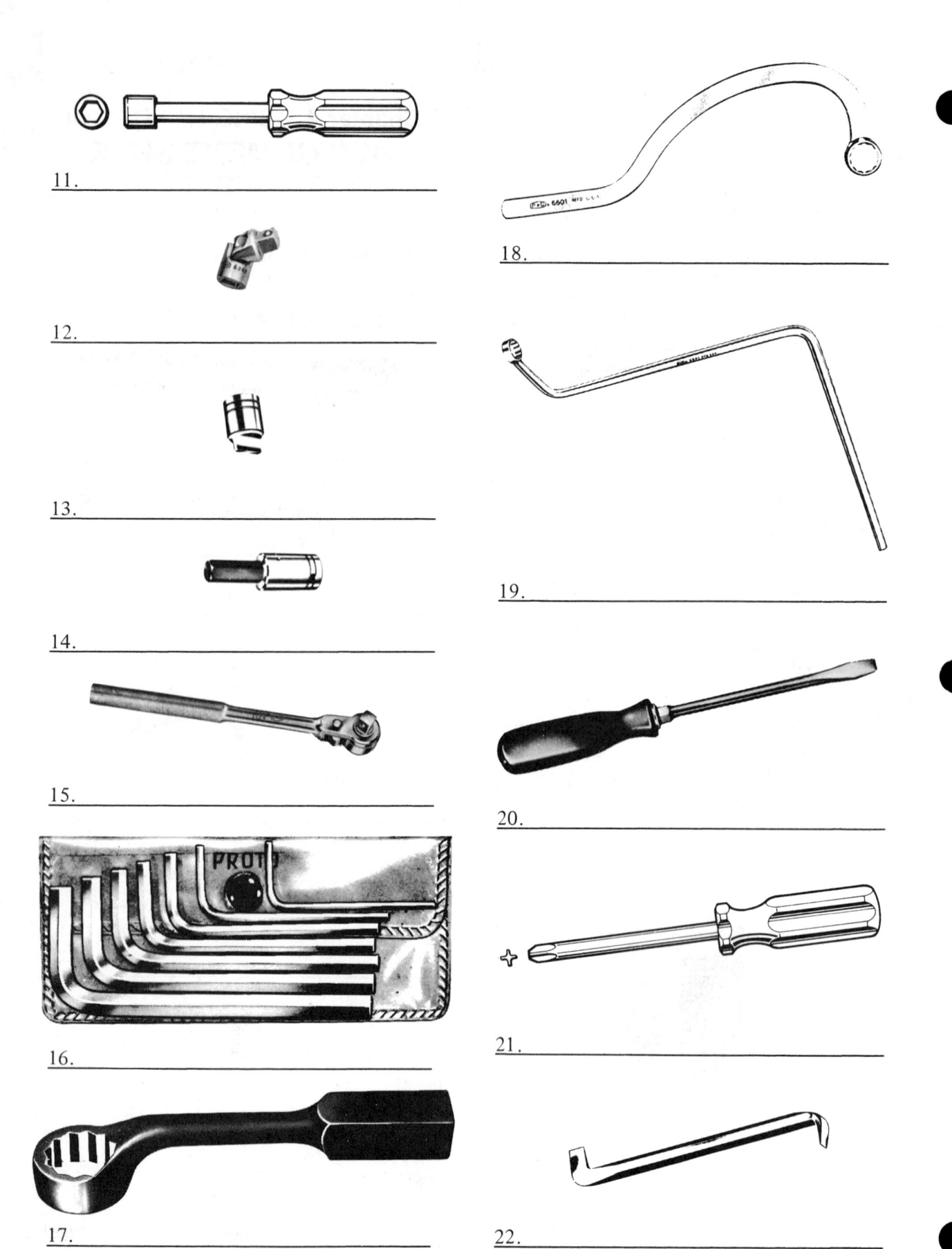

11. _____

12. _____

13. _____

14. _____

15. _____

16. _____

17. _____

18. _____

19. _____

20. _____

21. _____

22. _____

14

NAME _____ SECTION _____ DATE _____ SCORE _____

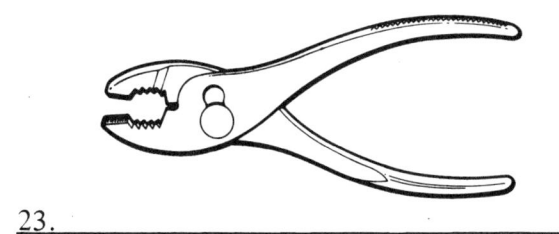

23. _____

24. _____

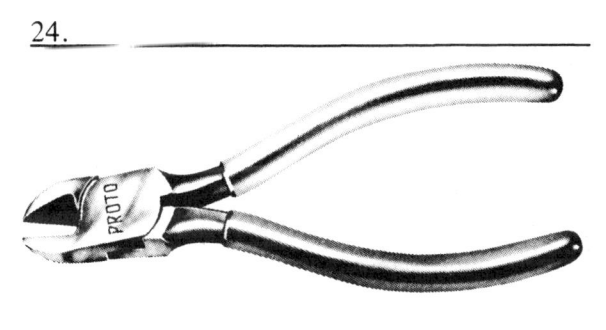

25. _____

26. _____

27. _____

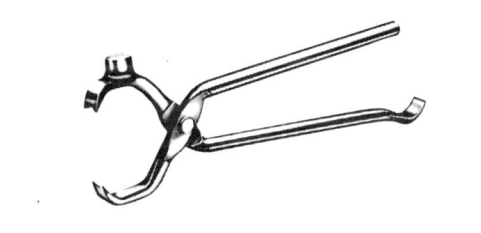

28. _____

15

Review of New Terms

For each definition in Column 2, select the term in Column 1 that best matches its meaning. Write the identifying *letter* of the term in the Answer column.

Column 1	Column 2	Answer
A. Box-end wrench	1. A wrench with one box end and one open end.	1. _____
B. Combination wrench	2. A tool designed to grip objects that wrenches or screwdrivers will not fit.	2. _____
C. Diagonal cutting pliers	3. A wrench designed to fit all the way around a bolt or nut.	3. _____
D. Hammer	4. A wrench that fits all the way around a bolt or nut which can be detached from a handle.	4. _____
E. Open-end wrench	5. A tool that is driven by a hammer and is used to remove or install pins.	5. _____
F. Pliers	6. A wrench designed to tighten bolts or nuts to a certain tightness.	6. _____
G. Phillips screwdriver	7. A wrench with an opening at the end which can slip onto the bolt or nut.	7. _____
H. Punch	8. A tool with cutting edges on the jaw for cutting cotter keys.	8. _____
I. Socket wrench	9. A tool with a point on the blade or tip used for driving Phillips head screws.	9. _____
J. Torque wrench	10. A tool used to drive or pound on an object.	10. _____

NAME _____ SECTION _____ DATE _____ SCORE _____

Chapter 5 USING POWER TOOLS AND EQUIPMENT
ASSIGNMENT SHEET 5

Identifying Power Tools

Before you begin: Read Chapter 5 in *Auto Mechanics*. Write the names of the power tools in the space provided below.

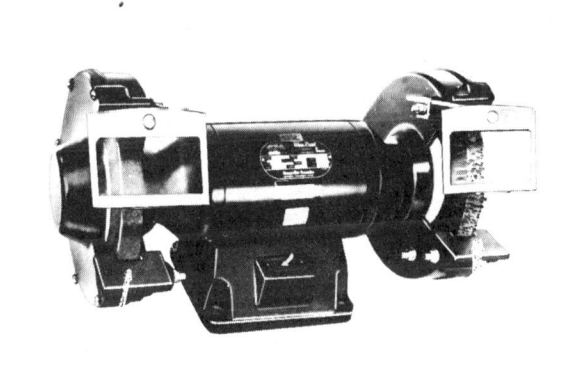

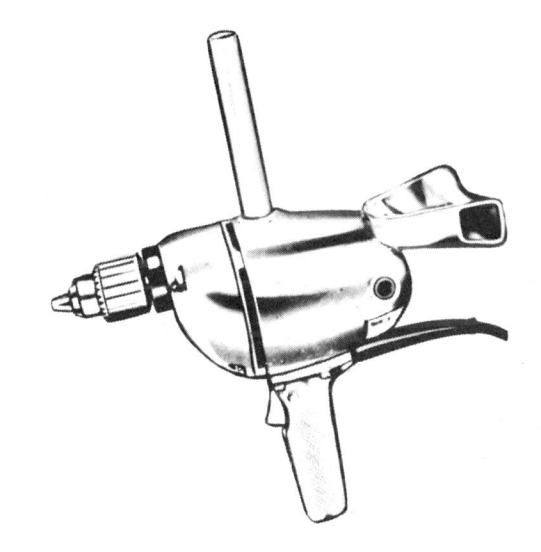

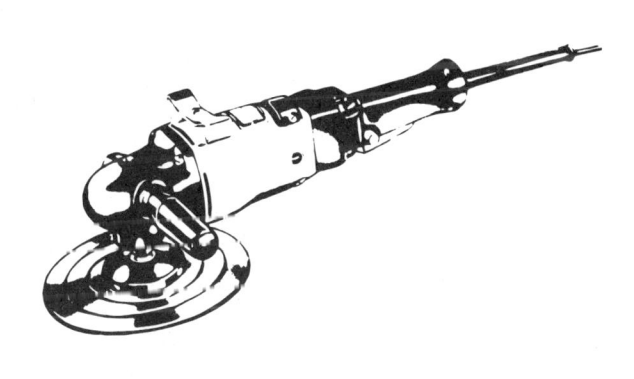

1. _____

3. _____

2. _____

4. _____

(Continued on next page)

17

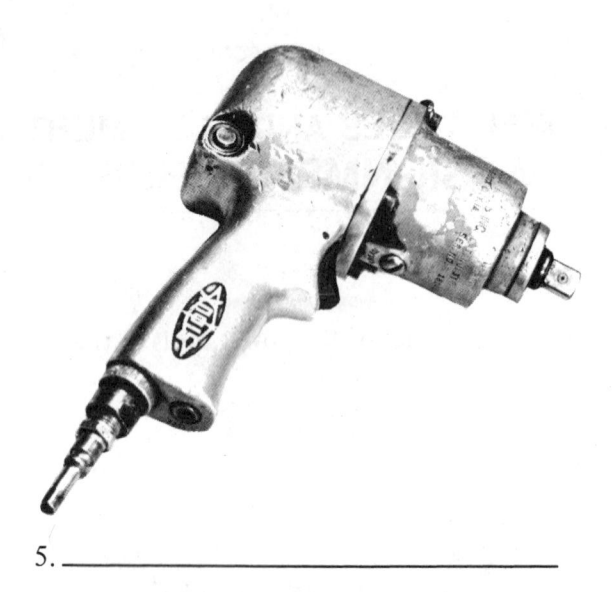

5. _____

6. _____

7. _____

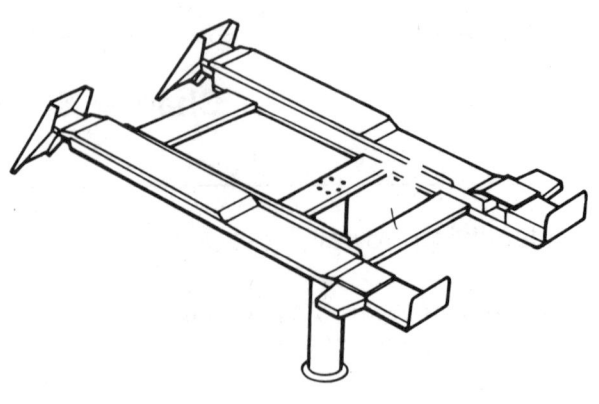

8. _____

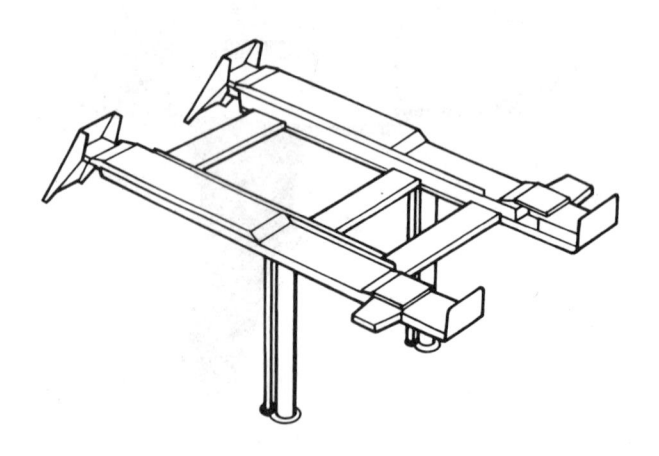

9. _____

10. _____

(Continued on next page)

18

NAME _____ SECTION _____ DATE _____ SCORE _____

11. _____

12. _____

13. _____

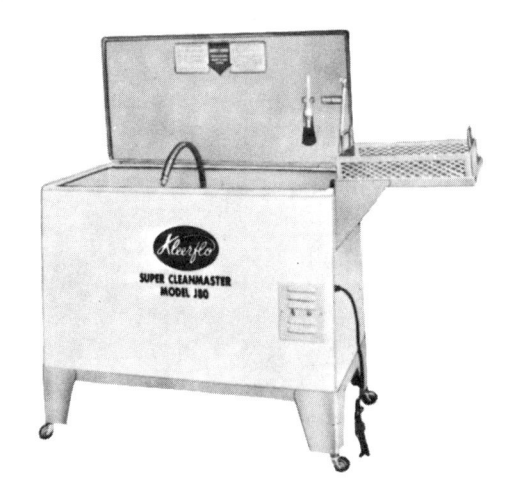

14. _____

15. _____

19

Review of New Terms

For each definition in Column 2, select the term in Column 1 that best matches its meaning. Write the identifying *letter* of the term in the Answer column.

Column 1	Column 2	Answer
A. Air impact wrench	1. A container in which a hot solution cleans ferrous metal parts such as cast iron or steel.	1. _____
B. Cold tank cleaner	2. Automotive cleaning equipment that uses a combination of steam and soap to clean parts.	2. _____
C. Floor jack		
D. Glass bead blaster	3. A container with a cold solution for cleaning nonferrous metal parts such as aluminum.	3. _____
E. Hot tank cleaner		
F. Hydraulic press	4. A hydraulically operated table used to push parts together or apart.	4. _____
G. Power tool	5. An electric light with a protective hood used to light dark areas of the automobile.	5. _____
H. Solvent cleaner		
I. Steam cleaner		
J. Trouble light	6. A wrench powered by compressed air.	6. _____
	7. Cleaning equipment in which compressed air drives small glass beads against the part to be cleaned.	7. _____
	8. A tool that uses electricity, compressed air, or hydraulic fluid.	8. _____
	9. A piece of equipment powered by air or hydraulic fluid used to raise an automobile.	9. _____
	10. A container in which cleaning solvent is used to wash off oil and grease from automotive parts.	10. _____

NAME _____ SECTION _____ DATE _____ SCORE _____

Chapter 6 USING METALWORKING TOOLS
ASSIGNMENT SHEET 6

Identifying Metalworking Tools

Before you begin: Read Chapter 6 in *Auto Mechanics*. Write the name of the metalworking tools in the spaces provided below.

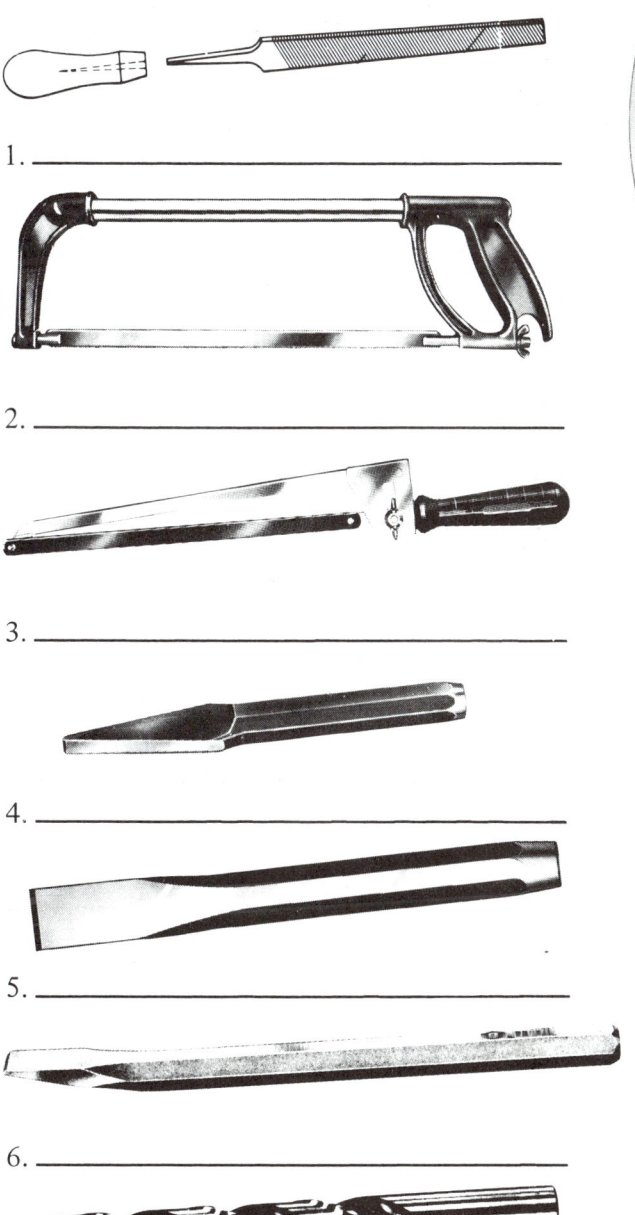

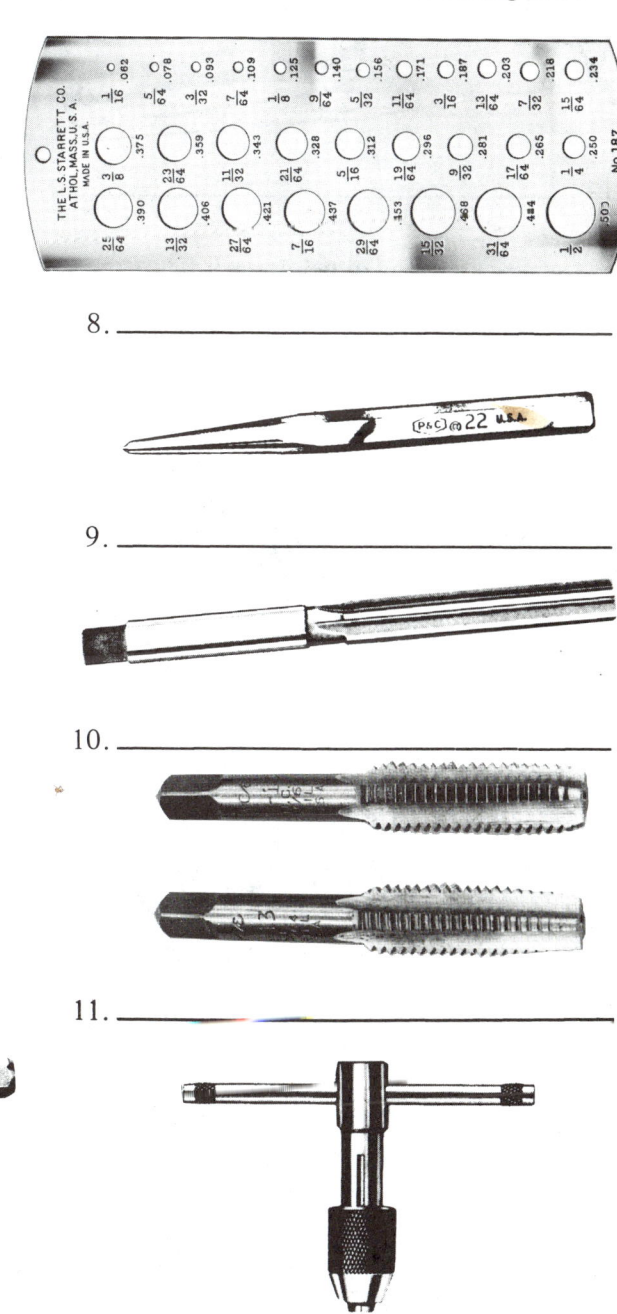

1. _____

2. _____

3. _____

4. _____

5. _____

6. _____

7. _____

8. _____

9. _____

10. _____

11. _____

12. _____

21

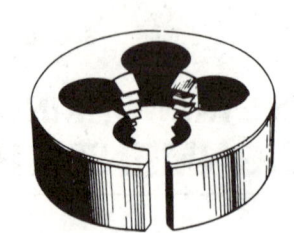

13. _____

14. _____

15. _____

In the spaces provided below each figure, describe the steps used to remove a broken stud or bolt.

1. _____
   _____
   _____

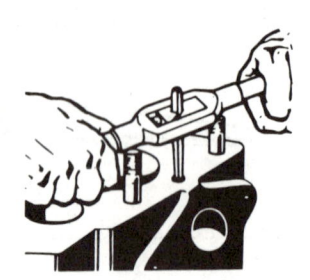

2. _____
   _____
   _____

3. _____
   _____
   _____

22

NAME _____ SECTION _____ DATE _____ SCORE _____

Review of New Terms

For each definition in Column 2, select the term in Column 1 that best matches its meaning. Write the identifying *letter* of the term in the Answer column.

Column 1

A. Chisel
B. Die
C. File
D. Hacksaw
E. Metal-working tools
F. Reamer
G. Screw extractor
H. Tap
I. Twist drill

Column 2

1. A tool used to remove broken bolts or studs from automotive parts.
2. A hardened steel tool with rows of cutting edges used to remove metal for polishing, smoothing, or shaping.
3. A tool with cutting edges used to remove a small amount of metal from a drilled hole.
4. A bar of hardened steel with a cutting edge ground on one end. It is driven with a hammer to cut metal.
5. A hardened cutting tool made to cut or drill a hole.
6. A tool used to cut external threads.
7. Tools used to cut or shape metal.
8. A tool used to cut internal threads.
9. A saw for cutting metal.

Answer

1. _____
2. _____
3. _____
4. _____
5. _____
6. _____
7. _____
8. _____
9. _____

NAME _____ SECTION _____ DATE _____ SCORE _____

Chapter 7 USING MEASURING SYSTEMS AND TOOLS
ASSIGNMENT SHEET 7

Identifying Measuring Tools

Before you begin: Read Chapter 7 in *Auto Mechanics*. Write the names of the measuring tools in the spaces provided below.

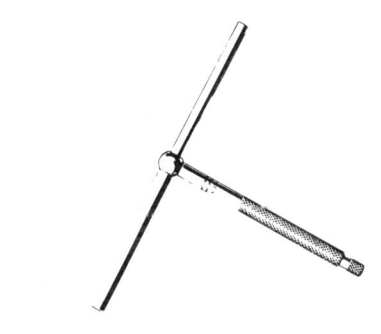

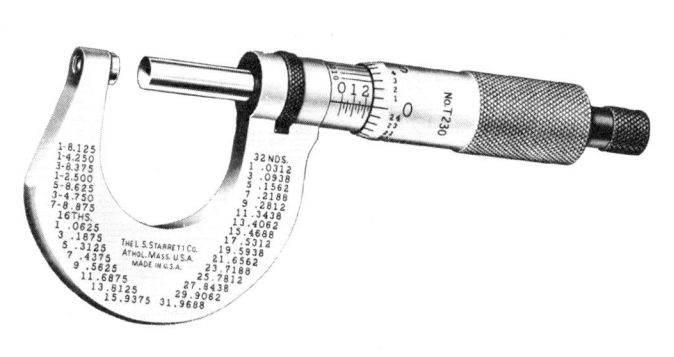

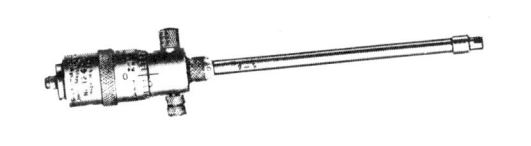

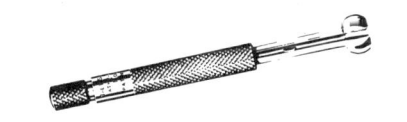

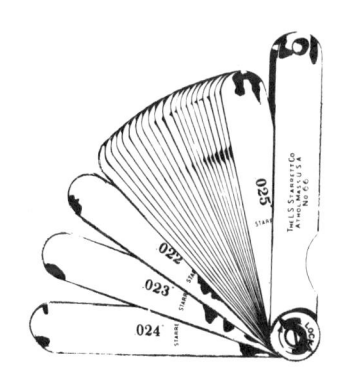

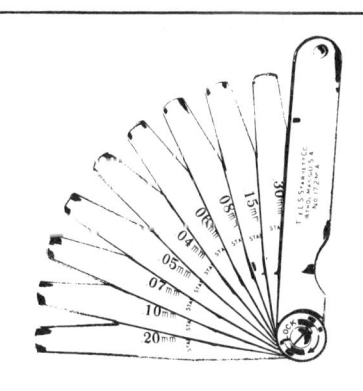

1. _____

2. _____

3. _____

4. _____

5. _____

6. _____

7. _____

8. _____

25

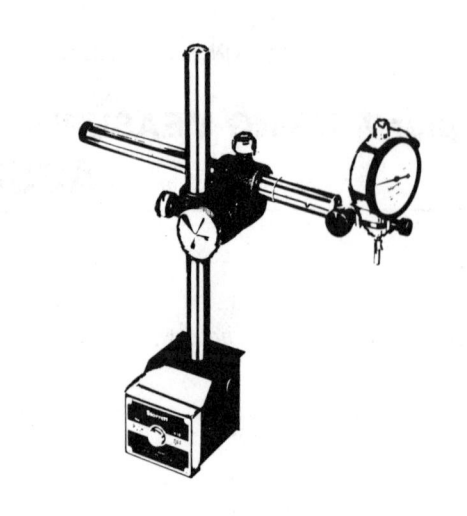

9. _____

Measurement Practice

Write each of the micrometer measurements in the spaces provided below.

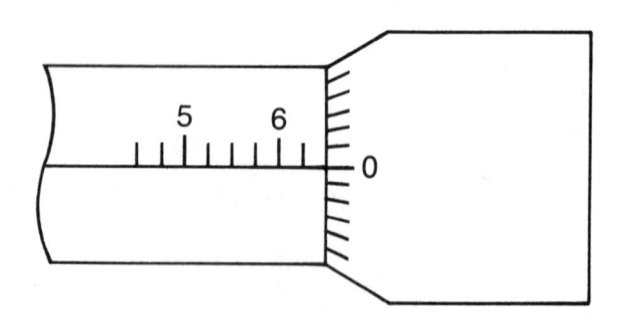

1. _____

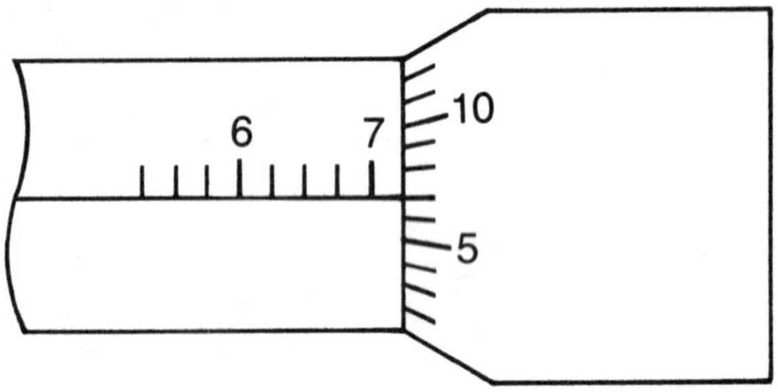

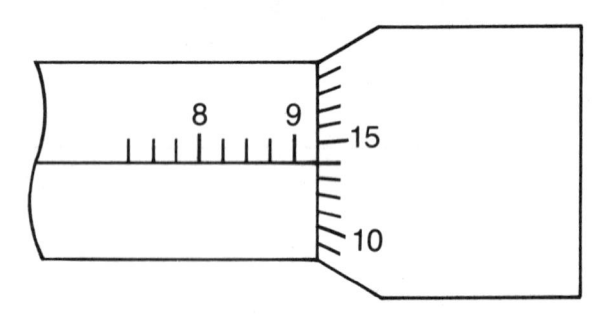

2. _____

3. _____

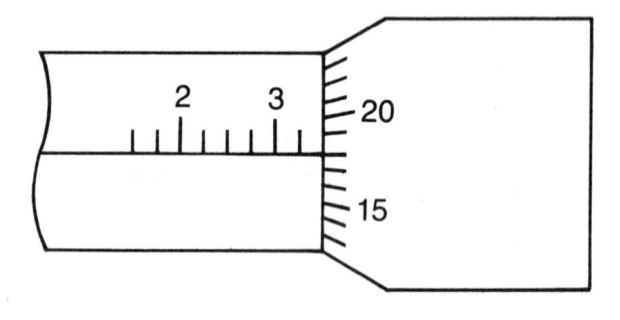

4. _____

NAME _____ SECTION _____ DATE _____ SCORE _____

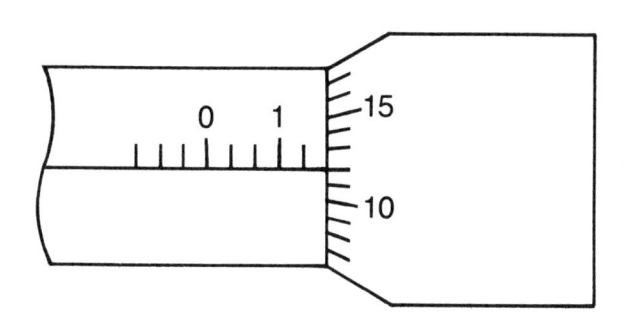

5. _____

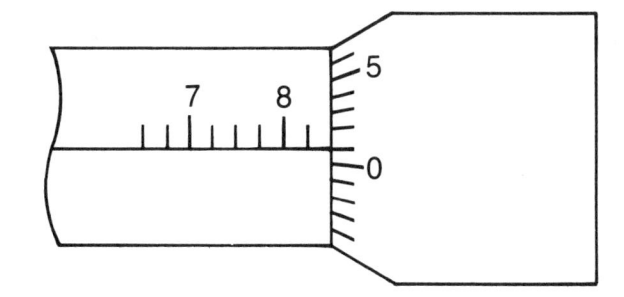

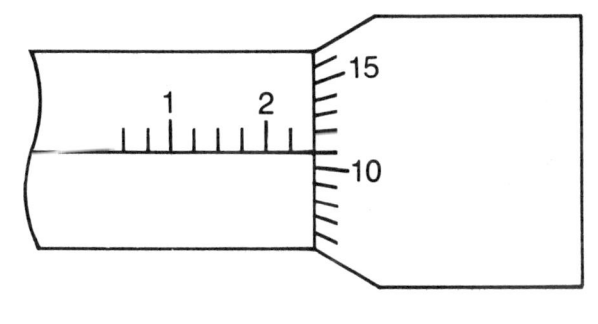

6. _____

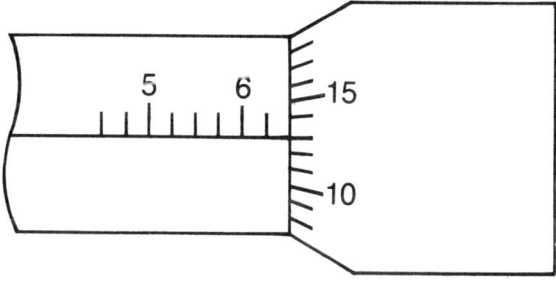

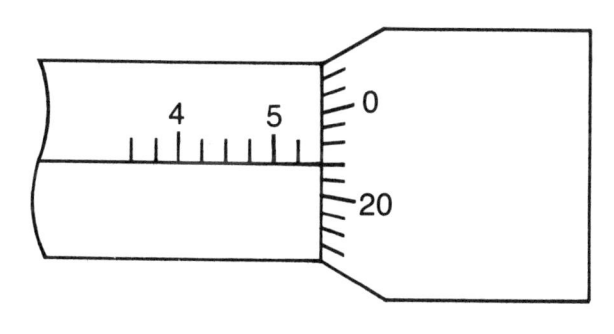

7. _____

8. _____

9. _____

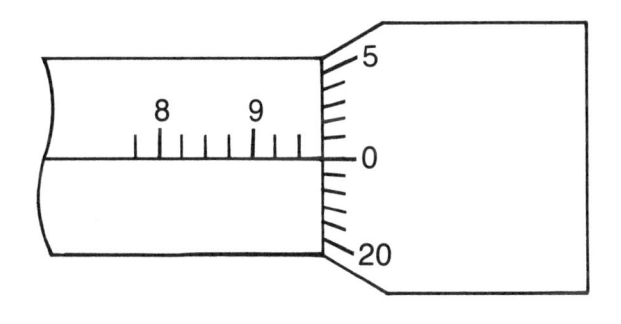

10. _____

Review of New Terms

For each definition in Column 2, select the term in Column 1 that best matches its meaning. Write the identifying *letter* of the term in the Answer column.

Column 1

A. Dial indicator
B. English measuring system
C. Feeler gauge
D. Inside micrometer
E. Metric measuring system
F. Metric units
G. Outside micrometer
H. Rule
I. Small hole gauge
J. Telescoping gauge

Column 2

1. A flat length of wood, plastic, or metal divided into a number of measuring units.
2. A gauge used to measure movement or play and contour or runout of an automobile part.
3. A tool used to measure the size of holes, such as an automotive engine cylinder.
4. A tool with a spring-loaded piston that telescopes within a cylinder, used to measure the inside of a hole.
5. One of the two main measuring systems in use in the world that is most commonly used in the United States.
6. A tool used to measure the outside of an object such as a crankshaft or piston.
7. A tool used to measure the space between two surfaces.
8. Standard units based upon the metre and decimal steps of the metre.
9. A tool consisting of a split sphere with an internal wedge used to measure the inside of small holes such as valve guides.
10. One of the main measuring systems in use in the world, now being slowly adopted in the United States.

Answer

1. _____
2. _____
3. _____
4. _____
5. _____
6. _____
7. _____
8. _____
9. _____
10. _____

NAME _____ SECTION _____ DATE _____ SCORE _____

Chapter 8 USING FASTENERS
ASSIGNMENT SHEET 8

Identifying Fasteners

Before you begin: Read Chapter 8 in *Auto Mechanics*. Write the names of the fasteners in the spaces provided below.

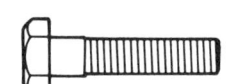

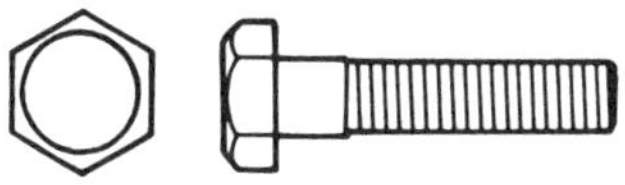

1. _____

2. _____

3. _____

4. _____

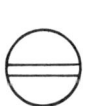

5. _____

6. _____

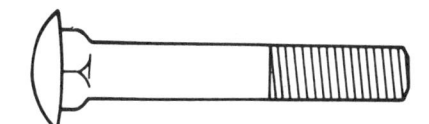

7. _____

8. _____

9. _____

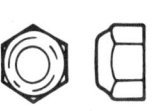

10. _____

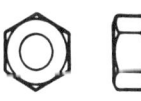

11. _____

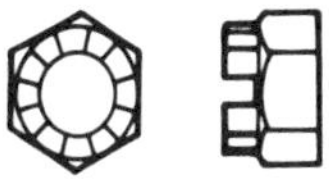

12. _____

29

13. _____

14. _____

15. _____

16. _____

17. _____

18. _____

Review of New Terms

For each definition in Column 2, select the term in Column 1 that best matches its meaning. Write the identifying *letter* of the term in the Answer column.

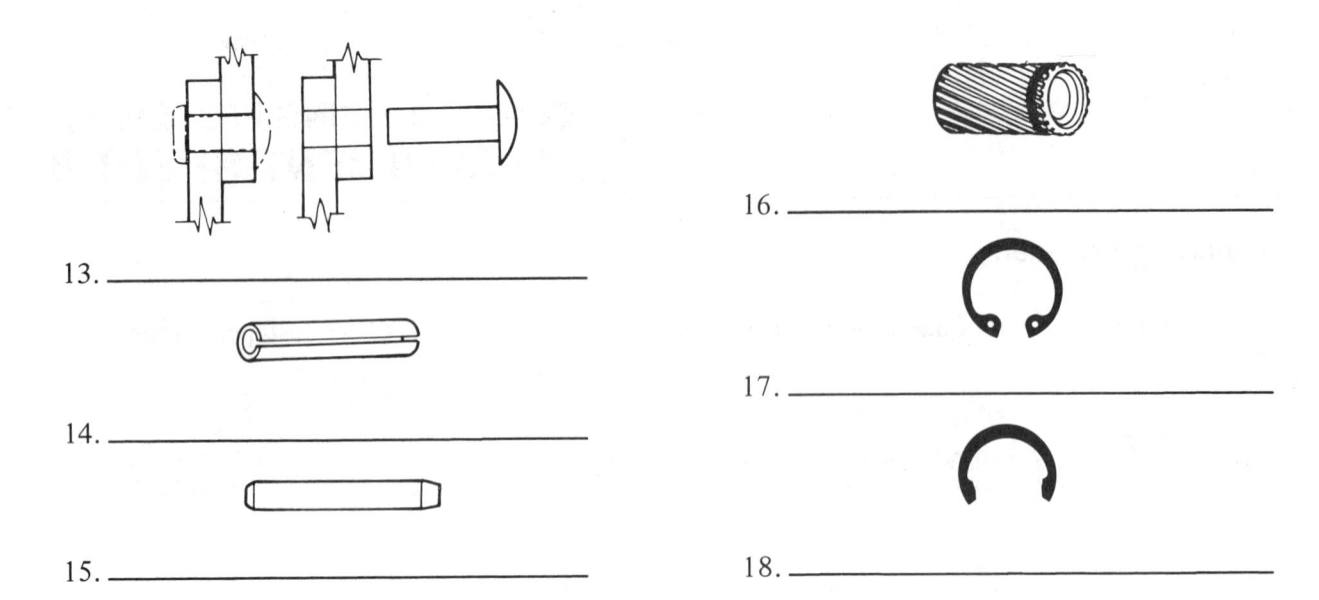

Column 1	Column 2	Answer
A. Bolt	1. A threaded fastener that fits into a threaded hold in an automotive component.	1. _____
B. Grade markings	2. A threaded fastener used with a nut to hold automotive parts together.	2. _____
C. Nonthreaded fasteners	3. A small fastener with internal threads used with bolts and screws.	3. _____
D. Nut	4. Fasteners that use threads to hold automotive parts together.	4. _____
E. Pitch gauge	5. Markings on threaded fasteners used to identify their quality and strength.	5. _____
F. Screw	6. A tool used to measure the thread size of a threaded fastener.	6. _____
G. Stud	7. A fastener used with bolts, screws, studs, and nuts to distribute the clamping force and to prevent fasteners from vibrating loose.	7. _____
H. Thread designation	8. The system used to indicate the size of the threads on fasteners.	8. _____
I. Threaded fasteners	9. Fasteners that hold automotive parts together without the use of threads.	9. _____
J. Washer	10. A fastener with threads at both ends.	10. _____

NAME _____ SECTION _____ DATE _____ SCORE _____

Chapter 9 USING SERVICE MANUALS
ASSIGNMENT SHEET 9

Looking Up Specifications

Before you begin: Read Chapter 9 in *Auto Mechanics.* Use the manual page shown below to look up the assigned specifications at the bottom of this page.

BRAKES

SECTION 5

TORQUE SPECIFICATIONS

	Chevrolet and 125" W.B. Wagons	Chevelle and 116" W.B. Wagons and Monte Carlo	Camaro	Nova	Corvette
Main Cylinder to Dash	24 ft. lbs.	24 ft. lbs.	24 ft. lbs.	24 ft. lbs.	24 ft. lbs.
Main Cylinder to Booster	24 ft. lbs.	24 ft. lbs.	24 ft. lbs.	24 ft. lbs.	24 ft. lbs.
Vacuum Cylinder to Dash	25 ft. lbs.	25 in. lbs.	25 ft. lbs.	25 in. lbs.	22 ft. lbs.
Push Rod to Clevis		14 in. lbs.		14 ft. lbs.	14 ft. lbs.
Primary Brake Pipe Nut	150 in. lbs.	150 in. lbs.	150 in. lbs.	150 in. lbs.	150 in. lbs.
Secondary Brake Pipe Nut	150 in. lbs.	150 in. lbs.	150 in. lbs.	150 in. lbs.	150 in. lbs.
Brake Line to Frame Screw	100 in. lbs.	100 ft. lbs.	100 in. lbs.	100 in. lbs.	100 in. lbs.
Brake Shoe Anchor Pin	120 ft. lbs.	120 ft. lbs.	120 ft. lbs.	120 ft. lbs.	—
Wheel Cylinder to Backing Plate	50 ft. lbs.	50 ft. lbs.	50 ft. lbs.	50 ft. lbs.	—
Parking Brake Equalizer	60 in. lbs.	90 in. lbs.	90 in. lbs.	90 in. lbs.	70 in. lbs.
Parking Brake Assembly Attachment	150 in. lbs.	100 in. lbs.	100 in. lbs.	100 in. lbs.	100 in. lbs.
Flex Hose to Wheel Cylinder		22 ft. lbs.	—	22 ft. lbs.	—
Tubing to Flex Hose	120 in. lbs.	120 in. lbs.	120 in. lbs.	120 in. lbs.	120 in. lbs.
Caliper Mounting Bolt	35 ft. lbs.	35 ft. lbs.	35 ft. lbs.	35 ft. lbs.	70 ft. lbs.
Caliper Housing Bolt	—	—	—	—	130 ft. lbs.
Flex Hose to Caliper	22 ft. lbs.	22 ft. lbs.	22 ft. lbs.	22 ft. lbs.	22 ft. lbs.
Support Plate to Steering Knuckle (Upper Bolt)	140 in. lbs.	140 ft. lbs.	140 in. lbs.	140 ft. lbs.	—
Support Plate/Steering Arm to Knuckle Nuts	—	70 ft. lbs.	—	70 ft. lbs.	—
Shield to Steering Knuckle Nuts (Hold Bolt)		70 ft. lbs.		70 ft. lbs.	
Shield to Steering Knuckle Bolt (Hold Nut)		95 ft. lbs.		95 ft. lbs.	
Pedal Mounting Pivot Bolt (Nut)	30 ft. lbs.	—	30 ft. lbs.	—	
Combination Valve Mounting	150 ft. lbs.	100 in. lbs.	150 in. lbs.	150 in. lbs.	—

1. Torque for Camaro vacuum cylinder to dash _____

2. Torque for Nova push rod to clevis _____

3. Torque for Corvette main cylinder to dash _____

4. Torque for Chevelle brake shoe anchor pin _____

5. Torque for Chevrolet caliper mounting bolt _____

6. Torque for Corvette caliper housing bolt _____

Use the annual page shown below to look up the assigned specifications at the bottom of this page.

Exc. Chevette, Monza & Vega — CHEVROLET

TUNE UP SPECIFICATIONS

The following specifications are published from the latest information available. This data should be used only in the absence of a decal affixed in the engine compartment.

★ When using a timing light, disconnect vacuum hose or tube at distributor and plug opening in hose or tube so idle speed will not be affected.

● When checking compression, lowest cylinder must be within 80 percent of highest.

▲ Before removing wires from distributor cap, determine location of the No. 1 wire in cap, as distributor position may have been altered from that shown at the end of this chart.

Year	Spark Plug		Distributor		Ignition Timing ★			Carb. Adjustments					
	Type	Gap Inch	Point Gap Inch	Dwell Angle Deg.	Firing Order Fig. ▲	Timing BTDC ①	Mark Fig.	Hot Idle Speed ③		Air Fuel Ratio		Idle "CO" %	
								Std. Trans.	Auto. Trans.	Std. Trans.	Auto. Trans.	Std. Trans.	Auto. Trans.
CAMARO													
6-250④	R46TS	.035	—	—	H	6°	B	③	—	—	—	—	—
6-250⑪	R46TS	.035	—	—	H	8°⑤	B	—	600	—	—	—	—
8-305	R45TS	.045	—	—	I	8°⑥	B	700	500/650	—	—	—	—
8-350④	R45TS	.045	—	—	I	8°	B	700	—	—	—	—	—
8-350⑪	R45TS	.045	—	—	I	8°	B	—	500/650	—	—	—	—

For a 1977 Camaro:

1. Type of spark plug for a six cylinder engine _____

2. Spark plug gap for a 305 engine _____

3. Spark plug gap for a 350 engine _____

4. Hot idle speed for a 305 engine with standard transmission _____

5. Hot idle speed for a 305 engine with an automatic transmission _____

6. Timing specification for a 350 engine _____

NAME _____ SECTION _____ DATE _____ SCORE _____

Review of New Terms

For each definition in Column 2, select the term in Column 1 that best matches its meaning. Write the identifying *letter* of the term in the Answer column.

Column 1

A. Flat rate manual
B. Manufacturer's shop manual
C. Owner's manual
D. Repair manual
E. Service bulletins
F. Service literature
G. Specifications

Column 2

1. A description of a repair procedure not covered in a manufacturer's service manual.
2. A manual published by an automotive manufacturer to help the mechanic make repairs on a certain vehicle.
3. A guide to the operation and periodic service of an automobile that comes with a new automobile.
4. Measurements and dimensions the automobile manufacturer recommends for various parts (sometimes called specs).
5. A book that lists the cost of parts and labor for automotive repairs.
6. A manual published for mechanics that covers many years and makes of automobiles.
7. Books or manuals that provide the mechanic with step-by-step repair procedures and specifications.

Answer

1. _____
2. _____
3. _____
4. _____
5. _____
6. _____
7. _____

NAME _____ SECTION _____ DATE _____ SCORE _____

Chapter 10 FUNDAMENTALS OF ENGINE OPERATION
ASSIGNMENT SHEET 10

Four-Stroke-Cycle Operation

Before you begin: Read Chapter 10 in *Auto Mechanics*. In the spaces provided describe the action in each of the four strokes shown below.

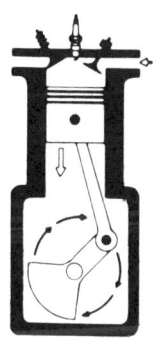

1. _____

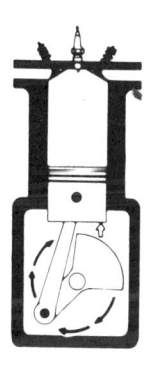

2. _____

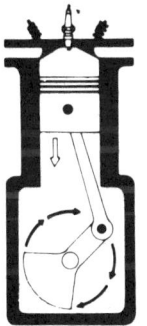

3. _____

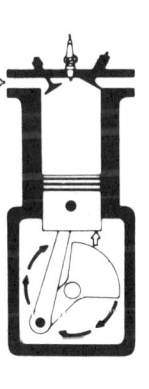

4. _____

Basic Parts Identification

Identify the numbered parts of each figure shown below by writing the correct names in the spaces provided.

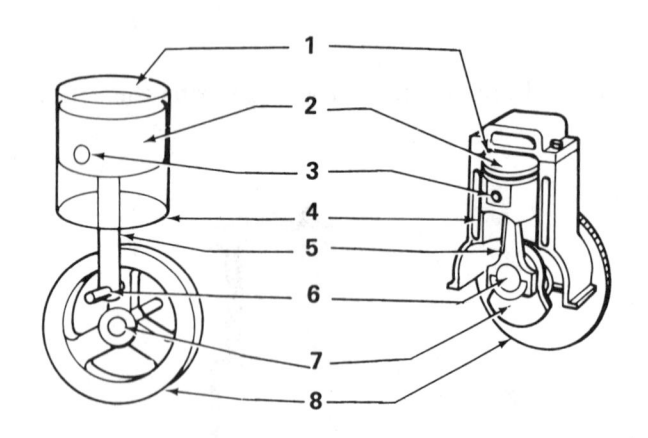

Basic engine parts

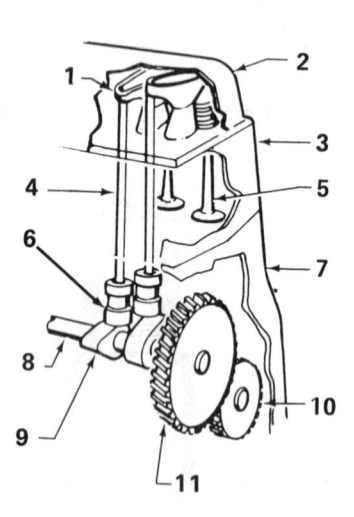

1. _____
2. _____
3. _____
4. _____
5. _____
6. _____
7. _____
8. _____

Valve train

1. _____
2. _____
3. _____
4. _____
5. _____
6. _____
7. _____
8. _____
9. _____
10. _____
11. _____

36

NAME _____ SECTION _____ DATE _____ SCORE _____

Review of New Terms

For each definition in Column 2, select the term in Column 1 that best matches its meaning. Write the identifying *letter* of the term in the Answer column.

Column 1

A. Combustion chamber
B. Compression stroke
C. Engine
D. Flywheel
E. Internal combustion engine
F. Power overlap
G. Reciprocating engine
H. Reciprocating motion
I. Rotary motion
J. Valve train

Column 2

1. A heavy wheel used to smooth out the power strokes.
2. An engine in which pistons go up and down.
3. One of the strokes of the four-stroke-cycle engine in which the air-fuel mixture is compressed.
4. Round-and-round motion.
5. An engine in which the burning of the fuel takes place inside the engine.
6. An assembly of engine parts that open and close the passageways for the intake of air and fuel as well as for the exhaust of burned gases.
7. Part of the engine in which the burning of air and fuel takes place.
8. Up-and-down motion.
9. The timing of power stokes of different cylinders in an engine for smooth operations.
10. A machine that converts heat energy into a usable form of energy.

Answer

1. ____
2. ____
3. ____
4. ____
5. ____
6. ____
7. ____
8. ____
9. ____
10. ____

NAME _____ SECTION _____ DATE _____ SCORE _____

Chapter 11 TYPES OF AUTOMOTIVE ENGINES
ASSIGNMENT SHEET 11

Two-Stroke-Cycle Diesel Engine Operation

Before you begin: Read Chapter 11 in *Auto Mechanics*. Describe the action in a two-stroke-cycle diesel in the spaces provided below each figure.

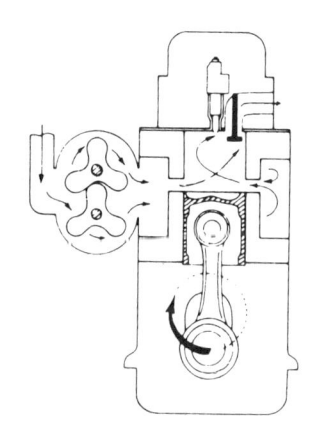

1. _____

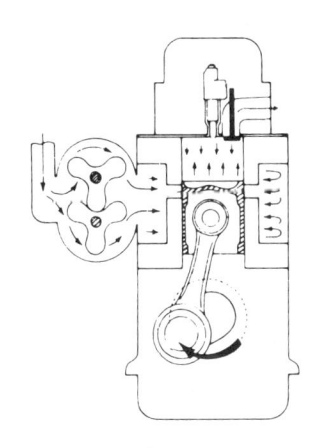

2. _____

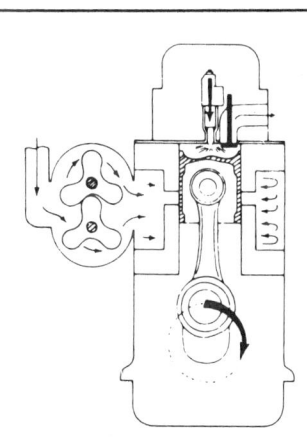

3. _____

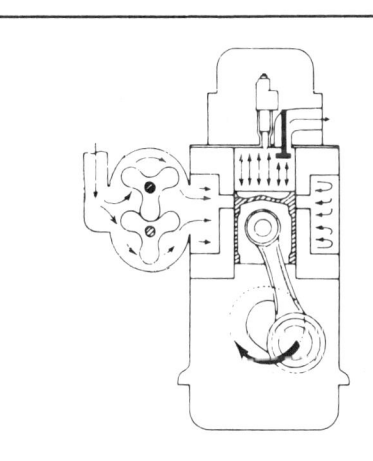

4. _____

39

Four-Stroke-Cycle Diesel Engine Operation

Describe the action in each of the four strokes of a four-stroke-cycle diesel operation in the spaces provided at the right of each figure

1. _____
_____
_____
_____
_____
_____

2. _____
_____
_____
_____
_____
_____

3. _____
_____
_____
_____
_____
_____

4. _____
_____
_____
_____
_____
_____

NAME _____ SECTION _____ DATE _____ SCORE _____

Review of New Terms

For each definition in Column 2, select the term in Column 1 that best matches its meaning. Write the identifying *letter* of the term in the Answer column.

Column 1

A. Air cooling
B. Flat engine
C. Hemispherical combustion chamber
D. In-line engine
E. Liquid-cooled engine
F. Overhead
G. Overhead camshaft
H. Spark ignition
I. V engine
J. Precombustion chamber
K. Wedge combustion chamber

Column 2

1. A combustion chamber in which the valves are located next to each other and the spark is mounted to one side.
2. An engine that is cooled by circulating a liquid around the hot parts.
3. A means of removing excessive heat from engine parts by circulating air around them.
4. A rounded combustion chamber.
5. The process by which the air-fuel mixture is ignited with an electrical spark.
6. An engine with cylinders arranged on a flat plane.
7. An engine whose cylinders are arranged in the shape of a V.
8. An engine design in which the camshaft is positioned on top of the cylinder head.
9. An engine in which the cylinders are arranged in a straight line.
10. A valve arrangement in which the valves are located over the piston on the cylinder head.
11. A small chamber connected to the main combustion chamber used to begin the combustion process.

Answer

1. _____
2. _____
3. _____
4. _____
5. _____
6. _____
7. _____
8. _____
9. _____
10. _____
11. _____

NAME _____ SECTION _____ DATE _____ SCORE _____

Chapter 12 PISTON ENGINE COMPONENTS: CRANKCASE, CYLINDERS, CRANKSHAFT AND BEARINGS
ASSIGNMENT SHEET 12

Cylinder Block Identification

Before you begin: Read Chapter 12 in *Auto Mechanics*. Identify the parts of the cylinder block in the spaces provided below.

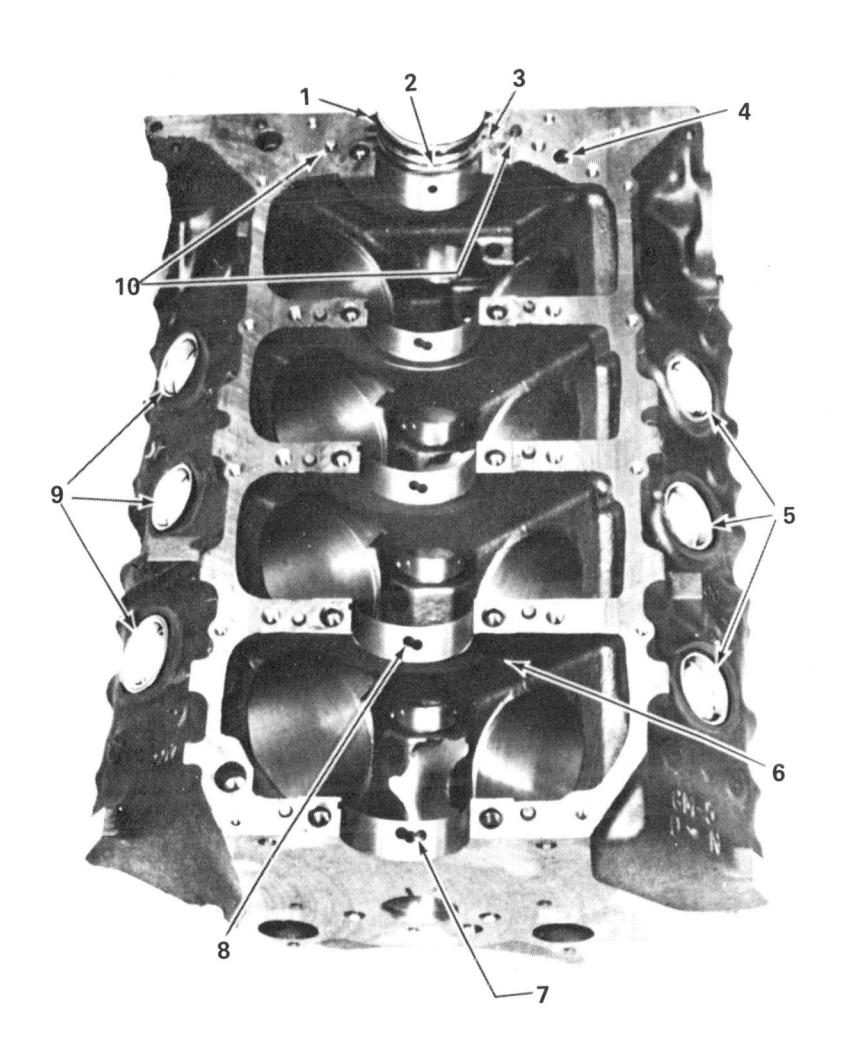

1. _____
   _____

2. _____
   _____

3. _____
   _____

4. _____
   _____

5. _____
   _____

6. _____
   _____

7. _____
   _____

8. _____
   _____

9. _____
   _____

10. _____
    _____

43

Crankshaft Identification

Identify the parts of the crankshaft in the spaces provided below.

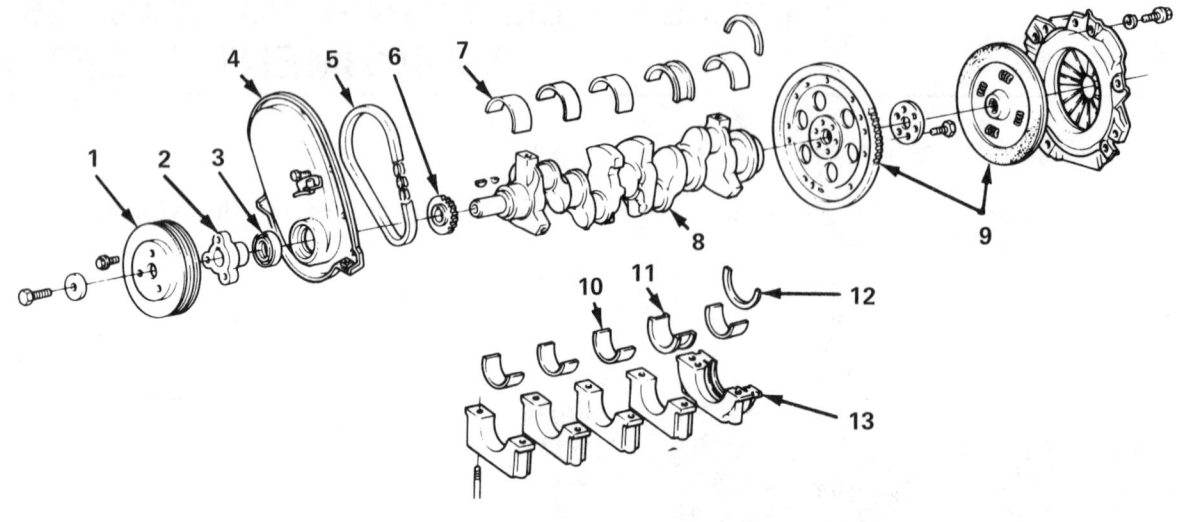

1. _____

2. _____

3. _____

4. _____

5. _____

6. _____

7. _____

8. _____

9. _____

10. _____

11. _____

12. _____

13. _____

NAME_____ SECTION_____ DATE_____ SCORE_____

Review of New Terms

For each definition in Column 2, select the term in Column 1 that best matches its meaning. Write the identifying *letter* of the term in the Answer column.

Column 1

A. Bearing
B. Bolt-on-cylinders
C. Bushing
D. Compatibility
E. Conformability
F. Embedability
G. Fatigue strength
H. Gasket
I. Insert
J. Journal
K. Lip seal
L. "O" ring
M. Oil clearance
N. Seal
O. Throw

Column 2

1. The ability of a bearing to absorb particles of dirt to prevent damage to the shaft.
2. A seal used to keep lubricant inside a bearing area.
3. The ability of a bearing to shape itself to minor irregularities.
4. A part used to reduce friction and wear between moving parts.
5. The bearing used between the connecting rod and the crankshaft.
6. Cylinders held in place with bolts or studs.
7. The space between a bearing and its journal provided for the flow of oil.
8. A bearing made in two half-round pieces to be inserted onto an automotive component.
9. A sleeve that fits into a hole or bore and acts as a bearing.
10. The ability of a bearing to resist failure due to stress.
11. A ring-shaped seal.
12. The part of a shaft on which a bearing is installed.
13. A soft material used between two automotive parts to form a pressure seal.
14. A device used to seal around a rotating shaft.
15. The offset part of the crankshaft to which the connecting rod is attached.

Answer

1. _____
2. _____
3. _____
4. _____
5. _____
6. _____
7. _____
8. _____
9. _____
10. _____
11. _____
12. _____
13. _____
14. _____
15. _____

NAME _____ SECTION _____ DATE _____ SCORE _____

Chapter 13 PISTON ENGINE COMPONENTS: PISTONS, RINGS, PINS, AND CONNECTING RODS
ASSIGNMENT SHEET 13

Piston Assembly Identification

Before you begin: Read Chapter 13 in *Auto Mechanics*. Identify the parts of the piston assembly in the spaces provided below.

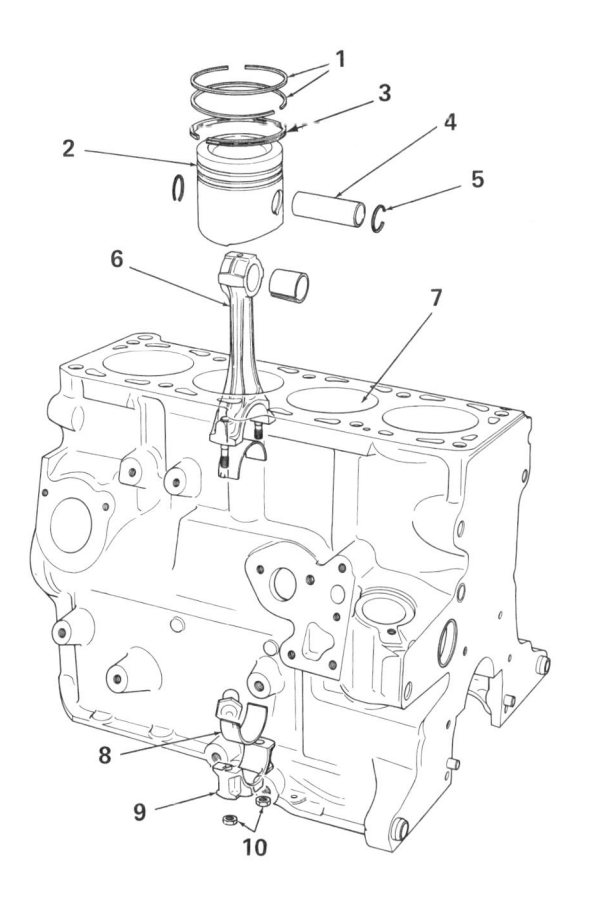

1. _____

2. _____

3. _____

4. _____

5. _____

6. _____

7. _____

8. _____

9. _____

10. _____

Piston Part Identification

Identify the parts of the piston in the spaces provided below.

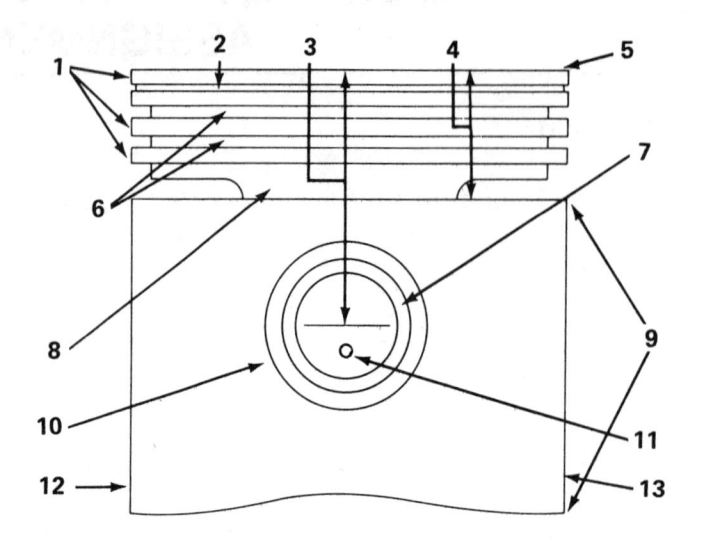

1. _____

2. _____

3. _____

4. _____

5. _____

6. _____

7. _____

8. _____

9. _____

10. _____

11. _____

12. _____

13. _____

NAME _____ SECTION _____ DATE _____ SCORE _____

Review of New Terms

For each definition in Column 2, select the term in Column 1 that best matches its meaning. Write the identifying *letter* of the term in the Answer column.

Column 1

A. Cam ground piston
B. Counterbored ring
C. End gap
D. Expander
E. Head land ring
F. Heat dam
G. Major thrust face
H. Piston clearance
I. Slipper skirt
J. T slot

Column 2

1. A spring placed behind a ring to increase its tension against a cylinder wall.
2. A type of skirt cut away to reduce weight and friction and to provide clearance for the crankshaft.
3. A groove cut around the top of the piston to prevent heat from making its way down the skirt.
4. A space cut in a piston for expansion control.
5. A piston ground to an oval shape that becomes round when it is heated.
6. The space between the piston skirt and the cylinder wall.
7. A ring constructed so that the top of the ring tips away from the cylinder except during the power stroke.
8. The face of the piston skirt that absorbs the load during the power stroke.
9. The space between the two ends of a ring when it is installed in a cylinder.
10. An L-shaped ring that covers the head land area of the piston and reduces exhaust emissions.

Answer

1. _____
2. _____
3. _____
4. _____
5. _____
6. _____
7. _____
8. _____
9. _____
10. _____

NAME _____ SECTION _____ DATE _____ SCORE _____

Chapter 14 PISTON ENGINE COMPONENTS: CYLINDER HEAD AND VALVE TRAIN
ASSIGNMENT SHEET 14

Camshaft Parts Identification

Before you begin: Read Chapter 14 in *Auto Mechanics*. Identify the parts of the camshaft in the spaces provided below.

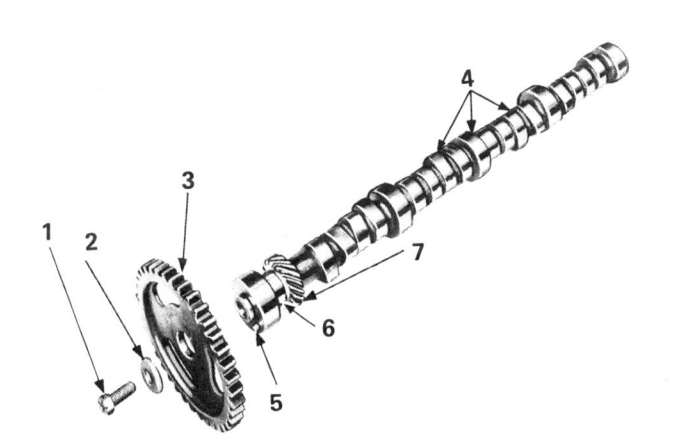

1. _____

2. _____

3. _____

4. _____

5. _____

6. _____

7. _____

Identify the parts of a cam lobe in the spaces provided below.

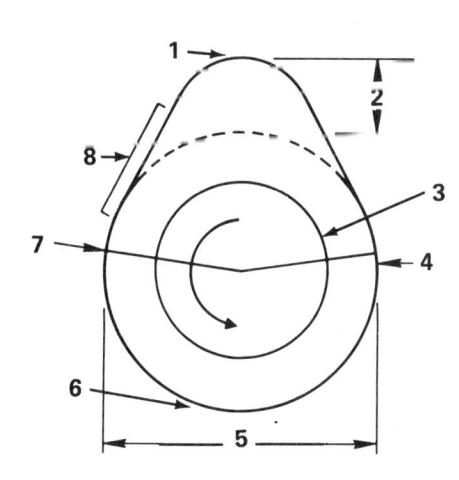

1. _____
2. _____
3. _____
4. _____
5. _____
6. _____
7. _____
8. _____

Valve Train Parts Identification

Identify the parts of the rocker shaft assembly in the spaces provided below.

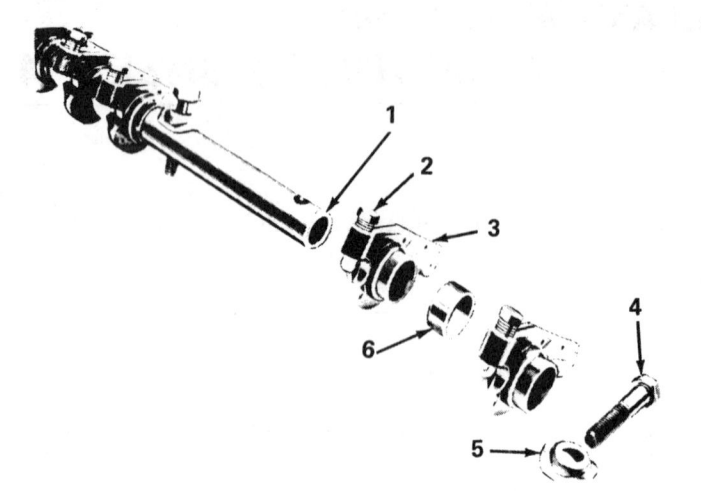

1. _____
2. _____
3. _____
4. _____
5. _____
6. _____

Identify the parts of the valve lifter in the spaces provided below.

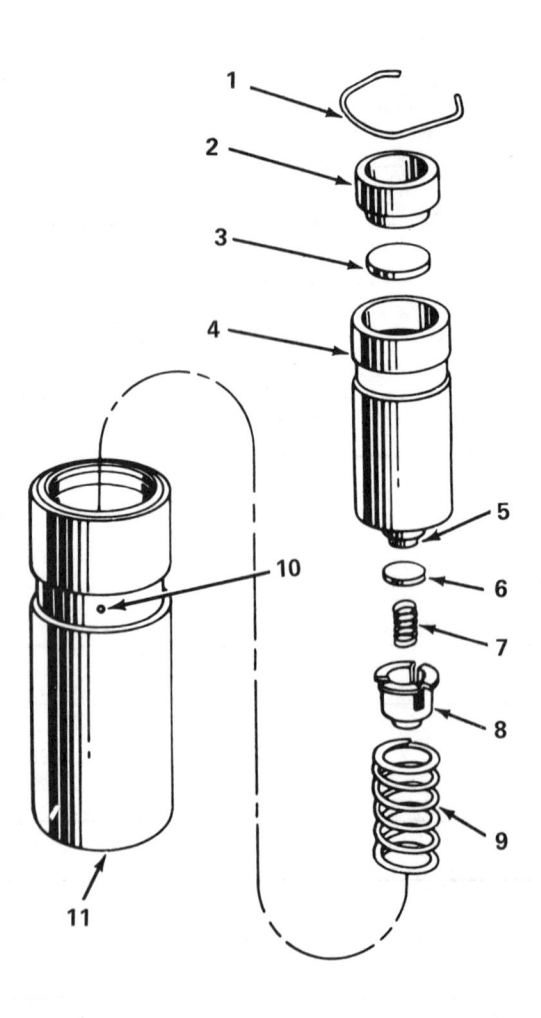

1. _____
2. _____
3. _____
4. _____
5. _____
6. _____
7. _____
8. _____
9. _____
10. _____
11. _____

NAME _____ SECTION _____ DATE _____ SCORE _____

Identify the parts of the valve spring and retainer assembly in the spaces provided below.

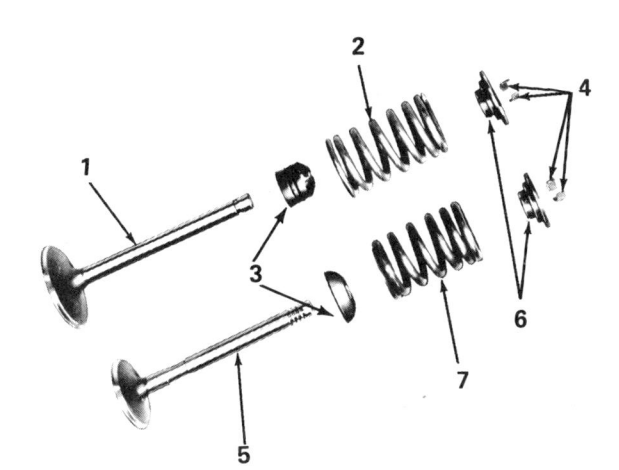

1. _____
2. _____
3. _____
4. _____
5. _____
6. _____
7. _____

Identify the parts of a rotator assembly in the spaces provided below.

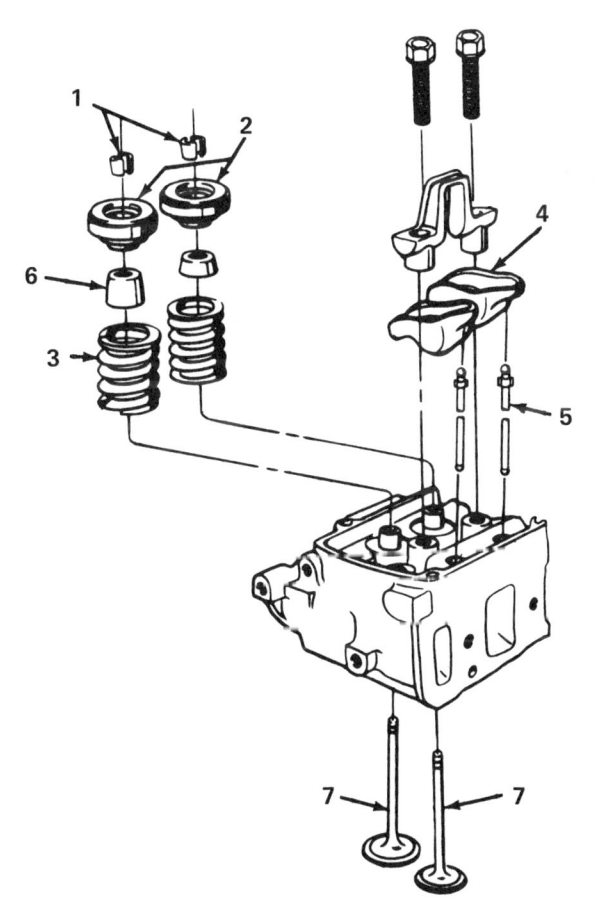

1. _____
2. _____
3. _____
4. _____
5. _____
6. _____
7. _____

53

Identify the parts of the valves in the spaces provided below.

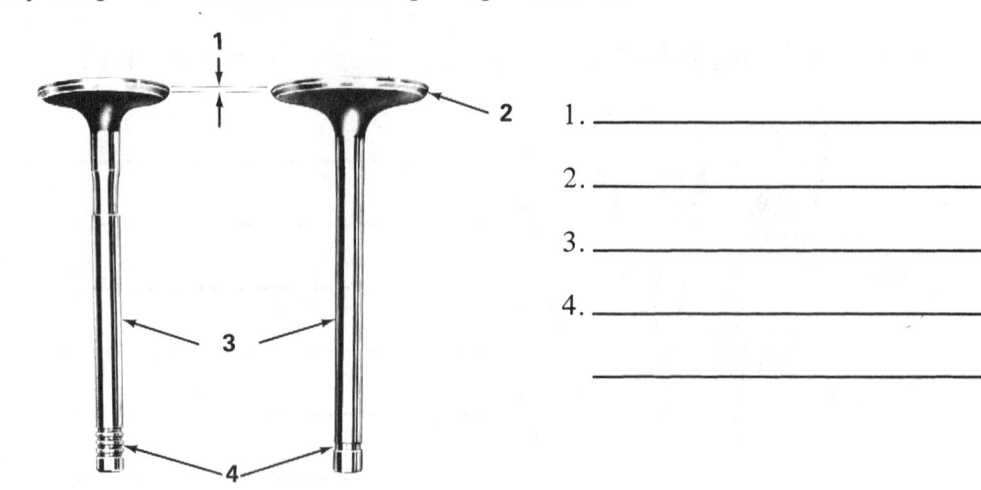

1. _____
2. _____
3. _____
4. _____

Identify the parts of the valve and valve seat in the spaces provided below.

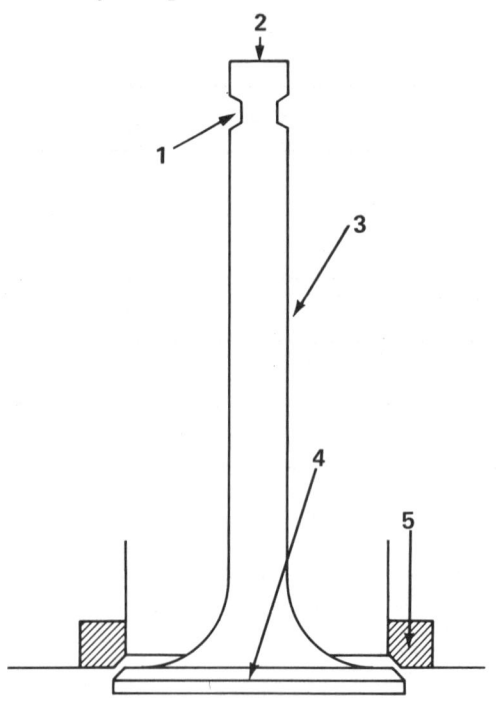

1. _____
2. _____
3. _____
4. _____
5. _____

NAME _____ SECTION _____ DATE _____ SCORE _____

Review of New Terms

For each definition in Column 2, select the term in Column 1 that best matches its meaning. Write the identifying *letter* of the term in the Answer column.

Column 1	Column 2	Answer
A. Cylinder head	1. The part of the cylinder head that the valve seals against.	1. _____
B. Exhaust ports	2. A valve lifter that controls valve lash or clearance hydraulically.	2. _____
C. Exhaust valve	3. The assembly of parts that opens and closes the ports of an engine.	3. _____
D. Hydraulic lifter	4. A lever mounted on the cylinder head that pushes the valves open.	4. _____
E. Lobe	5. Large casting bolted to the top of the engine that contains the combustion chamber and valves.	5. _____
F. Overlap	6. Opening and closing the valves at the correct time in relation to piston position.	6. _____
G. Pushrod	7. Valve used to control flow of burned exhaust gases from the cylinder.	7. _____
H. Rocker arm	8. The period of time when both valves in a cylinder are open.	8. _____
I. Solid lifter	9. Passages in the cylinder head used to route out burned gases from the cylinder.	9. _____
J. Valve	10. A device that rotates valves to prevent them from burning.	10. _____
K. Valve lash	11. A valve lifter that is solid and does not use hydraulic fluid to control valve lash.	11. _____
L. Valve rotator	12. Space or clearance in the valve train for heat expansion.	12. _____
M. Valve seat	13. A rod used to transfer camshaft motion to the rocker arm.	13. _____
N. Valve timing	14. A part installed in the cylinder head to support and guide the valve.	14. _____
O. Valve train	15. A raised section on the camshaft used to lift the valve.	15. _____

55

NAME _____ SECTION _____ DATE _____ SCORE _____

Chapter 15 PISTON ENGINE SERVICE
JOB SHEET 1

Measure Engine Compression

Before you begin: Read Chapter 15 in *Auto Mechanics*.

Student _____ Section _____ Date _____

Make of Car _____ Model _____ Year _____

Time Started _____ Time Finished _____ Total Time _____

Flat Rate Time _____

Special Tools, Equipment, Parts, and Materials

Compression-testing gauge   _____

Spark-plug socket   _____

Torque wrench   _____

Spark-plug gaskets   _____

_____   _____

References

Manufacturer's Shop Manual _____

Repair Manual _____

Service Bulletin _____

Specifications

Look up the following compression testing specifications for the vehicle and record them in the spaces provided below.

Manufacturer's compression pressure _____

Allowable variation _____

Label cylinder numbering pattern:

NOTE: To avoid error, always write the specifications down and do not rely on memory.

_____
Instructor's Check

Procedure

1. Run the engine until normal operating temperature is reached.

2. Stop the engine and loosen all spark plugs about one turn to break loose any accumulated carbon.

3. Start the engine again and accelerate slightly to blow out loosened carbon from the combustion chamber. Stop the engine. Clean the area around the spark plug with compressed air.

4. Remove the spark plugs.

5. Remove the air cleaner and block the throttle and choke in the wide open position.

    NOTE: This ensures an adequate supply of air. It also prevents too much fuel from being drawn from the carburetor idle circuit, which could wash oil off the cylinder walls and lower the compression readings.

6. Disconnect the ignition system primary distributor lead. *Safety Caution:* Failure to disconnect the primary lead could result in a shock from one of the secondary wires. If the car uses an electronic ignition, check the service manual for the correct way to disconnect the system.

7. Insert the compression gauge firmly into the spark plug hole. Crank the engine through at least four compression strokes to obtain the highest possible reading on the gauge. (Check and record the compression readings in the space provided below.)

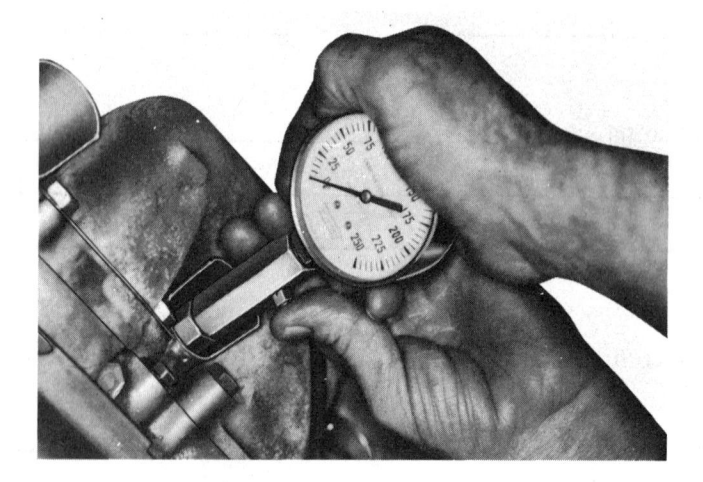

8. Test the compression in the remaining cylinders, following steps 6 and 7, and making a note of the highest compression point for each cylinder.

9. Install the spark plugs, tightening them by hand. Be sure that the gaskets are in place on the plugs.

10. Use a torque wrench and tighten the plugs to the correct torque.

11. Submit the recommended and the actual compression readings to your instructor.

NAME _____ SECTION _____ DATE _____ SCORE _____

NOTE: A cylinder that is below specifications and varies more than 20 pounds per square inch or 1 kilogram per square centimetre from the highest cylinder reading is considered abnormal. An abnormal reading along with low-speed missing indicates an improperly seated valve or worn or broken piston rings. Worn piston rings are indicated by low compression on the first stroke which tends to build up on the following strokes. A further indication of worn rings is an improved reading when oil is added to the cylinder. Valve problems are indicated by a low compression reading on the first stroke which does not rapidly build up on following strokes and is not changed by the addition of oil. Leaking head gaskets give nearly the same test results as valve problems but may also be recognized by coolant in the crankcase. Head gasket leakage between two cylinders will give low readings on each of the cylinders.

_____
Instructor's Check

Results (in psi or kPa):

Cylinder No.

1 _____ (1st) _____ (4th)

2 _____ (1st) _____ (4th)

3 _____ (1st) _____ (4th)

4 _____ (1st) _____ (4th)

5 _____ (1st) _____ (4th)

6 _____ (1st) _____ (4th)

7 _____ (1st) _____ (4th)

8 _____ (1st) _____ (4th)

NOTES

Date Completed _____ Instructor's Check _____

NAME_____ SECTION_____ DATE_____ SCORE_____

Chapter 15 PISTON ENGINE SERVICE
JOB SHEET 2

Adjust valves

Before you begin: Read Chapter 15 in *Auto Mechanics*.

Student _____ Section _____ Date _____

Make of Car _____ Model _____ Year _____

Time Started _____ Time Finished _____ Total Time _____

Flat Rate Time _____

Special Tools, Equipment, Parts, and Materials

Feeler gauge   _____

Valve cover gasket(s)   _____

Sealant   _____

_____   _____

_____

References

Manufacturer's Shop Manual _____

Repair Manual _____

Service Bulletin _____

Specifications

Look up the following valve adjustment specifications for the vehicle and record them in the spaces provided below.

Valves adjusted: Hot _____ or Cold _____

Measured at: Rocker Arm _____ Lifter and Cam (Overhead Cam) _____

Intake Valve Clearance _____

Exhaust Valve Clearance _____

Instructor's Check

61

Procedure

1. For a cold setting, allow the engine to cool down completely before starting work.

2. For a hot setting, run the engine until the normal operating temperature is reached. Set the throttle to the lowest idling speed.

3. Remove the valve cover(s).

4. In an I-head engine with adjustable rocker arms, valve lash is measured by inserting a feeler gauge between the rocker arm and valve stem

    NOTE: The clearance must be measured when the lifter is resting on the heel of the cam. If the valve is adjusted when it is not on the heel of the cam, a large error in the clearance will result. This could lead to damaged valves. The service manual will specify how to position the engine so that the valves are in the correct position for adjustment. A feeler gauge is selected that is the same as the clearance specification. If the feeler gauge does not slide into the space, the adjustment screw must be turned to increase the valve clearance. If the feeler gauge fits into the space too loosely, the adjustment screw must be turned to reduce the clearance. The feeler gauge should fit with a light drag.

5. Ball and stud rocker arm assemblies are adjusted by turning the nut on top of the stud.

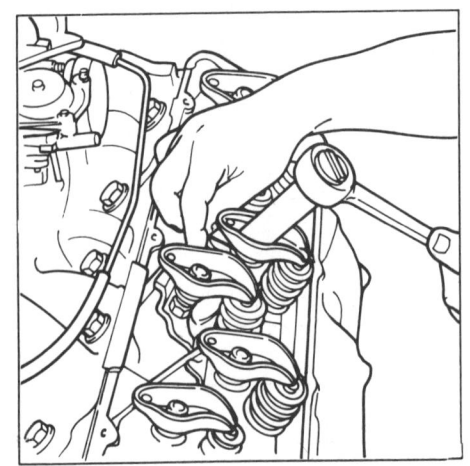

6. Most overhead camshaft engines have adjustable lifters or adjustable rocker arms. The feeler gauge is positioned between the valve stem and rocker arm. Loosen the lock nut and adjust the clearance by rotating the rocker arm adjustment screw.

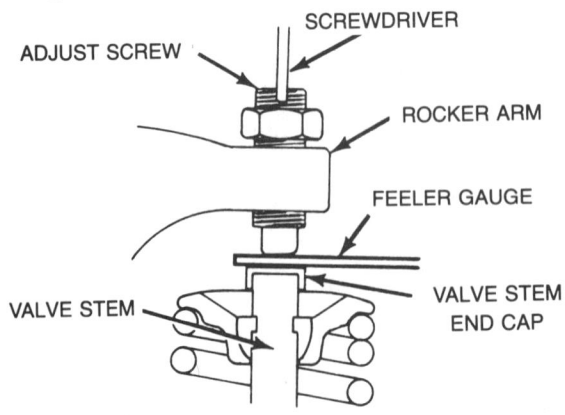

7. Some overhead camshaft engines use valve adjusting discs between the cam follower or lifter and the camshaft lobe. Thicker or thinner discs are installed by pushing down the follower and compressing the valve spring with a special tool. Use a small magnet to pull out the disc. Insert the feeler gauge between the cam and the lifter. Remember: the camshaft must be turned so the heel of the cam lobe is on the lifter.

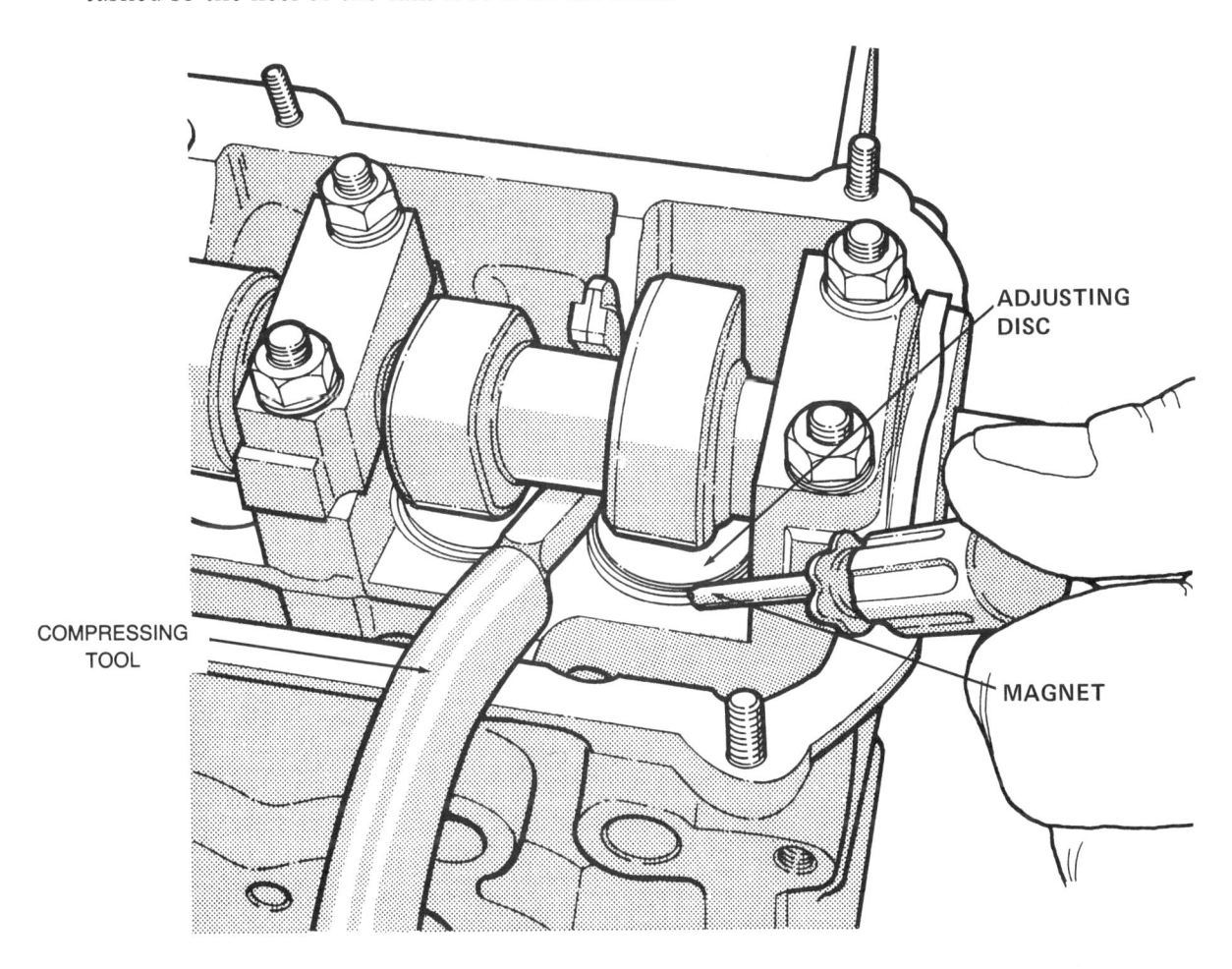

8. Using the above procedure, adjust all the other valves.

9. Clean all gasket surfaces.

10. Clean the valve cover thoroughly.

11. Oil lightly all moving parts of the rocker-arm assembly.

12. After the valves are adjusted, a new gasket is fitted on and the valve cover is replaced. (Use sealant if necessary.) Retaining screws are tightened to the correct torque with a torque wrench.

Date Completed_____ Instructor's Check_____

NAME_____ SECTION_____ DATE_____ SCORE_____

Chapter 16 ENGINE SIZE AND PERFORMANCE MEASUREMENT
ASSIGNMENT SHEET 15

Engine Measurement

Before you begin: Read Chapter 16 in *Auto Mechanics*. Look up the engine size specifications for your vehicle in an owner's manual. Record the information in the spaces provided below.

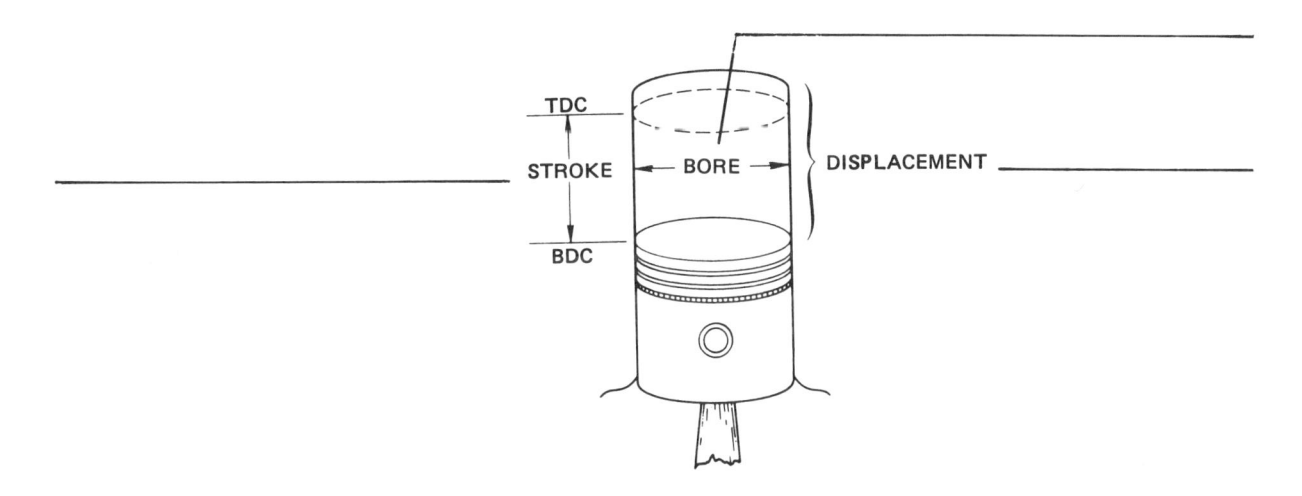

_____   TDC
                                                  STROKE |— BORE —| DISPLACEMENT _____
                                                  BDC

Applied Mathematics

1. Determine the amount of work done.

    PROBLEM: Determine how much work is done if a 650 pound engine is lifted 6 feet in the air with a chain hoist.

    SOLUTION: Distance x Force = Work

    6 feet x 650 pounds = _____

2. Determine the horsepower needed to move an object.

    PROBLEM: How much horsepower is needed to pull a stalled 1,750 pound automobile 5,000 feet in 6 minutes.

    SOLUTION: The distance (L) times the weight (W) divided by 33,000 foot-pounds times the time (T) = horsepower.

    Horsepower = $\dfrac{L \times W}{33,000 \times T}$ $\dfrac{5,000 \times 1,750}{33,000 \times 6}$ = _____

65

3. Calculate horsepower of an automobile engine.

   PROBLEM: Find the approximate brake horsepower (BHP) of a Thunderbird V-8 engine that, at 4,600 rpm, registers 135 pounds at the end of a Prony brake arm 2-1/2 feet long.

   SOLUTION: Find twice the product of π, the length (L) of the arm in feet, and number (N) of revolutions per minute, and the registered weight (W) in pounds; then divide the results by 33,000 foot-pounds.

   $$BHP = \frac{2\pi \times LNW}{33,000} \qquad BHP = \frac{6.28 \times 2.5 \times 135 \times 4,600}{33,000}$$

   BHP = _____

4. Determine the torque developed.

   PROBLEM: A starter motor develops a turning effort of 65 pounds on a flywheel that has a diameter of one foot. How much torque is delivered at the crankcase?

   SOLUTION: Torque is measured in pound-feet. The force (F) times the lever arm length (L) equals torque.

   Torque = F × L

   Torque = 65 × 0.50

   Torque = _____

5. Compute total piston displacement of an engine.

   PROBLEM: A 300-horsepower 1962 Corvette has a bore of 4.00 inches, a stroke of 3.25 inches, and a V-8 engine. What is the total displacement?

   SOLUTION: When D^2 = the bore squared, L = the stroke, and N = the number of cylinders, the total piston displacement is computed as follows:

   $$D = \frac{\pi \times D^2 \times L}{4} \times N$$

   $$PD = \frac{3.14 \times (4 \times 4) \times 3.25}{4} \times 8$$

   D = _____

NAME _____ SECTION _____ DATE _____ SCORE _____

6. Calculate compression ratio.

   PROBLEM: Calculate the compression ratio for a 1958 Plymouth Fury with a bore of 3.91 inches and a stroke of 3.31 inches. Allow combustion chamber space (CCS) or clearance volume of 4.84 cubic inches.

   SOLUTION: Compression ratio is the ratio of the total volume of the cylinder with the piston at bottom dead center (piston displacement plus clearance volume) to the volume of the combustion chamber when the piston is at top dead center (clearance volume).

   $$CR = \frac{\pi R^2 H + CCS}{CCS}$$

   $$CR = \frac{3.14 \times (1.96)^2 \times 3.31 + 4.84}{4.84}$$

   CR = _____

Review of New Terms

For each definition in Column 2, select the term in Column 1 that best matches its meaning. Write the identifying *letter* of the term in the Answer column.

Column 1	Column 2	Answer
A. Bore	1. The amount the air-fuel mixture is compressed during the compression stroke.	1. _____
B. Brake horsepower	2. The diameter of a cylinder.	2. _____
C. Compression ratio	3. A measure of how well an engine changes the chemical energy in gasoline to heat energy.	3. _____
D. Displacement	4. A turning or twisting effort or force.	4. _____
E. Horsepower	5. The cylinder volume displaced by the pistons of an engine.	5. _____
F. Stroke	6. The ratio of an engine's cylinder volume actually filled by air and fuel during engine operation.	6. _____
G. Thermal efficiency	7. The movement of the piston in the cylinder controlled and measured by the offset of the crankshaft.	7. _____
H. Torque	8. Power measured at the engine's flywheel.	8. _____
I. Vehicle efficiency	9. A measure of how well the power developed by the engine is used to drive the vehicle.	9. _____
J. Volumetric efficiency	10. A unit used to describe the power developed by an engine.	10. _____

NAME_____ SECTION_____ DATE_____ SCORE_____

Chapter 17 THE LUBRICATION SYSTEM
ASSIGNMENT SHEET 16

Oil Pump Part Identification

Before you begin: Read Chapter 17 in *Auto Mechanics*. Identify the parts of the gear-type oil pump in the spaces provided below.

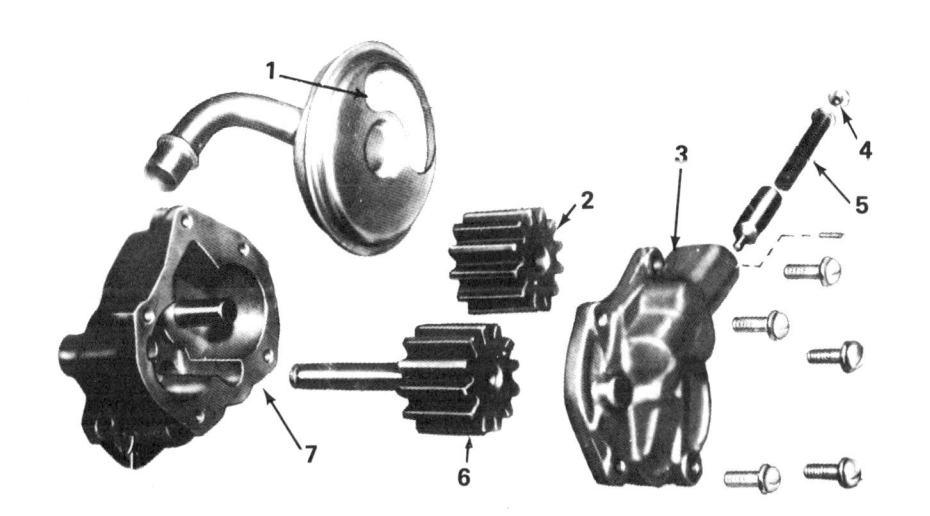

1. _____
2. _____
3. _____
4. _____
5. _____
6. _____
7. _____

Identify the parts of a rotor-type oil pump in the spaces provided below.

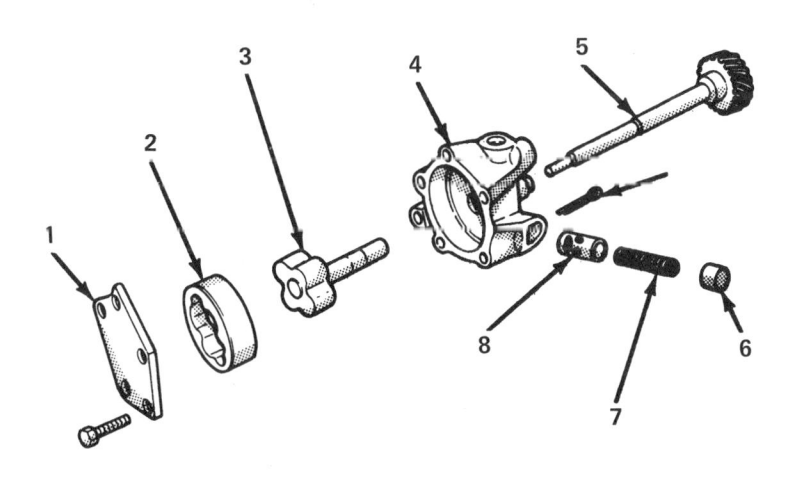

1. _____
2. _____
3. _____
4. _____
5. _____
6. _____
7. _____
8. _____

INDUSTRIAL ARTS DEPARTMENT
WICHITA HIGH SCHOOL EAST

Review of New Terms

For each definition in Column 2, select the term in Column 1 that best matches its meaning. Write the identifying *letter* of the term in the Answer column.

Column 1	Column 2	Answer
A. Oil additives	1. An instrument used to measure the amount of oil pressure in an engine.	1. _____
B. Oil filter	2. A device to filter out dirt and other foreign matter from the oil.	2. _____
C. Oil pan	3. Oil made from a material other than petroleum.	3. _____
D. Oil pressure gauge	4. A spring-loaded part used to regulate the pressure in the lubrication system.	4. _____
E. Pickup screen	5. Materials mixed with oil to improve its lubricating ability.	5. _____
F. Relief valve	6. The amount that oil thickness or thinness changes with changing temperatures.	6. _____
G. Service rating	7. A metal container covering the bottom of the engine used to store oil for lubrication.	7. _____
H. Synthetic oil	8. The thickness or thinness of an oil.	8. _____
I. Viscosity	9. A screen in the oil pan that prevents any large particles from entering the oil pump.	9. _____
J. Viscosity index	10. A system of determining how well an oil stands up under wear and tear, established by the American Petroleum Institute.	10. _____

NAME _____ SECTION _____ DATE _____ SCORE _____

Chapter 18 LUBRICATION SYSTEM SERVICE
JOB SHEET 3

Changing Engine Oil and Filter

Before you begin: Read Chapter 18 in *Auto Mechanics*.

Student _____ Section _____ Date _____

Make of Car _____ Model _____ Year _____

Time Started _____ Time Finished _____ Total Time _____

Flat Rate Time _____

Special Tools, Equipment, Parts, and Materials

Adjustable wrench   _____

New oil   _____

New oil filter   _____

Oil filter tool   _____

_____

References

Manufacturer's Shop Manual _____

Repair Manual _____

Service Bulletin _____

Specifications

Look up the recommended amount of oil required for this engine when the oil and filter are changed. Record the amount in the space provided below.

Oil Capacity _____

_____
Instructor's Check

Procedure

1. Warm up the engine to normal operating temperature.

2. Raise the vehicle on a lift or support on jack stands.

3. Set the emergency brake; put the transmission in "Park."

4. Use an oil drain pan that will hold five or six quarts. Look for the engine drain plug.

    Safety Caution: Do not confuse the engine drain plug with the transmission plug, which is located in the bottom of the transmission.

5. When the plug is located, place the correct size open-end wrench snugly on the drain plug. Have the pan ready. Turn the drain plug couterclockwise to loosen it. Pull it out quickly, allowing the oil to drain into the pan.

    Safety Caution: Be careful. The oil is hot!

6. While the oil is draining, locate the filter. Put a pan or drain under the filter, to catch the oil which will come out. Put the oil filter tool around the filter cartridge. Turn it counterclockwise with the tool until it can be turned by hand. Set the filter in the pan to drain and then throw it away.

7. With a rag, wipe the mounting surface on the engine where the filter fits. Put a light coat of grease or oil on the rubber gasket of the new filter. Fill the new filter with oil. Screw the filter on by turning it clockwise. Tighten it snugly by hand. Do not use the tool to tighten it.

8. Allow the oil time to drain. Replace the drain plug, turning it clockwise by hand. Tighten it with the wrench.

    NOTE: If torque specifications are available, use a torque wrench to tighten the drain plug.

9. Remove the oil filler cap. Push the oil spout into an oil can and pour oil into the engine until the recommended amount has been added.

    NOTE: An additional amount of oil will be required if the filter is changed.

    Check the oil level with the dipstick. Replace the filler cap. Check the drain plug for leaks.

10. After the oil change is completed and the required amount of oil is added, start the engine. Watch the filter for leaks. If it leaks, shut off the engine quickly. Either the filter is not tight enough or the filter gasket is defective. Take it off, clean up the gasket area, and try again. Installing another filter may be necessary to solve the problem.

11. Lower the vehicle.

Date Completed _____   Instructor's Check _____

NAME_____ SECTION_____ DATE_____ SCORE_____

Chapter 18 LUBRICATION SYSTEM SERVICE
JOB SHEET 4

Overhaul an Oil Pump

Before you begin: Read Chapter 18 in *Auto Mechanics*.

Student _____ Section _____ Date _____

Make of Car _____ Model _____ Year _____

Time Started _____ Time Finished _____ Total Time _____

Flat Rate Time _____

Special Tools, Equipment, Parts, and Materials

Straightedge

Feeler gauge

Outside micrometer

Inside micrometer

References

Manufacturer's Shop Manual _____

Repair Manual _____

Service Bulletin _____

Specifications

Look up the following clearance specifications for the pump being serviced and record them in the spaces provided below.

End clearance _____ Side clearance _____

Others _____

Instructor's Check

Procedure

1. Disassemble the oil pump and relief valve assembly and wash it in solvent.

2. Inspect each of the parts for wear.

    NOTE: The mating face of the oil pump cover should be smooth. If it is excessively scratched or grooved, it should be replaced.

3. Test cover-to-rotor wear by laying a straightedge across the cover surface. Use a feeler gauge to determine cover flatness.

    NOTE: No feeler gauge thicker than the service manual's specification should be able to slide under the straightedge.

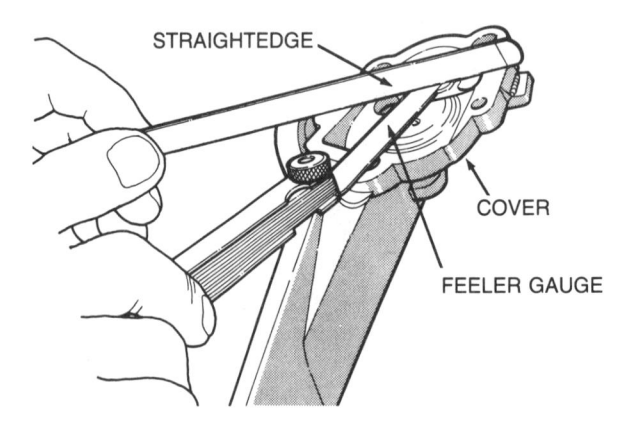

4. Measure the diameter and thickness of the outer rotor with an outside micrometer. If the dimensions are less than specified in the service manual, replace the outer rotor.

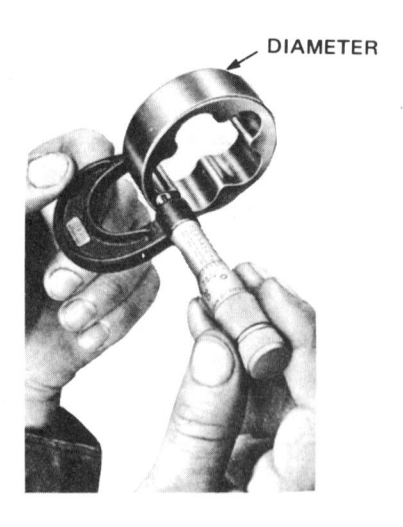

NAME_____ SECTION_____ DATE_____ SCORE_____

5. Measure the inner rotor thickness with an inside micrometer. If the dimensions are less than specifications, replace the inner rotor.

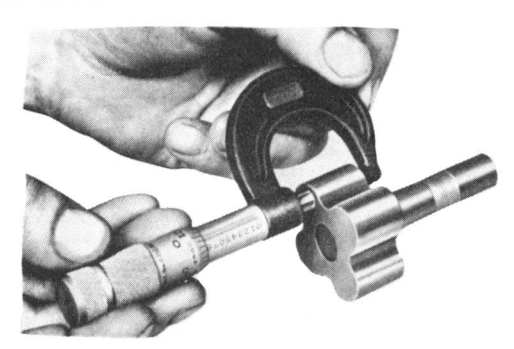

6. Measure the clearance between the outer rotor and the pump body with a feeler gauge. If the measurement is larger than the specifications call for, replace the pump body.

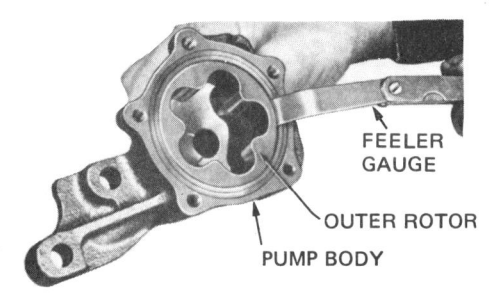

7. Measure the clearance between the outer and inner rotor with a feeler gauge. If the clearance is beyond specifications, replace the inner and outer rotors.

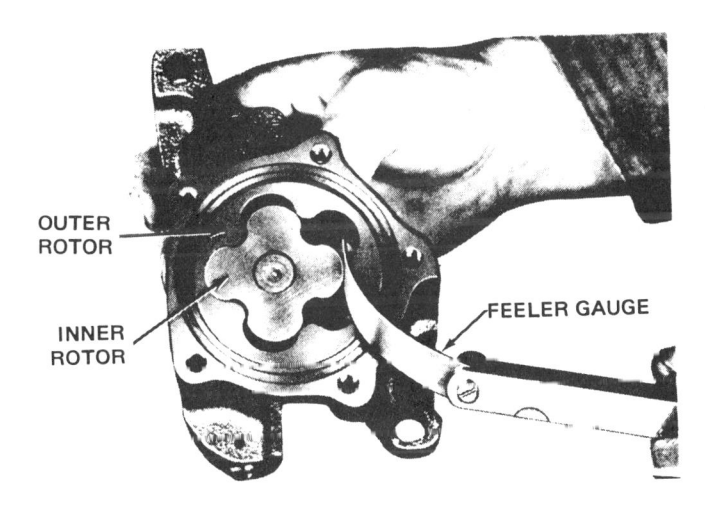

8. Place a straightedge across the pump housing over the assembled rotors and measure the clearance over the rotors with a feeler gauge. A measurement beyond specifications means that the pump body should be replaced.

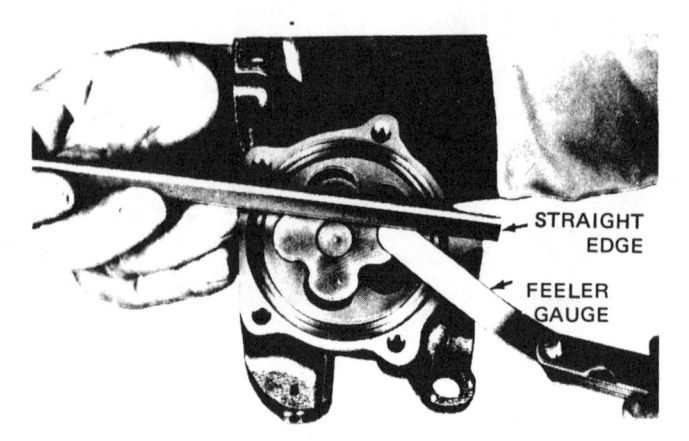

9. Inspect the relief ball or plunger and bore for scratches and scoring. If there is any evidence of damage, replace the plunger or ball.

10. Measure the length of the relief valve spring and compare against specifications. Replace springs that fail to meet specifications.

11. Reassemble components that pass these tests. Check the relief valve for free operation in its bore. If it moves freely, the retainer that holds the relief valve assembly in its bore may be replaced.

_____
Instructor's Check

NOTES

Date Completed _____ INSTRUCTOR'S Check _____

NAME _____ SECTION _____ DATE _____ SCORE _____

Chapter 19 THE COOLING SYSTEM
ASSIGNMENT SHEET 17

Cooling System Part Identification

Before you begin: Read Chapter 19 in *Auto Mechanics*. Identify the parts of the coolant pump in the spaces provided below.

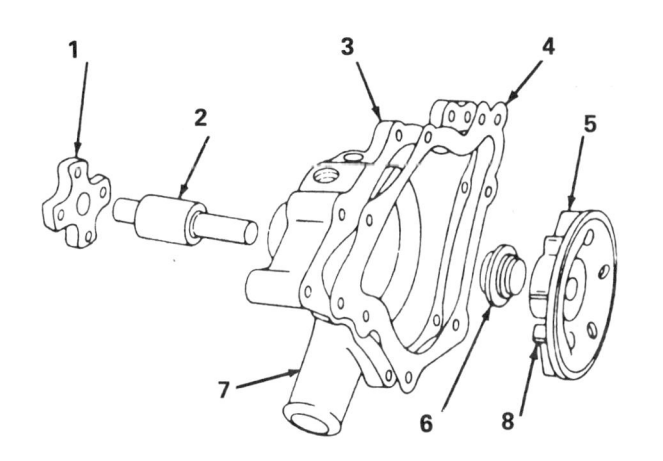

1. _____
2. _____
3. _____
4. _____
5. _____
6. _____
7. _____
8. _____

Identify the parts of the thermostat in the spaces provided below.

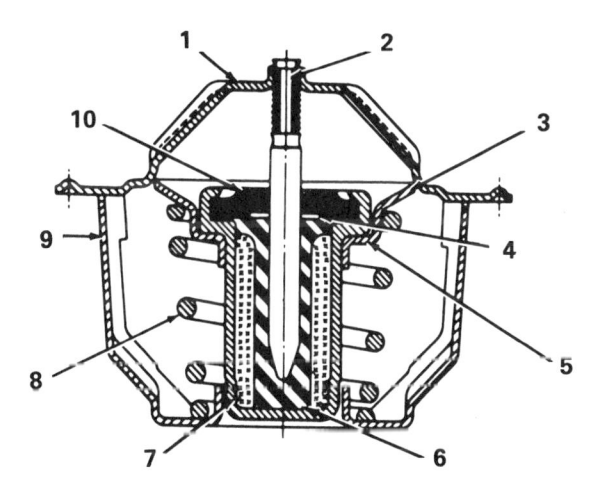

1. _____
2. _____
3. _____
4. _____
5. _____
6. _____
7. _____
8. _____
9. _____
10. _____

77

Review of New Terms

For each definition in Column 2, select the term in Column 1 that best matches its meaning. Write the identifying *letter* of the term in the Answer column.

Column 1	Column 2	Answer
A. Air pump	1. Liquid used in liquid cooling system to carry away heat; usually a mixture of ethylene glycol and water.	1. _____
B. Coolant	2. Pump used with an air cooling system to force air around hot parts.	2. _____
C. Cooling fins	3. A system connected to the radiator that catches overflow and sends it back into the radiator.	3. _____
D. Fan	4. Metal objects used to move heat away from parts of an air-cooled engine.	4. _____
E. Heat sensor	5. The part on the top of the radiator used to regulate radiator pressure and vacuum.	5. _____
F. Pressure cap	6. The part on the instrument panel that is used to warn the driver of too high a temperature in the engine.	6. _____
G. Recovery system	7. Passages in the cylinder block and head for coolant flow.	7. _____
H. Temperature warning light	8. A device in the cooling system used to control the flow of coolant.	8. _____
I. Thermostat	9. A part in the block used to monitor engine temperature.	9. _____
J. Water jackets	10. A device used to direct air over the radiator when the automobile is not moving.	10. _____

NAME _____ SECTION _____ DATE _____ SCORE _____

Chapter 20 COOLING SYSTEM SERVICE
JOB SHEET 5

Remove and Replace a Thermostat

Before you begin: Read Chapter 20 in *Auto Mechanics.*

Student _____ Section _____ Date _____

Make of Car _____ Model _____ Year _____

Time Started _____ Time Finished _____ Total Time _____

Flat Rate Time _____

Special Tools, Equipment, Parts, and Materials

Putty knife or scraper   Thermostat-housing gasket

Coolant drain pan   Emery cloth, No. 00

Replacement thermostat   _____

Coolant   _____

_____

_____

References

Manufacturer's Shop Manual _____

Repair Manual _____

Service Bulletin _____

Specifications

Look up the following specifications and record them in the spaces provided below.

Thermostat setting _____   Coolant capacity _____

Coolant type _____

_____
Instructor's Check

79

Procedure

1. Raise the vehicle on a hoist or support on jack stands.

   Safety Caution: Make sure the engine is cold to avoid burns from hot coolant.

2. Remove radiator drain plug to drain coolant.

   Safety Caution: Coolant solution is poisonous. Swallowing it can cause serious illness or death.

3. Remove upper radiator hose by removing the two hose clamps.

4. Remove cap screws that hold thermostat housing to front of engine.

5. Lift off the thermostat housing and gasket.

6. Pull the thermostat out of the engine.

7. Use a gasket scraper to clean the surfaces on the engine and on the thermostat housing.

8. Check the number and temperature setting on the old thermostat and compare it with the replacement. If they are not the same, show your instructor.

9. Install the new thermostat back into the engine.

10. Install the thermostat housing using a new gasket.

11. Replace and tighten the thermostat housing cap screws with a torque wrench.

12. Install the radiator hose and hose clamps.

13. Replace and tighten the radiator drain plug.

14. Fill the cooling system with the recommended type and amount of coolant.

15. Start the engine and check for leaks.

16. Check the engine operating temperature to be sure the thermostat is working properly.

17. Lower the vehicle.

Date Completed _____ Instructor's Check _____

NAME _____ SECTION _____ DATE _____ SCORE _____

Chapter 20 COOLING SYSTEM SERVICE
JOB SHEET 6

Replace Radiator Hoses

Before you begin: Read Chapter 20 in *Auto Mechanics*.

Student _____ Section _____ Date _____

Make of Car _____ Model _____ Year _____

Time Started _____ Time Finished _____ Total Time _____

Flat Rate Time _____

Special Tools, Equipment, Parts, and Materials

Scale, 12 inch [150mm]   Coolant drain pan

Screwdriver   _____

Hose clamps   _____

_____

_____

References

Manufacturer's Shop Manual _____

Repair Manual _____

Service Bulletin _____

Specifications

Look up the following specifications and record them in the spaces provided below.

Radiator hose diameter _____ Coolant capacity _____

Coolant type _____

_____

Instructor's Check

Procedure

1. Raise the vehicle on a hoist or position it on jack stands.

    Safety Caution: Allow the engine to cool to avoid burns from hot coolant.

2. Place a pan under the radiator and remove the radiator drain plug.

3. Remove radiator hose clamps from the hose to be replaced.

4. Work the radiator hose back and forth to free it at both ends.

5. Remove the radiator hose from the block and radiator.

6. Use emery cloth to clean the connectors where the new hose will fit.

7. Select the proper diameter and length of the new radiator hose.

8. Install the new radiator hose in position.

9. Install new radiator hose clamps on the hose. Position the clamps about ¼ inch [6.35mm] from the ends of the hose.

10. Replace the radiator drain plug.

11. Lower the vehicle.

12. Refill the cooling system with the recommended type and amount of coolant.

13. Start the engine and allow it to warm up. Check the new hose for leaks.

_____
Instructor's Check

NOTES

Date Completed _____ Instructor's Check _____

NAME _____ SECTION _____ DATE _____ SCORE _____

Chapter 21 THE FUEL SYSTEM
ASSIGNMENT SHEET 18

Fuel System Parts Identification

Before you begin: Read Chapter 21 in *Auto Mechanics*. Identify the parts of a fuel tank using the spaces provided below.

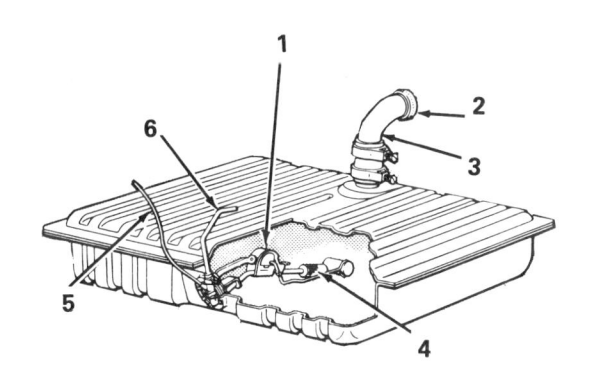

1. _____
2. _____
3. _____
4. _____
5. _____
6. _____

Identify the parts of the fuel pump using the spaces provided below.

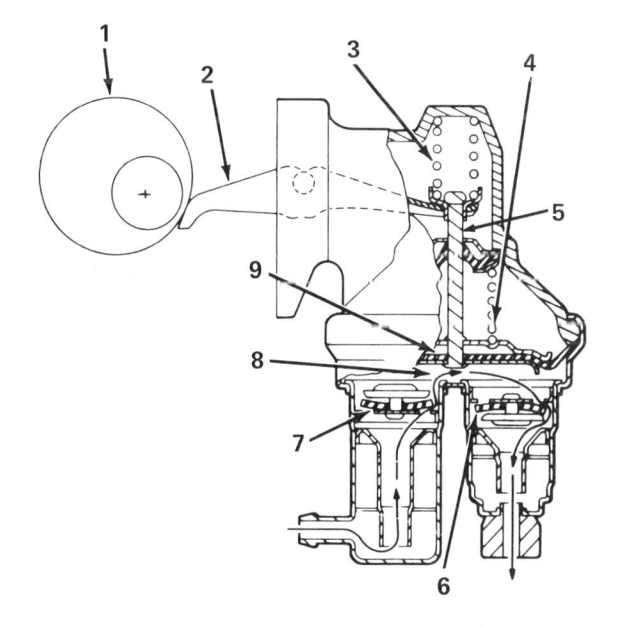

1. _____
2. _____
3. _____
4. _____
5. _____
6. _____
7. _____
8. _____
9. _____

83

Carburetor Parts Identification

Identify the parts of the carburetor using the spaces provided below.

1. _____
2. _____
3. _____
4. _____
5. _____
6. _____
7. _____

Draw arrows to show air and fuel flow through an idle circuit and use the spaces below to explain how the circuit works.

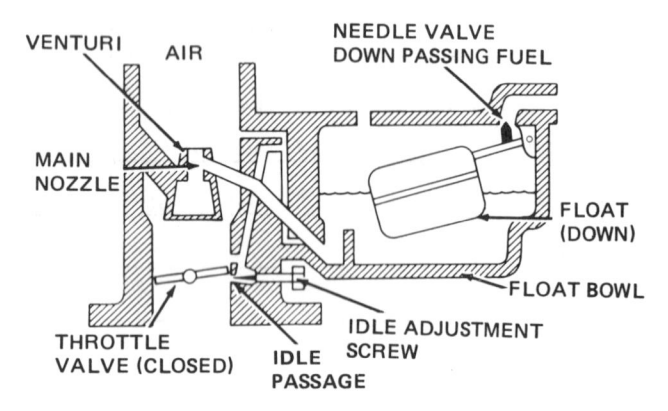

_____
_____
_____
_____
_____
_____

Carburetor Operation

Draw arrows on the figure below to show air and fuel flow in a low speed circuit. Use the spaces below to explain how it works.

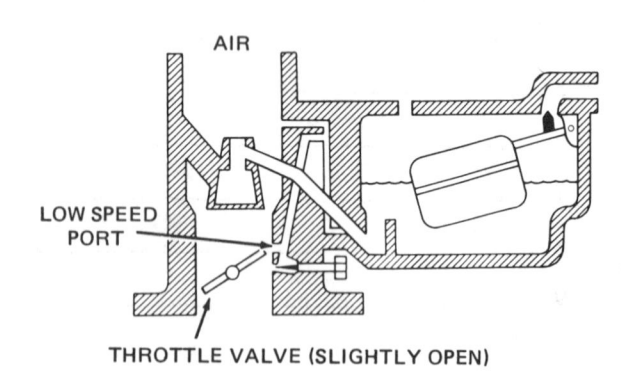

_____
_____
_____
_____
_____
_____
_____

NAME _____ SECTION _____ DATE _____ SCORE _____

Draw arrows on the figure below to show air and fuel flow in a main metering circuit. Use the spaces below to explain how it works.

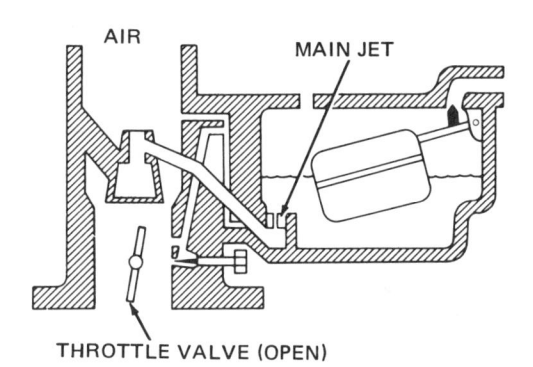

Draw arrows on the figure below to show air and fuel flow in a high speed circuit. Use the spaces below to explain how it works.

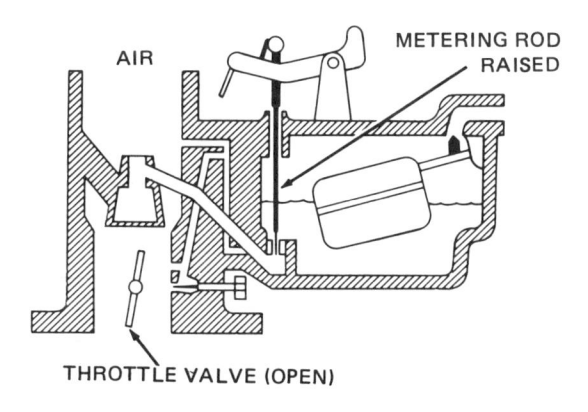

Draw arrows on the figure below to show air and fuel flow in an accelerator circuit. Use the spaces below to explain how it works.

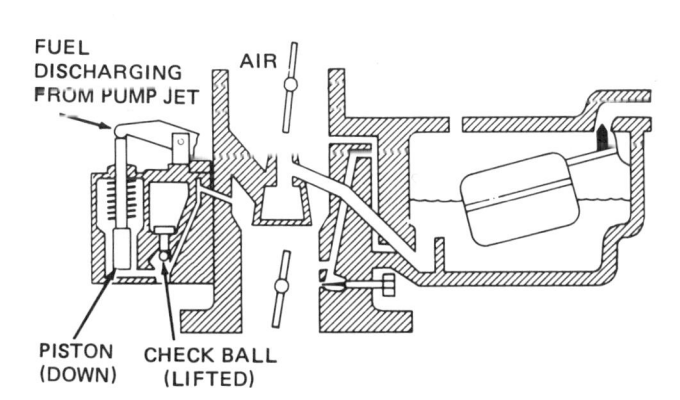

85

Review of New Terms

For each definition in Column 2, select the term in Column 1 that best matches its meaning. Write the identifying *letter* of the term in the Answer column.

Column 1

A. Atomization
B. Choke circuit
C. De-icers
D. Detonation
E. Fuel injection
F. Octane
G. Preignition
H. Supercharger
I. Turbocharger
J. Volatility
K. Needle valve
L. Injection pump
M. Mechanical injector nozzle
N. Mechanical fuel injection

Column 2

1. Chemicals added to the fuel to prevent ice from forming in the carburetor.
2. A rating of a fuel's antiknock ability.
3. The ease with which a fuel vaporizes.
4. Abnormal combustion in which something other than the ignition system explodes the air-fuel mixture.
5. Breaking the liquid fuel into small drops.
6. A pump used to force air into an engine.
7. A circuit in the carburetor used for cold starts.
8. A fuel mixing device that places the fuel directly into the cylinders or intake manifold.
9. A supercharger driven by the exhaust gas of an engine.
10. Abnormal combustion in which a portion of the mixture explodes during combustion.
11. Diesel fuel injection system in which a single pump provides fuel to all cylinders in a manner similar to that used in an ignition distributor.
12. Fuel injection component that delivers fuel to the injector nozzle.
13. Device mounted in the diesel engine combustion chamber and used to spray fuel for ignition.
14. Valve in an injector nozzle that opens to allow fuel to spray into the combustion chamber.

Answer

1. _____
2. _____
3. _____
4. _____
5. _____
6. _____
7. _____
8. _____
9. _____
10. _____
11. _____
12. _____
13. _____
14. _____

NAME _____ SECTION _____ DATE _____ SCORE _____

Chapter 22 FUEL SYSTEM SERVICE
JOB SHEET 7

Service an Air Cleaner

Before you begin: Read Chapter 22 in *Auto Mechanics*.

Student _____ Section _____ Date _____

Make of Car _____ Model _____ Year _____

Time Started _____ Time Finished _____ Total Time _____

Flat Rate Time _____

Special Tools, Equipment, Parts, and Materials

Replacement air filter   _____

Eye protection   _____

_____   _____

References

Manufacturer's Shop Manual _____

Repair Manual _____

Service Bulletin _____

                                                _____
                                                Instructor's Check

Procedure

1. Unscrew the wing nut on the air cleaner cover. Remove the cover.

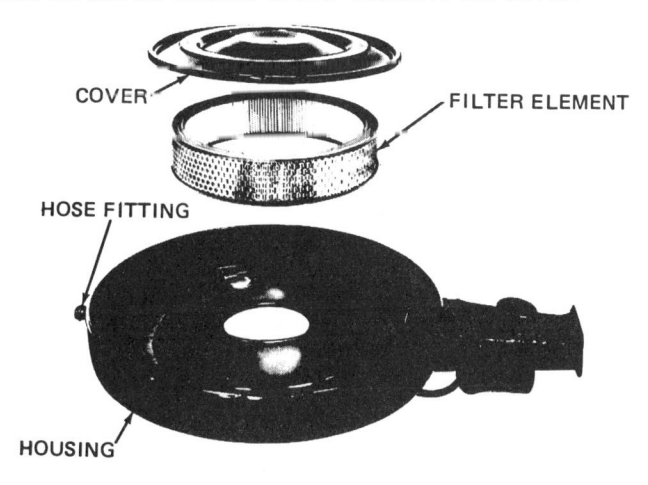

2. Lift out the filter element.

   NOTE: A dusty paper element air cleaner can be cleaned by blowing compressed air through the element from the inside out. Use low pressure and hold the air nozzle at least three inches from the element to avoid rupturing the element. An extremely dirty or oil-soaked element should be replaced.

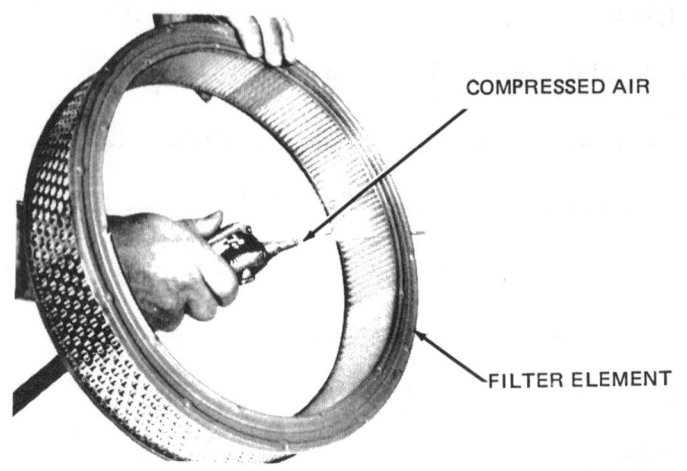

3. To service a polyurethane element, remove the cover wing nut, cover, and filter element. Visually check the element for tears or rips and replace if necessary. Clean all dirt and grime from the air cleaner bottom and cover.

   NOTE: Inspect, clean, and oil the element regularly, depending upon how dirty the air is.

4. Remove the support screen and wash the element in kerosene or mineral spirits. Squeeze out excess solvent.

   Safety Caution: Do not use a hot degreaser, acetone, or any solvent containing acetone. Dip the element into light engine oil and squeeze out the excess oil. Do not shake, swing, or wring the element. The polyurethane material may tear.

5. Install the element on the screen support. Using a new gasket, replace the air cleaner body over the carburetor air horn. Place the element in the air cleaner. Take care that the lower lip of the element is properly placed in the assembly.

   NOTE: If the filter material is folded or creased in any manner, it may cause a bad seal. Make sure in replacing the cover that the upper lip of the element is in the proper position.

6. On units that have one, remove and clean the flame arrestor with a suitable solvent.

7. Replace the cover and wing nut.

Date Completed _____ Instructor's Check _____

NAME _____ SECTION _____ DATE _____ SCORE _____

Chapter 22 FUEL SYSTEM SERVICE
JOB SHEET 8

Test a Fuel Pump

Before you begin: Read Chapter 22 in *Auto Mechanics*.

Student _____ Section _____ Date _____

Make of Car _____ Model _____ Year _____

Time Started _____ Time Finished _____ Total Time _____

Flat Rate Time _____

Special Tools, Equipment, Parts, and Materials

Fuel pump tester   _____

Eye protection   _____

_____

References

Manufacturer's Shop Manual _____

Repair Manual _____

Service Bulletin _____

Specifications

Look up the fuel pump specifications for the vehicle on which you are working and record them in the spaces provided below.

Fuel Pump Volume _____   Fuel Pump Pressure _____

_____
Instructor's Check

Procedure

1. Remove the air cleaner and disconnect the main fuel line at the carburetor, or at the "T" or junction if there is more than one carburetor.

2. Mount the tester to the carburetor inlet with the gauge vertical and facing the operator. Use adapters supplied with the tester.

3. Connect the fuel line to the fitting on the fuel pump tester hose.

4. Close the shutoff valve on the fuel discharge hose of the tester.

5. Start the engine and adjust the speed to approximately 500 rpm, unless specified otherwise. Insert the volume test hose into a graduated container and open the shutoff clamp. When fuel reaches the 4 ounce level in the container, submerge the end of the hose in the fuel and look for bubbles.

   Safety Caution: Use care to prevent combustion from fuel spillage.

   Note the time required to pump one pint of fuel. Then close the shutoff clamp securely.

   Safety Caution: Be sure to dispose of fuel in the graduated container to avoid fire hazard.

6. With the engine still running at test speed, note the gauge pressure reading on the fuel pump tester.

7. Compare volume and pressure test readings with the vehicle's specifications.

   NOTE: If pressure is too low or too high or if it changes a great deal at different speeds, the pump should be replaced

8. Remove the gauge and reconnect the fuel line to the carburetor.

9. Inspect fuel lines for kinks and bends and check all connections for leaks.

Instructor's Check

NOTES

Date Completed_____ Instructor's Check_____

NAME _____ SECTION _____ DATE _____ SCORE _____

Chapter 23 ELECTRICAL SYSTEMS AND FUNDAMENTALS
ASSIGNMENT SHEET 19

Electrical Circuits

Before you begin: Read Chapter 23 in *Auto Mechanics*. In the spaces provided identify the circuit below and describe its purpose.

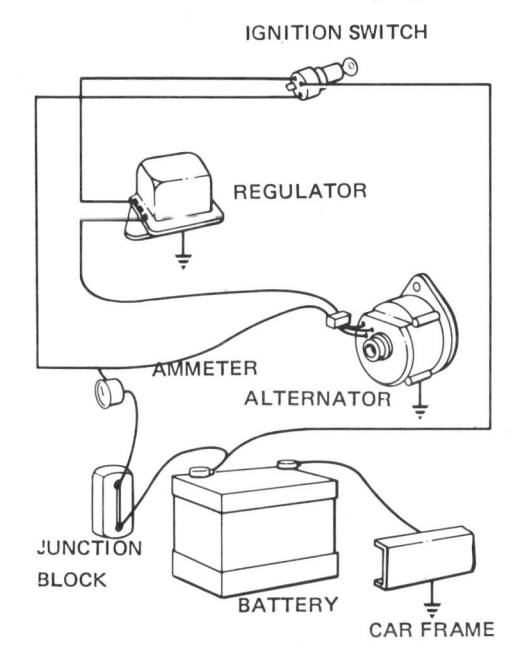

1. _____

In the spaces provided identify the circuit below and describe its purpose.

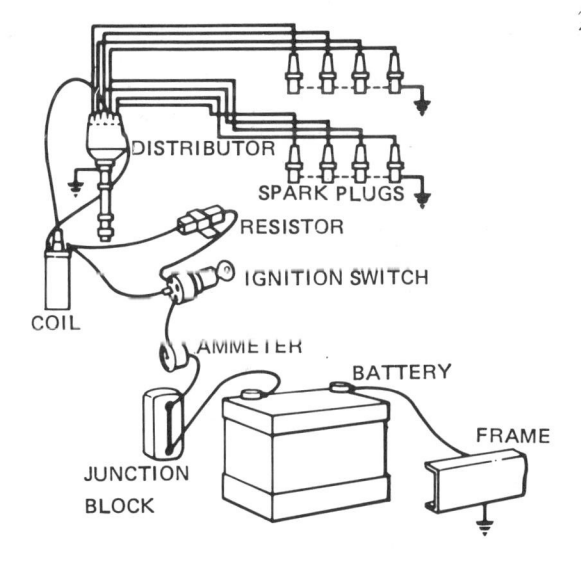

2. _____

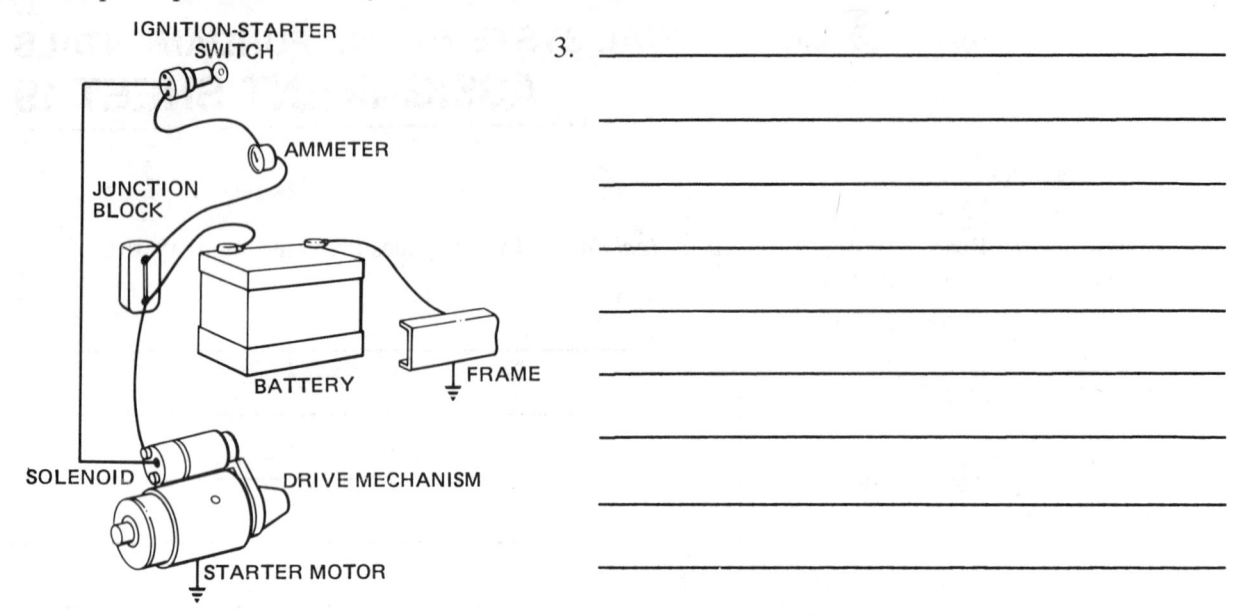

In the spaces provided identify the circuit below and describe its purpose.

3. _____

IGNITION-STARTER SWITCH
AMMETER
JUNCTION BLOCK
BATTERY
FRAME
SOLENOID
DRIVE MECHANISM
STARTER MOTOR

In the spaces provided identify the circuit below and describe its purpose.

4. _____

LIGHT SWITCH
TAIL LIGHTS
DIMMER SWITCH
HEAD LAMPS
BEAM INDICATOR LAMP
PARKING LIGHTS

92

Review of New Terms

For each definition in Column 2, select the term in Column 1 that best matches its meaning. Write the identifying *letter* of the term in the Answer column.

Column 1

A. Atom
B. Conductor
C. Current
D. Diode
E. Electronics
F. Induction
G. Insulator
H. Magnetic field
I. Semiconductor
J. Transistor
K. Printed circuit

Column 2

1. The transfer of energy from one object to another without the objects touching.
2. A semiconductor device used to control current flow.
3. A semiconductor that allows current flow in only one direction.
4. The small particle that is the basis of all matter.
5. A branch of electricity concerned with the flow of electronics through vacuum tubes and semiconductors.
6. A material that allows electrical current flow.
7. Tiny solid state devices that are half conductor and half insulator.
8. A material that prevents the flow of electricity.
9. The flow of electrons in an electrical circuit.
10. Printed board, which in place of wiring, has thin metallic conductors on one side.
11. An area of force surrounding a magnet.

Answer

1. _____
2. _____
3. _____
4. _____
5. _____
6. _____
7. _____
8. _____
9. _____
10. _____
11. _____

NAME _____ SECTION _____ DATE _____ SCORE _____

Chapter 24 STORAGE BATTERY
ASSIGNMENT SHEET 20

Battery Parts and Operation

Before you begin: Read Chapter 24 in *Auto Mechanics*. Write the names of the chemical symbols in the proper spaces of the figure below and describe the operation of the battery in the spaces provided.

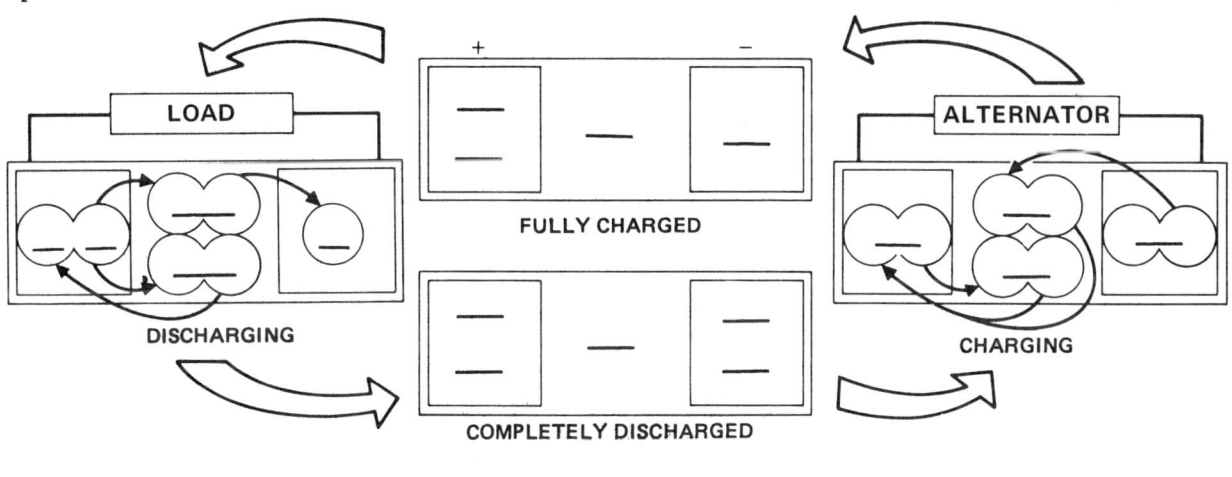

_____
_____
_____
_____
_____

Identify the plate groups and separators in the spaces provided below.

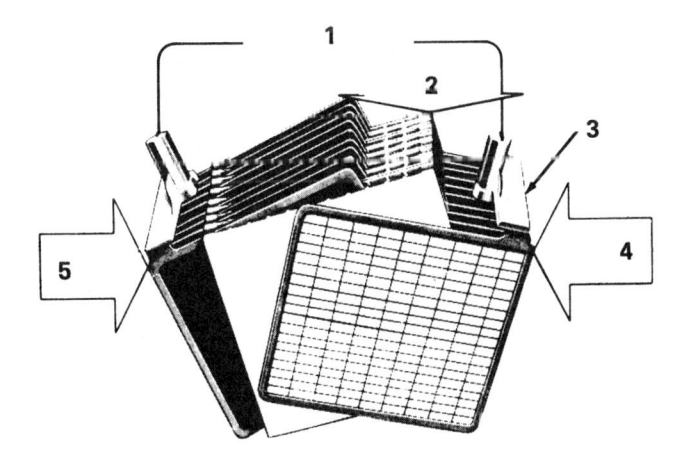

1. _____
2. _____
3. _____
4. _____
5. _____

Identify the battery parts in the spaces provided below.

1. _____
2. _____
3. _____
4. _____
5. _____

Review of New Terms

For each definition in Column 2, select the term in Column 1 that best matches its meaning. Write the identifying *letter* of the term in the Answer column.

Column 1

A. Cell
B. Deep cycling
C. Electrolyte
D. Overcharging
E. Plate
F. Separators
G. Sponge lead
H. Twenty-hour rating
I. Voltage rating
J. Watt

Column 2

1. A condition in which the battery is severely discharged before it is recharged.
2. The part of the battery on which the active material is spread.
3. A test of a battery's capacity to deliver current for twenty-four hours.
4. A test of how many volts a battery can deliver.
5. The active material on the negative plates in a cell.
6. A basic unit of the battery capable of developing about 2 volts.
7. A condition in which the battery is charged at too high rate.
8. An electrical unit of power computed by multiplying volts times amperes.
9. Sheets of insulation placed between the plates of a battery.
10. The acid solution in a battery cell.

Answer

1. _____
2. _____
3. _____
4. _____
5. _____
6. _____
7. _____
8. _____
9. _____
10. _____

NAME _____ SECTION _____ DATE _____ SCORE _____

Chapter 25 STORAGE BATTERY SERVICE
JOB SHEET 9

Battery Hydrometer Test

Before you begin: Read Chapter 25 in *Auto Mechanics*.

Student _____ Section _____ Date _____

Make of Car _____ Model _____ Year _____

Time Started _____ Time Finished _____ Total Time _____

Flat Rate Time _____

Special Tools, Equipment, Parts, and Materials

Battery hydrometer with a
temperature/correction scale

Brush or cloth

Baking soda

Eye protection

References

Manufacturer's Shop Manual _____

Repair Manual _____

Service Bulletin _____

Instructor's Check

Procedure

1. Clean the top of the battery with a brush or cloth saturated in a solution of baking soda, or ammonia, and water. Do not let the alkali solution leak inside of the battery.

    Safety Caution: Battery servicing can be dangerous unless the mechanic takes certain safety precautions. Since electrolyte contains sulphuric acid, if it is spilled, it will damage clothing, upholstery, or paint. More important, it is extremely harmful if spilled on the skin or splashed in the eyes. Safety glasses must always be worn when servicing batteries. If electrolyte is splashed in the eyes, flush them with cool clean water immediately for about five minutes and notify a doctor.

2. Unscrew the caps on the battery cells.

3. Place the hydrometer into the cell through the vent cap hole. Squeeze the bulb and release to suck electrolyte into the glass tube.

    NOTE: Numbered marks on the float allow the mechanic to note its level. On the specific scale, pure water is 1.000. Numbers bigger the 1.000 mean a higher specific gravity or more sulphuric acid. Most hydrometer scales read from 1.160 to 1.320 in gradations of 0.005.

4. To read a hydrometer, hold it vertically and carefully suck electrolyte into the hydrometer about halfway up the glass tube. Then sight directly across the electrolyte level to the marking on the float that lines up with the electrolyte level. Note and record the number on the float. Repeat this procedure for each of the other cells.

Specific Gravity

Cell 1 _____	Cell 4 _____
Cell 2 _____	Cell 5 _____
Cell 3 _____	Cell 6 _____

5. If the specific gravity is below 1.225, the battery should be recharged. A reading of 1.250 to 1.300 indicates that the battery is in satisfactory condition. If the reading is over 1.300, consult with your instructor, for adjustments should be made in the electrolytic solution.

6. Write in the percentage that represents this battery's state of charge _____

Date Completed _____   Instructor's Check _____

NAME _____ SECTION _____ DATE _____ SCORE _____

Chapter 25 STORAGE BATTERY SERVICE
JOB SHEET 10

Battery Load Testing

Before you begin: Read Chapter 25 in *Auto Mechanics*.

Student _____ Section _____ Date _____

Make of Car _____ Model _____ Year _____

Time Started _____ Time Finished _____ Total Time _____

Flat Rate Time _____

Special Tools, Equipment, Parts, and Materials

Battery Load Tester

Eye protection

References

Manufacturer's Shop Manual _____

Repair Manual _____

Service Bulletin _____

Specifications

Look up the following specification and record it in the space provided below.

Battery ampere-hour rating _____

_____
Instructor's Check

Procedure

Safety Caution: On vented batteries some of this gas escapes through the vent plugs. If ventilation around the battery is poor, an explosive mixture can remain around the battery for several hours after it has been charged. A spark or flame can ignite the mixture and cause an explosion.

Charge and service batteries in a well-ventilated area. Avoid breaking any live circuits that may cause a spark around the battery. Attach booster or jumper cables, tester, and charger leads carefully to avoid a loose connection that could cause a spark. Do not smoke near a battery.

1. Connect the load tester to the battery following instructions on the tester. Make sure the ammeter and load leads are connected to the correct battery post. Batteries with side terminals require special adapters for this connection.

2. Turn the load control on the tester until the reading is three times the ampere-hour rating of the battery.

3. Hold the load for 15 seconds while observing the tester ammeter.

4. Record the voltage registered on the tester voltmeter. The battery voltage should not drop below 9.5 volts. Write the voltage in the space provided. Voltage _____

5. A battery that fails to hold a charge and fails the load test should be replaced.

6. A battery that passes the load test is in satisfactory condition. Check one: the battery passed _____ failed _____

7. Disconnect the tester leads from the battery.

_____
Instructor's Check

NOTES

Date Completed _____   Instructor's Check _____

NAME _____ SECTION _____ DATE _____ SCORE _____

Chapter 26 THE STARTING SYSTEM
ASSIGNMENT SHEET 21

Starter Motor Parts Identification

Before you begin: Read Chapter 26 in *Auto Mechanics*. Identify the parts of the starter motor in the spaces provided below.

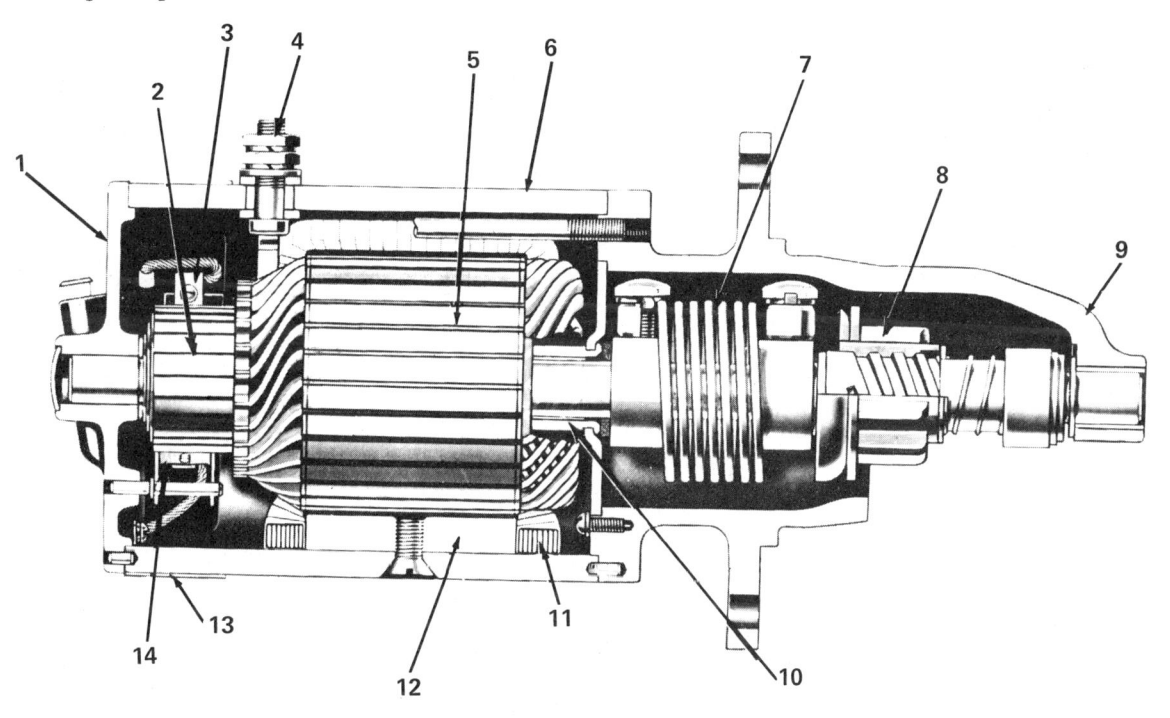

1. _____
2. _____
3. _____
4. _____
5. _____
6. _____
7. _____
8. _____
9. _____
10. _____
11. _____
12. _____
13. _____
14. _____

101

Starter Motor Circuits

Complete the circuits for each of the starter motors shown below by drawing lines representing the wires.

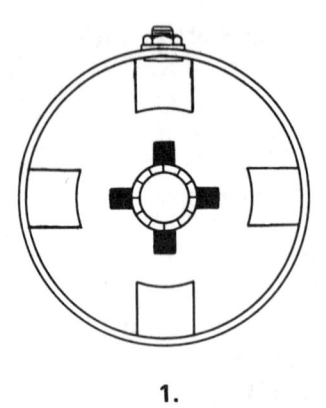

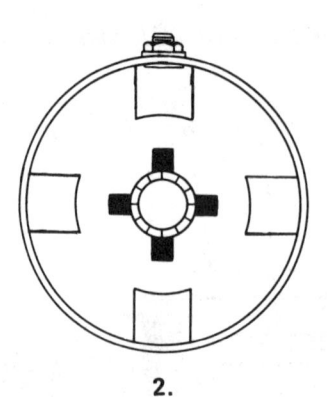

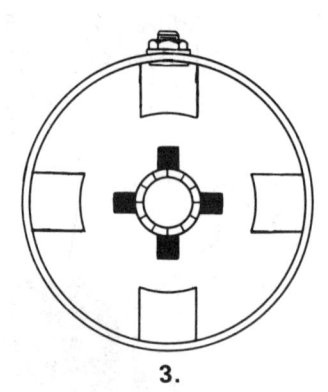

1.

2.

3.

Starter Motor Drives

In the spaces provided below identify the parts of the starter drives.

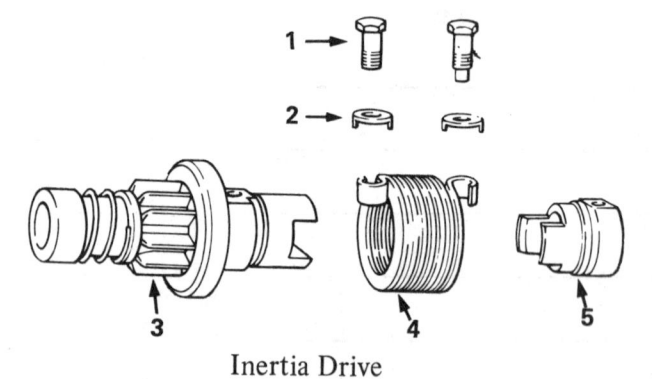

Inertia Drive

1. _____   4. _____

2. _____   5. _____

3. _____

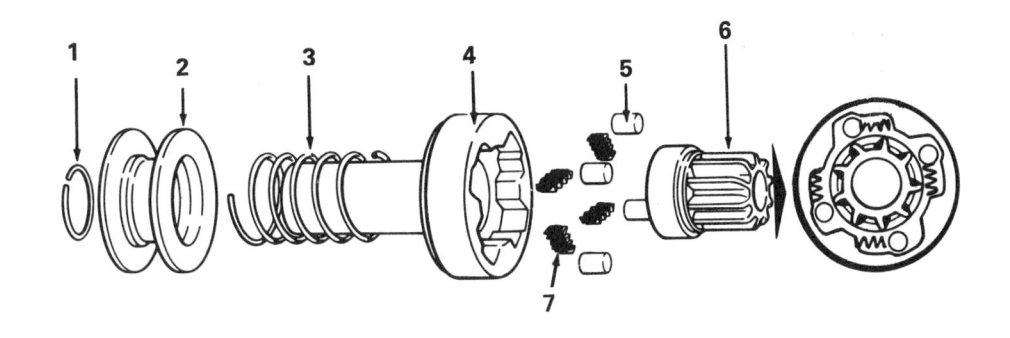

Overrunning clutch drive

1. _____   5. _____

2. _____   6. _____

3. _____   7. _____

4. _____

Solenoid Parts Identification

Identify the parts of the solenoids in the spaces provided below.

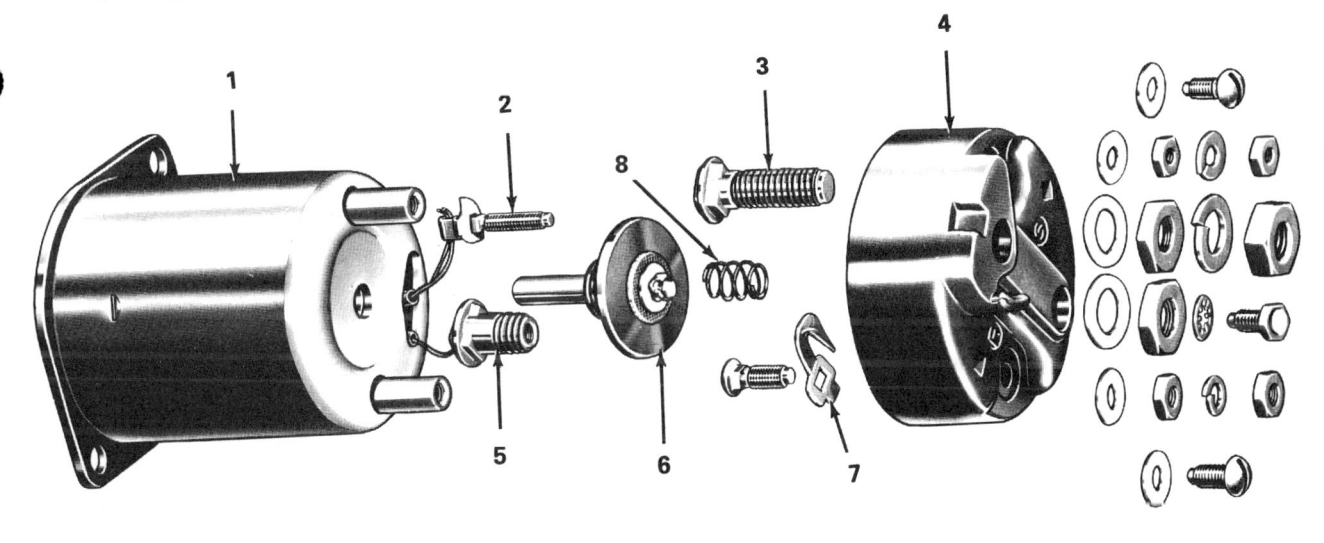

Exploded view of a solenoid

1. _____   5. _____

2. _____   6. _____

3. _____   7. _____

4. _____   8. _____

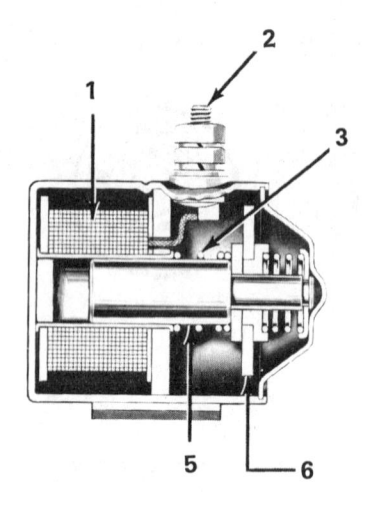

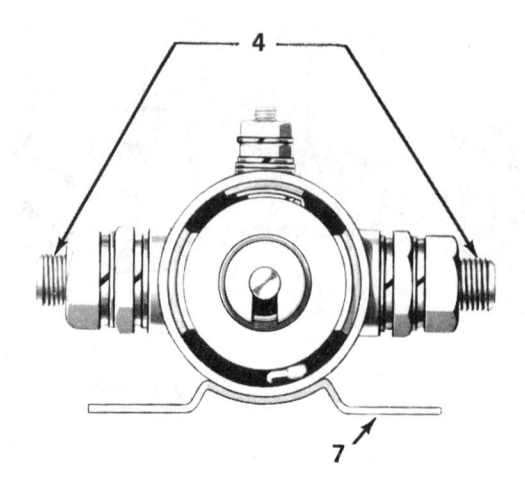

Magnetic switch

1. _____   5. _____
2. _____   6. _____
3. _____   7. _____
4. _____

Review of New Terms

For each definition in Column 2, select the term in Column 1 that best matches its meaning. Write the identifying *letter* of the term in the Answer column.

Column 1	Column 2	Answer
A. Field winding	1. A starter motor drive that uses an overrunning clutch to disconnect the drive pinion from the flywheel ring gear.	1. _____
B. Inertia drive	2. The part of the starter motor that creates a magnetic field.	2. _____
C. Overrunning clutch drive	3. The gear driven by the starter motor that rotates the flywheel.	3. _____
D. Pinion	4. A magnetic switch that controls the circuit between the starter motor and battery.	4. _____
E. Solenoid	5. A starter motor drive that uses the force of inertia to engage the drive pinion.	5. _____
F. Neutral switch	6. A starting system control switch used to prevent operation of the starting system if the car is in gear.	6. _____

NAME _____ SECTION _____ DATE _____ SCORE _____

Chapter 27 STARTING SYSTEM SERVICE
JOB SHEET 11

Starter Motor Testing

Before you begin: Read Chapter 27 in *Auto Mechanics*.

Student _____ Section _____ Date _____

Make of Car _____ Model _____ Year _____

Time Started _____ Time Finished _____ Total Time _____

Flat Rate Time _____

Special Tools, Equipment, Parts, and Materials

Amperage Draw Tester   _____

Eye protection   _____

_____   _____

References

Manufacturer's Shop Manual _____

Repair Manual _____

Service Bulletin _____

Specifications

Look up the following specification and record it in the space provided below.

Starter Motor Amperage Draw _____

Instructor's Check

Procedure

1. Connect the starter load tester to the vehicle starter motor following the instructions on tester.

2. Set the tester voltage switch to the correct vehicle voltage.

3. Set the test selector switch to the starter motor load position.

4. Crank the engine while observing the tester ammeter. Note the ammeter reading. Record the reading in the space provided: Amperage draw _____

    NOTE: Never operate the starter longer than 15 seconds without pausing to allow it to cool for at least 2 minutes. Too much cranking can overheat and damage the starter motor.

5. Compare the amperage reading while cranking to the specifications for the vehicle. Is the reading Too high _____ Too low _____ Correct _____

6. A reading that is too high means there is a problem in the starter motor or in the engine. Use a wrench to turn the engine. If the engine turns freely, the problem is in the starter motor.

7. A reading that is too low indicates the problem is in the starter motor. The starter motor must be disassembled and serviced as explained in Job Sheet 12.

8. Disconnect the tester.

_____
Instructor's Check

NOTES

Date Completed _____ Instructor's Check _____

NAME_____ SECTION_____ DATE_____ SCORE_____

Chapter 27 STARTING SYSTEM SERVICE
JOB SHEET 12

Overhauling a Starter Motor

Before you begin: Read Chapter 27 in *Auto Mechanics*.

Student _____ Section _____ Date _____

Make of Car _____ Model _____ Year _____

Time Started _____ Time Finished _____ Total Time _____

Flat Rate Time _____

Special Tools, Equipment, Parts, and Materials

Bushing driving tool   Brush hook

Armature tester with test lamp   Starting-motor brushes

                                              Armature end washers

_____   _____

_____   _____

_____   _____

References

Manufacturer's Shop Manual _____

Repair Manual _____

Service Bulletin _____

                                              _____
                                              Instructor's Check

107

Procedure

1. Disconnect the battery cables.

   Safety Caution: Make sure the battery cables are disconnected when working on a starter motor or injury may be caused by the engine cranking.

2. Disconnect any accessories that interfere with starter motor removal.

3. Remove the bolts that hold the starter motor to the engine.

4. Remove the battery and solenoid leads from the starter motor.

5. Remove the starter motor from the engine.

6. Remove the through bolts and separate the end frames from the motor housing.

7. Disconnect the leads to the brushes.

8. Remove the drive mechanism and clean all parts for inspection.

9. Locate opens by inspecting the points where the conductors are joined to the commutator for loose connections.

   NOTE: Poor connections cause arcing and burning of the commutator. If the segments are not badly burned, resolder the leads in the riser segments and turn the commutator down in a lathe. Then undercut the insulation between the commutator segments 1/32 inch [0.80mm].

10. Detect grounds in the armature with a test lamp. If the lamp lights with one test prod on the commutator and the other test prod on the armature core or shaft, the armature is grounded.

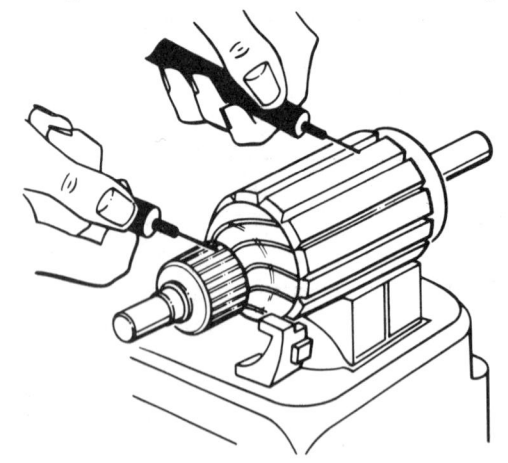

    NOTE: If the commutator is worn, dirty, out of round, or has high insulation, the commutator should be turned down and undercut.

11. Check the field coils for grounds and opens with a test lamp. Disconnect field coil ground connections. Connect one test prod to the field frame and the other to the field connector. If the lamp lights, the field coils are grounded and must be repaired or replaced.

12. Connect test lamp prods to the ends of the field coils. If the lamp does not light, the field coils are open. To remove them for repair or replacement, use a pole shoe spreader and pole shoe screwdriver.

    NOTE: Care should be taken in replacing the field coils to prevent grounding or shorting them as they are tightened into place. Where the pole has a long lip on the side, it should be assembled in the direction of armature rotation.

13. Reassemble the starter motor.

14. Test the starter motor by operating it.

15. Install and reconnect the starter motor on the engine.

Instructor's Check

NOTES

Date Completed _____ Instructor's Check _____

NAME _____ SECTION _____ DATE _____ SCORE _____

Chapter 28 THE CHARGING SYSTEM
ASSIGNMENT SHEET 22

Alternator Parts Identification

Before you begin: Read Chapter 28 in *Auto Mechanics*. Identify the parts of the alternator in the spaces provided below.

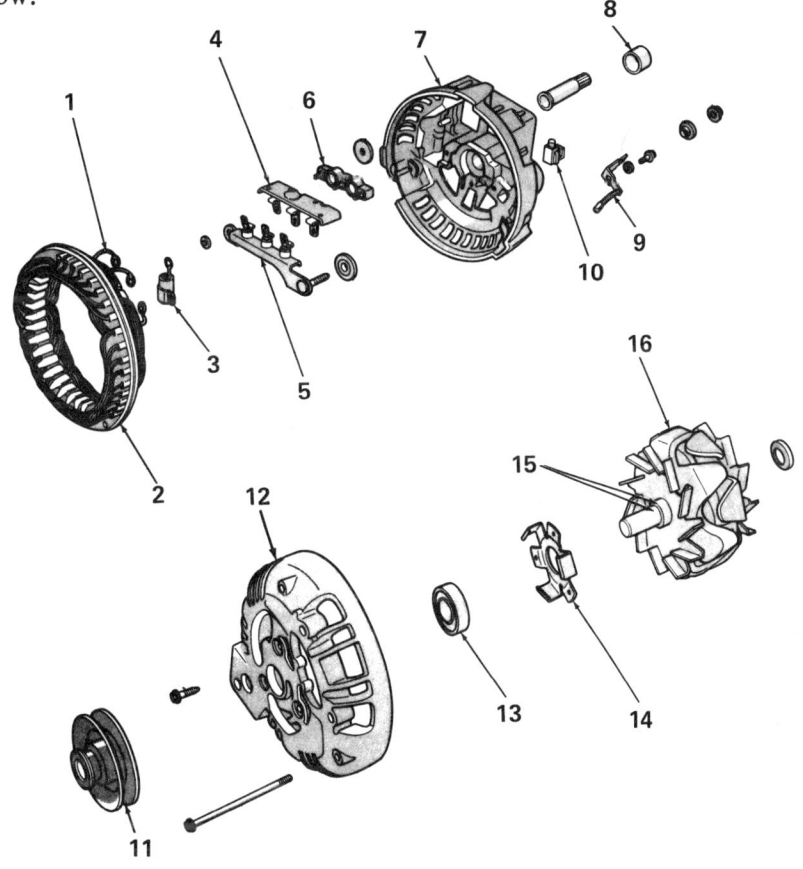

1. _____
2. _____
3. _____
4. _____
5. _____
6. _____
7. _____
8. _____
9. _____
10. _____
11. _____
12. _____
13. _____
14. _____
15. _____
16. _____

111

Alternator Wiring

In each of the figures below connect the stator to the battery by drawing in the correct wiring circuitry.

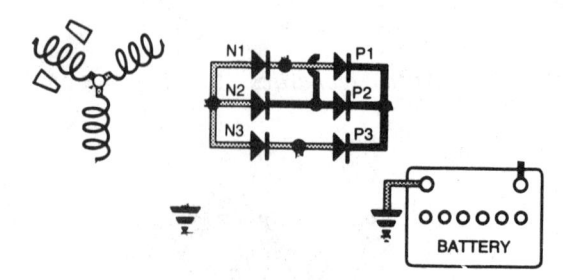

Review of New Terms

For each definition in Column 2, select the term in Column 1 that best matches its meaning. Write the identifying *letter* of the term in the Answer column.

Column 1

A. Current regulation

B. Direct current

C. Field relay

D. Inductive reactance

E. Integral regulator

F. Mechanical voltage regulator

G. Rectifier

H. Slip rings

I. Transistorized voltage regulator

J. Voltage regulation

Column 2

1. An induced voltage that opposes current flow in the stator windings.

2. Electrical current that flows in one direction.

3. A part of the rotor assembly on which brushes ride.

4. The limiting of alternator output to a safe voltage.

5. The limiting of the current developed by the alternator.

6. A voltage regulator mounted inside the alternator.

7. A magnetic switch in the regulator that controls the circuit between the voltage regulator and the battery.

8. The part that uses solid state components to limit voltage.

9. The part of an alternator that changes alternating current to direct current.

10. The part that uses magnetically controlled switches to control voltage.

Answer

1. _____
2. _____
3. _____
4. _____
5. _____
6. _____
7. _____
8. _____
9. _____
10. _____

NAME_____ SECTION_____ DATE_____ SCORE_____

Chapter 29 CHARGING SYSTEM SERVICE
JOB SHEET 13

Testing an Alternator

Before you begin: Read Chapter 29 in *Auto Mechanics*.

Student _____ Section _____ Date _____

Make of Car _____ Model _____ Year _____

Time Started _____ Time Finished _____ Total Time _____

Flat Rate Time _____

Special Tools, Equipment, Parts, and Materials

Alternator Tester

Eye protection

_____

_____

_____

References

Manufacturer's Shop Manual _____

Repair Manual _____

Service Bulletin _____

Specifications

Look up the following specifications and record it in the spaces provided below.

Alternator Output _____ Specified rpm _____

_____

Instructor's Check

Procedure

1. Connect an alternator tester to the charging circuit. The tester manual will explain the proper connections as well as the test procedure. Different connections are required for different wiring systems.

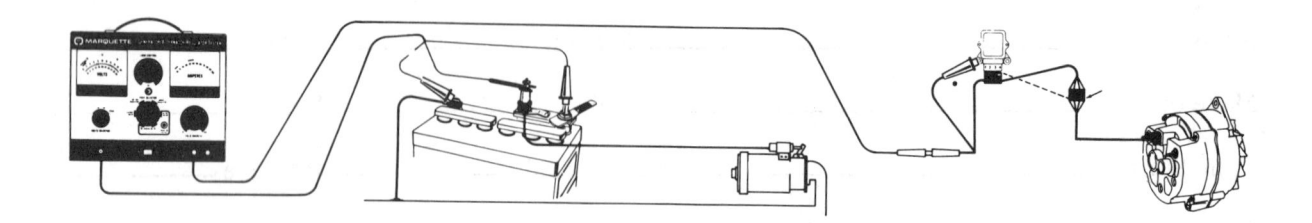

   NOTE: Never operate an alternator on open circuit. The alternator must never be operated with the output terminal disconnected when the rotor (field) is energized. This allows the alternator to operate without any resistance, which could lead to damage from too much output.

2. Connect a tachometer to the engine.

3. Start the engine and adjust the idle speed screw on the carburetor to 2,000 rpm.

4. Set the test selector switch to alternator output position.

5. Observe the ammeter scale. When the output is lower than specified slowly rotate the load increase knob on the tester until the highest ammeter reading is obtained. Record the reading in the space provided. _____ Amps

   NOTE: Excessive load will cause an unwanted drop in voltage.

6. Return the load knob to the off position.

7. Compare ammeter reading to specifications. If the alternator is within specifications the alternator is in satisfactory condition. Is your alternator output too low _____ too high _____ correct _____

8. If the alternator tests above specifications 5 amps or more, test the voltage regulator. Instructor's Check _____

9. If the alternator tests below specifications check for a slipping drive belt or loose electrical connection. Did you find: loose electrical connections _____ slipping belt _____

10. Return idle speed to normal and turn ignition off.

11. Connect the tester field control to the alternator.

12. Start engine and activate field control switch. Slowly increase engine speed and observe ammeter for the highest reading.

    NOTE: Do not increase engine speed any further if voltmeter reads 16 volts.

13. If ammeter reading shows specified output the regulator is at fault.

14. If output is low or there is no output the alternator must be removed for repair.

15. Based on your tests which component is at fault? Alternator _____
    Voltage regulator _____

16. Turn engine off.

17. Disconnect tester leads.

_____
Instructor's Check

NOTES

Date Completed _____ Instructor's Check _____

NAME _____ SECTION _____ DATE _____ SCORE _____

Chapter 29 CHARGING SYSTEM SERVICE
JOB SHEET 14

Overhaul an Alternator

Before you begin: Read Chapter 29 in *Auto Mechanics*.

Student _____ Section _____ Date _____

Make of Car _____ Model _____ Year _____

Time Started _____ Time Finished _____ Total Time _____

Flat Rate Time _____

Special Tools, Equipment, Parts, and Materials

Ohmmeter   _____

Special tools or test equipment   _____

as required by the manufacturer   _____

_____   _____

_____   _____

References

Manufacturer's Shop Manual _____

Repair Manual _____

Service Bulletin _____

                                                                                                   Instructor's Check

Procedure

1. Disconnect the battery ground cable.

    NOTE: The output terminal of the alternator always has battery voltage connected to it. Grounding the output terminal or the wire connected to it can result in a wiring harness burnout or damage to the alternator. To prevent these problems, the battery ground cable must be disconnected before removing the alternator.

2. Loosen the alternator mounting bolts and remove the adjusting arm for the alternator belt.

3. Remove the alternator belt.

4. Remove the alternator mounting bolts and spacers.

5. Lift the alternator to the fender apron area.

6. Use masking tape to mark each wire for proper reconnection to output, field, ground, and indicator lamp terminal.

7. Disconnect the wires and remove the alternator.

8. Disassemble the alternator by removing the four through-bolts. Separate the drive end housing and rotor assembly from the stator assembly by prying apart with a screwdriver at the stator slot.

9. To remove the drive end housing from the rotor, place the rotor in a vise and tighten only enough to permit removal of the shaft nut. Excessive tightening may distort the rotor. Remove the shaft nut, washer, pulley, fan, and collar. Then separate the drive end frame from the rotor shaft.

10. Inspect the slip rings on the rotor shaft for dirt and wear. Clean and finish dirty slip rings with 400 or finer abrasive paper. Mount the rotor in a lathe and spin while cleaning.

11. Individually mounted diodes can be replaced. The diodes are pressed into the heat sink or alternator housing. When removing the diodes, support the alternator housing or heat sink to prevent damage to these castings.

12. Noisy or rough bearings should be replaced. Some bearings are sealed. Others require lubrication with a special high-temperature lubricant. Instructions for lubrication normally are supplied with the replacement bearing. Removal and installation are done with an arbor or hydraulic press.

13. The reassembly procedure is the reverse of disassembly. New brushes will normally be installed in the brush holders before reassembly. To install the slip ring end housing assembly to the rotor and drive end housing assembly, remove the tape over the bearing and shaft. Make sure the shaft is perfectly clean after removing the tape. Insert wire through the holes to hold up the brushes. Carefully install the shaft into the slip ring end frame assembly to avoid damage to the seal. Tighten the through-bolts to the specified torque with a torque wrench. Then remove the brush retaining wire so that the brushes fall down onto the slip rings.

14. Connect the output, field, ground, and indicator lamp wire to the terminals of the alternator.

15. Place the alternator in the correct position on the engine and install the mojnting bolts finger tight.

16. Install the adjusting arm to the alternator belt.

17. Adjust the belt tension to manufacturer's specifications. Tighten the adjusting arm and mounting bolts.

18. Connect the battery ground cable.

Date Completed _____ Instructor's Check _____

NAME _____ SECTION _____ DATE _____ SCORE _____

Chapter 30 THE IGNITION SYSTEM
ASSIGNMENT SHEET 23

Ignition System Wiring

Before you begin: Read Chapter 30 in *Auto Mechanics*. Draw in the primary wires necessary to make the ignition system operate.

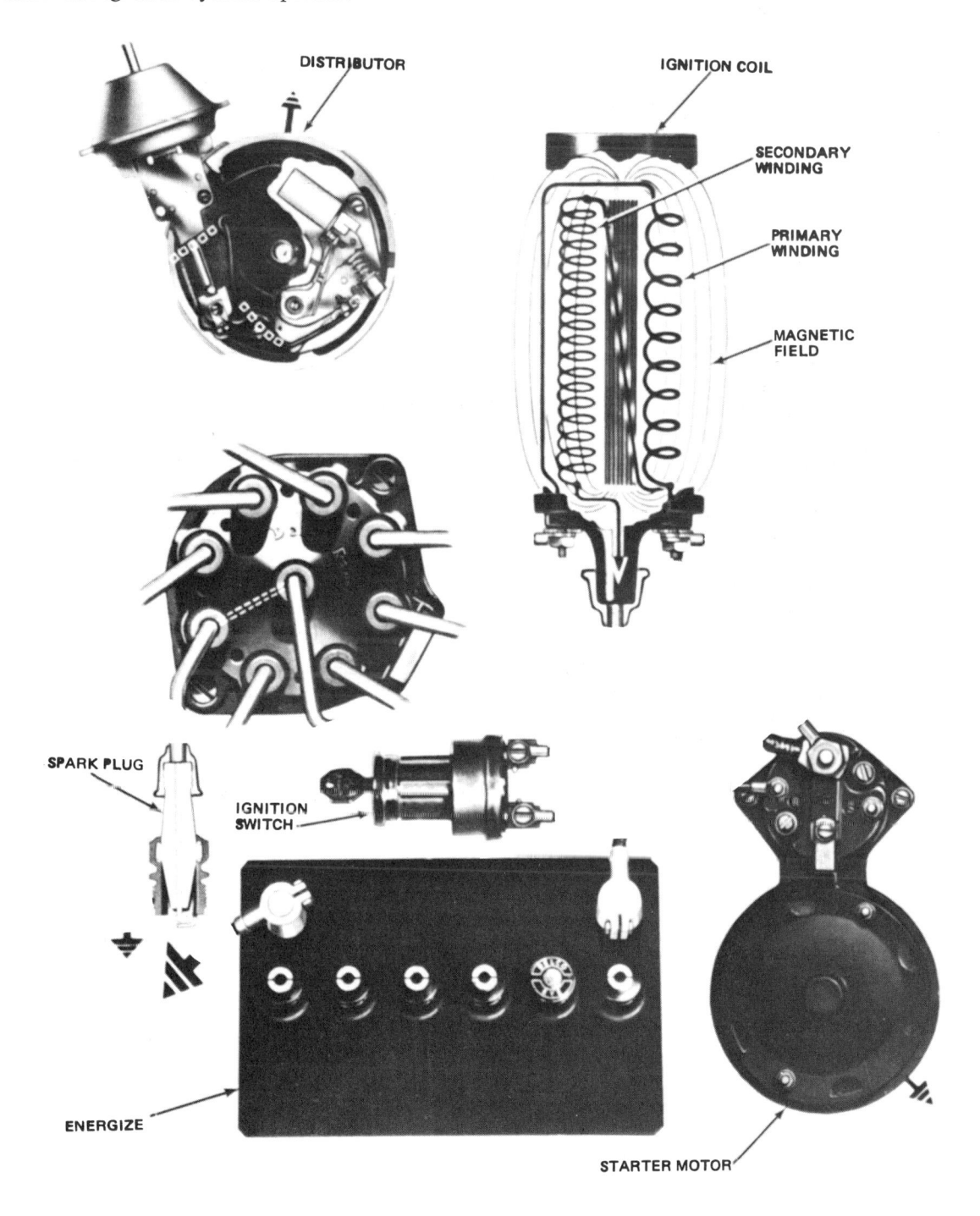

119

Ignition Coil Parts Identification

Identify the parts of the ignition coil by writing the names in the spaces provided below.

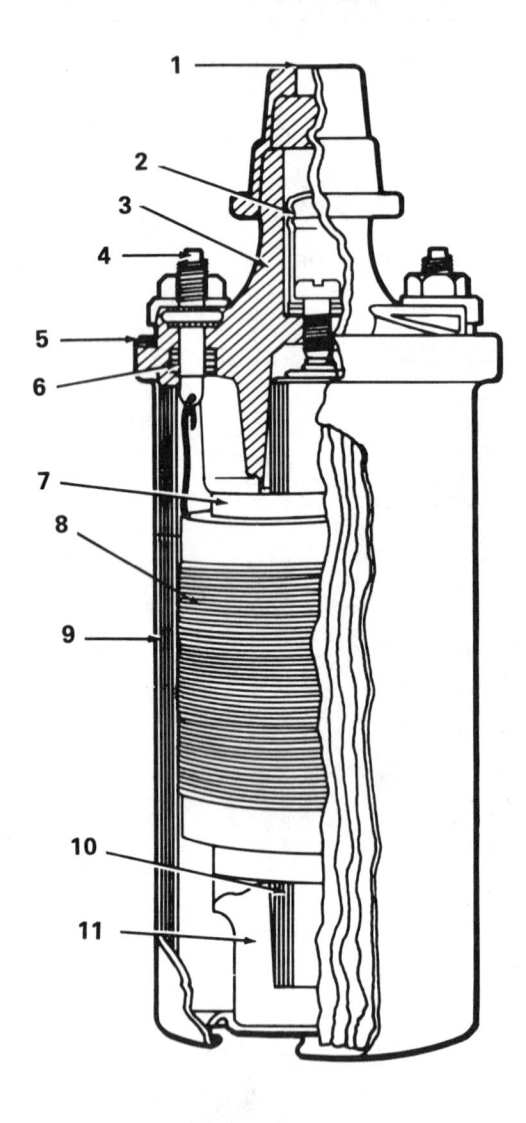

1. _____
2. _____
3. _____
4. _____
5. _____
6. _____
7. _____
8. _____
9. _____
10. _____
11. _____

NAME _____ SECTION _____ DATE _____ SCORE _____

Distribution Parts Identification

Identify the parts of the distributor in the spaces provided below

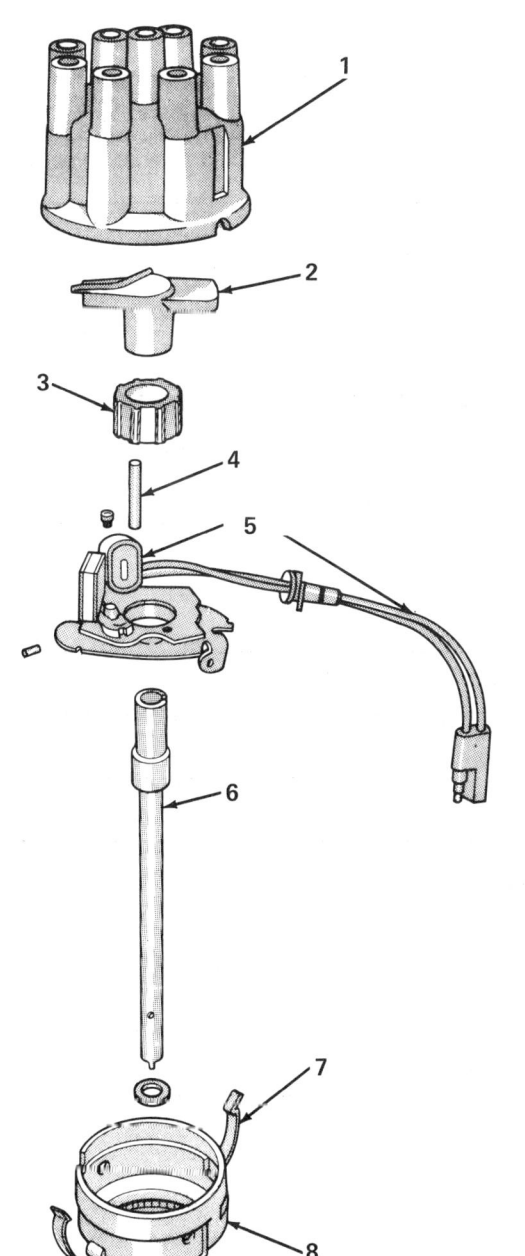

1. _____
2. _____
3. _____
4. _____
5. _____
6. _____
7. _____
8. _____
9. _____

121

Spark Plug Part Identification

Identify the parts of the spark plug in the spaces provided below.

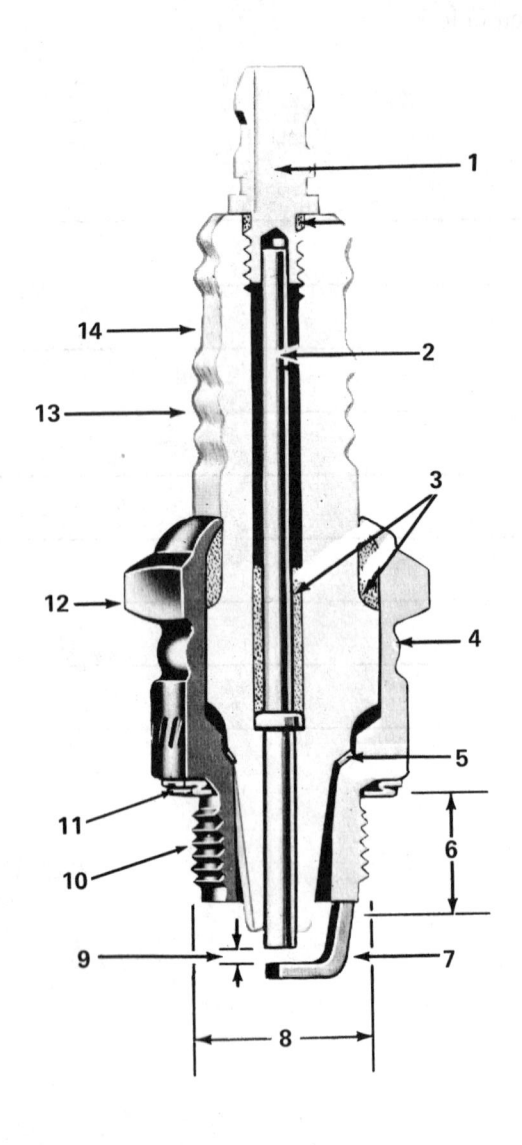

1. _____
2. _____
3. _____
4. _____
5. _____
6. _____
7. _____
8. _____
9. _____
10. _____
11. _____
12. _____
13. _____
14. _____

NAME_____ SECTION_____ DATE_____ SCORE_____

Chapter 30 THE IGNITION SYSTEM
ASSIGNMENT SHEET 24

Secondary Wiring

Before you begin: Read Chapter 30 in *Auto Mechanics*. Draw the secondary wires in the correct firing order on the six and eight cylinder engines shown below.

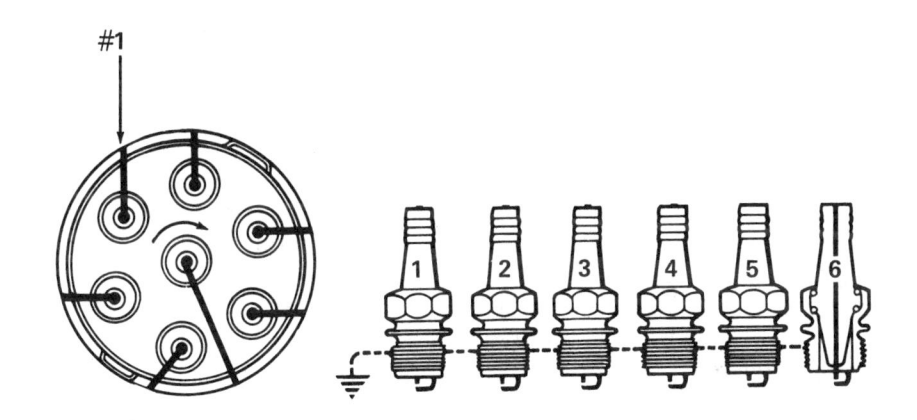

FIRING ORDER 1, 5, 3, 6, 2, 4

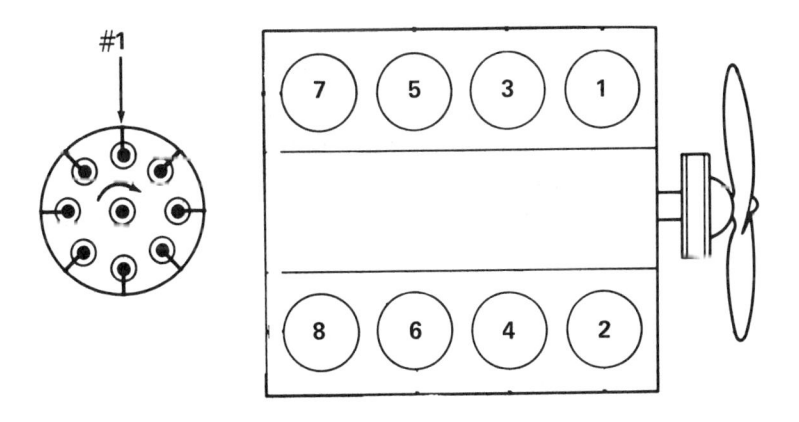

FIRING ORDER 1, 8, 4, 3, 6, 5, 7, 2

123

Review of New Terms

For each definition in Column 2, select the term in Column 1 that best matches its meaning. Write the identifying *letter* of the term in the Answer column.

Column 1

A. Capacitor
B. Capacitive discharge ignition system
C. Centrifugal advance
D. Heat range
E. Ignition timing
F. Inductive discharge system
G. Light-triggered inductive discharge system
H. Magnetically triggered inductive discharge system
I. Resistor bypass circuit
J. Unitized ignition
K. Hall effect ignition

Column 2

1. Providing the spark to the correct cylinder at the correct time for combustion.
2. An ignition system that uses a magnetic pulse to trigger the coil.
3. An electrical device that stores or soaks up a surge of electricity.
4. An ignition timing system that uses a set of weights controlled by centrifugal force.
5. An ignition system that combines the coil and distributor in one unit.
6. An ignition system that uses the energy stored in a capacitor to develop high voltage.
7. An ignition system that uses a beam of light to trigger the coil.
8. The circuit that sends ignition current through a resistor when the vehicle is started.
9. An ignition system that uses the energy stored in a coil for ignition.
10. How hot the plug gets during operation.
11. Breakerless electronic control switch the operation of which is based upon the Hall effect. In the case of electronic ignition systems, it is used as a pulse generator.

Answer

1. _____
2. _____
3. _____
4. _____
5. _____
6. _____
7. _____
8. _____
9. _____
10. _____
11. _____

NAME_____ SECTION_____ DATE_____ SCORE_____

Chapter 30 THE IGNITION SYSTEM
ASSIGNMENT SHEET 25

Hall Effect Ignition Circuit

Before you begin: Read Chapter 30 in *Auto Mechanics*. Connect the parts of the Hall effect ignition system by drawing the wires in the correct places on the figure below.

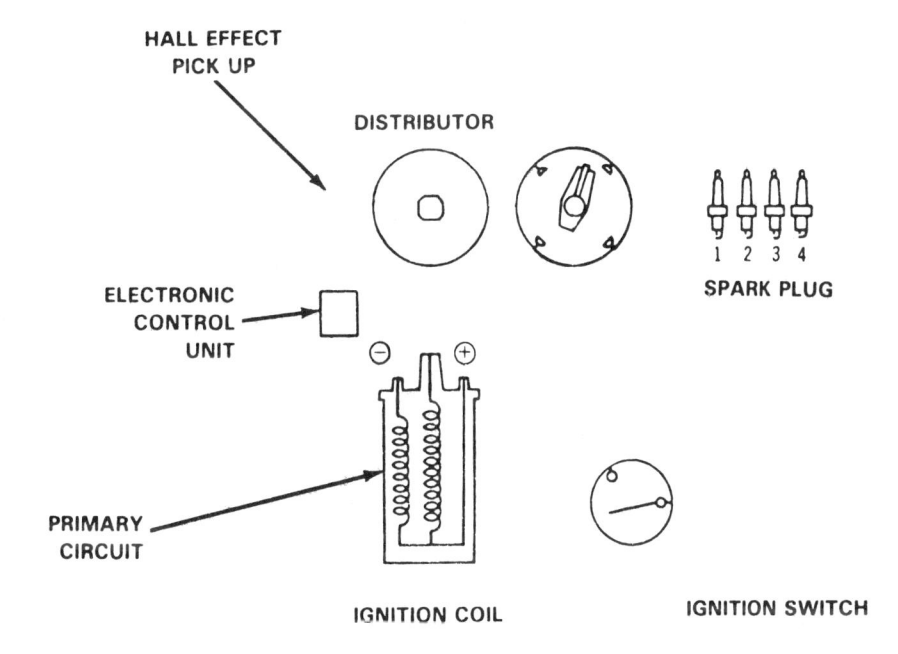

HALL EFFECT PICK UP

DISTRIBUTOR

SPARK PLUG
1 2 3 4

ELECTRONIC CONTROL UNIT

PRIMARY CIRCUIT

IGNITION COIL

IGNITION SWITCH

Ignition Cable Parts

Identify the parts of the ignition cable by writing the names in the spaces provided.

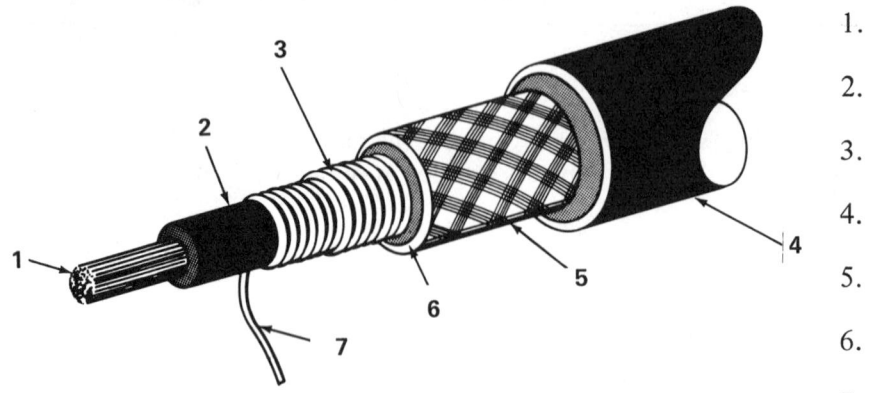

1. _____
2. _____
3. _____
4. _____
5. _____
6. _____
7. _____

Electronic Distributor

Identify the parts of the electronic distributor by writing the names in the spaces provided.

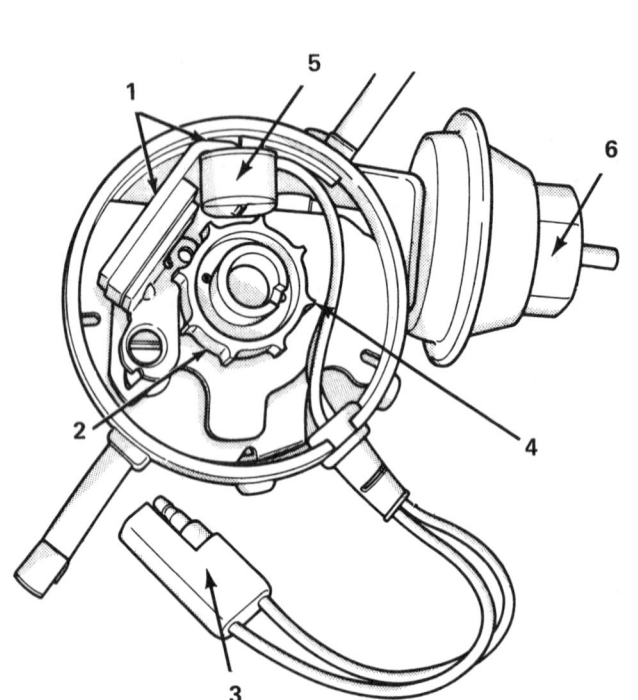

1. _____
2. _____
3. _____
4. _____
5. _____
6. _____

NAME _____ SECTION _____ DATE _____ SCORE _____

Unitized Ignition Parts Identification

Identify the parts of a unitized ignition in the spaces provided below.

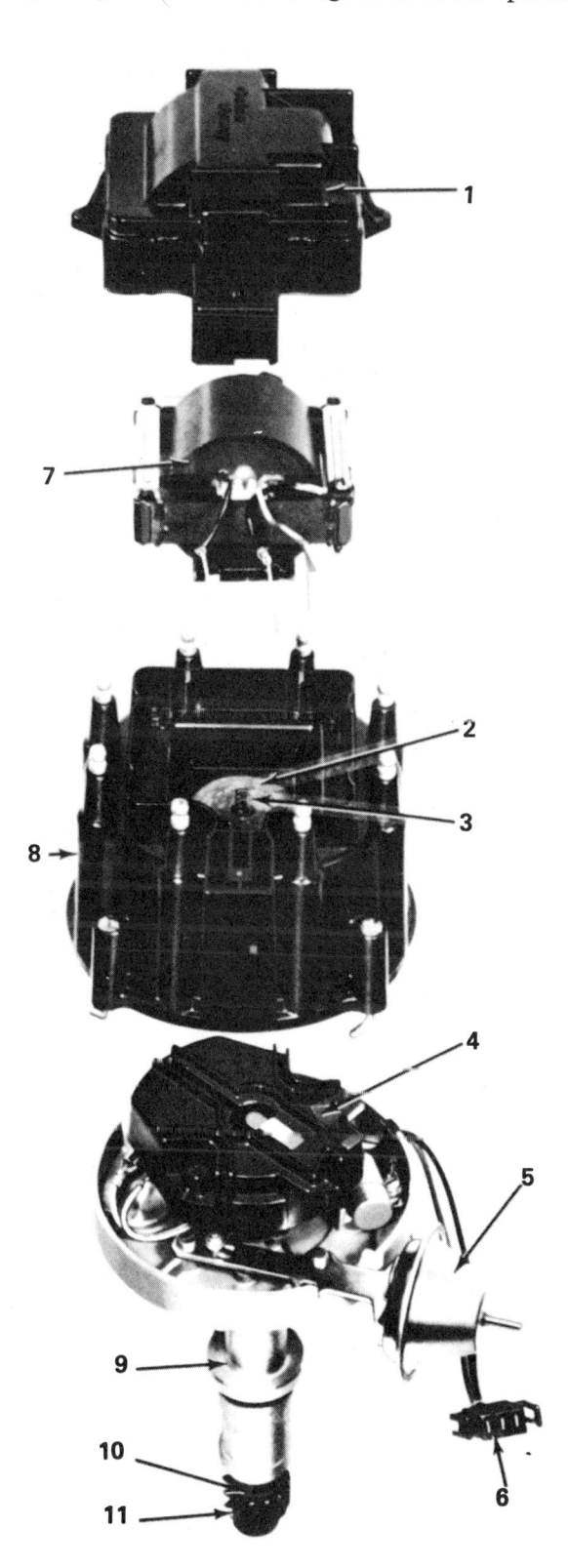

1. _____
2. _____
3. _____
4. _____
5. _____
6. _____
7. _____
8. _____
9. _____
10. _____
11. _____

NAME _____ SECTION _____ DATE _____ SCORE _____

Chapter 31 IGNITION SYSTEM SERVICE
JOB SHEET 15

Spark Plug Service

Before you begin: Read Chapter 31 in *Auto Mechanics*.

Student _____ Section _____ Date _____

Make of Car _____ Model _____ Year _____

Time Started _____ Time Finished _____ Total Time _____

Flat Rate Time _____

Special Tools, Equipment, Parts, and Materials

Correct spark plug socket   Spark plug testing maching

Torque wrench   Spark plug gaskets

Spark plug gap tool   _____

Spark plug cleaning machine   _____

_____   _____

References

Manufacturer's Shop Manual _____

Repair Manual _____

Service Bulletin _____

Specifications

Look up the following specifications and record them in the spaces provided below.

Spark plug type _____ Spark plug gap _____ Spark plug torque _____

_____
Instructor's Check

Procedure

1. Remove the wires from the spark plugs.

    NOTE: Be sure that each wire can be identified correctly when reconnecting.

2. Use an air hose to clean all dirt and grit from the area around the spark plugs.

3. Remove the spark plugs with the correct size spark plug socket.

    NOTE: Use a 6 point deep spark plug socket for spark plug removal and installation. Spark plug sockets are designed to hold the spark plug firmly so that it may be placed in the socket and started into the cylinder head by hand.

4. Remove the spark plugs (and gaskets, if used), placing each spark plug in order.

5. Inspect the appearance and condition of both ends of the insulator, the electrodes, seat gasket, and the shell of the plug.

6. Clean spark plugs, following the instructions of the cleaner manufacturer.

7. After cleaning, inspect the plug carefully for cracks or other defects which may not have been visible before. If the plug appears to be in good condition, the end of the center electrode should be filed lightly to provide a flat, square surface.

    NOTE: If blast cleaning has not removed all deposits from the electrodes, they should be cleaned with several strokes of fine abrasive or a file.

8. Replace spark plugs that have a cracked or broken insulator or burned or worn electrodes.

9. Regap the spark plugs to the exact specifications with a round wire feeler gauge.

NAME _____ SECTION _____ DATE _____ SCORE _____

GROUND ELECTRODE

WIRE GAUGE

    NOTE: In regapping, adjust only the side (ground) electrode. Never bend the center electrode; sidewise pressure on it may crack or break the insulator tip.

10. Test the spark plugs in a spark plug tester. Follow the manufacturer's instructions for the tester you are using.

11. Place a new spark plug seat gasket on each new or cleaned plug.

    NOTE: Be sure the cylinder head threads and plug seats are clean and free from any dirt which would prevent proper seating of the plug and gasket. Dirty cylinder head threads should be cleaned with a greased thread chaser of the proper size.

12. Screw the plug by hand all the way down until it seats on the gasket finger-tight.

    NOTE: Starting a spark plug with a wrench could cause cross threading and a ruined spark plug thread.

Then use a torque wrench and torque to the specification in the service manual. This specification is given for new gaskets, with spark plug and engine threads thoroughly clean.

    NOTE: Since spark plug torquing is frequently difficult because of inaccessibility, the following rule of thumb will produce plug installations that are neither too tight nor too loose. Tighten the spark plug finger-tight and then turn it with a spark plug wrench 1/2 to 3/4 turn.

NOTES

Date Completed _____ Instructor's Check _____

NAME _____ SECTION _____ DATE _____ SCORE _____

Chapter 31 IGNITION SYSTEM SERVICE
JOB SHEET 16

Replace Contact Points

Before you begin: Read Chapter 31 in *Auto Mechanics*.

Student _____ Section _____ Date _____

Make of Car _____ Model _____ Year _____

Time Started _____ Time Finished _____ Total Time _____

Flat Rate Time _____

Special Tools, Equipment, Parts, and Materials

Ignition-point aligning tool   Ignition feeler gauge

Ignition wrench set   Ignition pliers

_____   _____

_____   _____

_____   _____

References

Manufacturer's Shop Manual _____

Repair Manual _____

Service Bulletin _____

Specifications

Look up the following specification and record it in the space provided below.

Contact point gap _____

_____
Instructor's Check

133

Procedure

1. Remove the distributor cap and spark plug wires.

    NOTE: Most distributors have spring clips on each side of the cap that are unsnapped to free the cap.

2. Remove the rotor from the shaft by pulling it straight up.

3. Remove the screws that hold the contact points and condenser down.

4. Disconnect the wires from the distributor to the contact points.

5. Lift the point assembly out of the distributor.

6. Remove the new contact point set from the package.

    NOTE: Do not touch the point surfaces. Oil from the skin can coat the points and cause quick burning of the points.

7. Position the new contact point set in the distributor. Start the screws but do not tighten them.

8. Mount the new condenser. Reinstall the wires just as they were. Make sure the rubbing block of the new contact set is positioned on top of the cam lobe.

9. Choose the flat feeler gauge of the correct size and make sure it is perfectly clean. Slide it between the contact points. If the gap is accurate, there will be a slight drag.

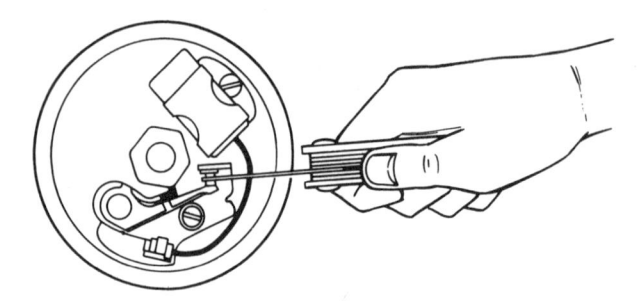

10. If the gap is too wide or too narrow, adjust the points by sliding the contact set around. When the adjustment is correct, tighten the contact point mounting screws. Recheck the spacing with the feeler gauge.

11. Recheck the wiring. If everything looks good, the shield, rotor, and cap can be replaced. The rotor is keyed to the distributor shaft so that it will fit in only one position. Look at the underside of the rotor for the key or groove.

12. Push the rotor on the distributor shaft and turn it until it engages the key.

13. Replace the distributor cap and spark plug wires.

Date Completed _____ Instructor's Check _____

NAME_____ SECTION_____ DATE_____ SCORE_____

Chapter 31 IGNITION SYSTEM SERVICE
JOB SHEET 17

Adjusting Dwell

Before you begin: Read Chapter 31 in *Auto Mechanics*.

Student _____ Section _____ Date_____

Make of Car _____ Model _____ Year_____

Time Started _____ Time Finished _____ Total Time_____

Flat Rate Time or Recommended Time _____

Special Tools, Equipment, Parts, and Materials

Dwell Meter

_____   _____
_____   _____
_____   _____
_____   _____

References

Manufacturer's Shop Manual _____

Repair Manual _____

Service Bulletin _____

Specifications

Look up the following specification and record it in the space provided below.

Dwell or Cam Angle _____

_____
Instructor's Check

135

Procedure

1. Connect the dwell meter to the ignition system following the instructions supplied for the dwell meter.

2. Calibrate the dwell meter following the instructions supplied for the dwell meter.

3. Turn the test selector switch on the dwell meter to the dwell position.

4. Turn the cylinder selection switch to the number of cylinders for the engine.

5. Start the engine. Observe the dwell reading on the dwell meter.

6. Compare the dwell reading to the specifications for the vehicle being tested. If the dwell is within specifications, no adjustment is necessary.

7. If the dwell is incorrect, an adjustment of the point spacing will be required.

8. Stop the engine.

9. Remove the distributor cap. Loosen the contact point hold-down screw.

10. Increase the point spacing to decrease dwell. Decrease the point spacing to increase dwell.

11. Recheck dwell by installing the rotor cap and starting the engine. Adjust dwell again if required.

12. Disconnect the dwell meter.

_____
Instructor's Check

NOTES

Date Completed _____ Instructor's Check _____

NAME _____ SECTION _____ DATE _____ SCORE _____

Chapter 31 IGNITION SYSTEM SERVICE
JOB SHEET 18

Adjust Ignition Timing

Before you begin: Read Chapter 31 in *Auto Mechanics*.

Student _____ Section _____ Date _____

Make of Car _____ Model _____ Year _____

Time Started _____ Time Finished _____ Total Time _____

Flat Rate Time _____

Special Tools, Equipment, Parts, and Materials

Timing light

Tachometer

_____   _____

_____   _____

_____   _____

_____

References

Manufacturer's Shop Manual _____

Repair Manual _____

Service Bulletin _____

Specifications

Look up the following specification and write it in the space provided below.

Ignition timing specification _____

Make a sketch of the timing marks on the pulley of the flywheel for this engine in the space below:

_____
Instructor's Check

137

Procedure

1. Locate the ignition timing marks on the engine front pulley (or flywheel of some front drive cars).

    NOTE: On some cars it is necessary to disconnect the vacuum line at the distributor before making timing adjustments.

2. Disconnect and plug the distributor vacuum advance line if required. (There may be more than one vacuum line attached to the distributor.)

3. Clean the area around the ignition timing marks, so that the marks will be easily seen in the flash of the timing light.

4. Connect the timing light and tachometer according to the manufacturer's instructions.

    Safety Caution: Take care not to get the timing light wires caught in the fan or belts.

5. Start the engine.

6. Adjust the engine idling speed (using a tachometer) to the manufacturer's specifications.

7. Direct the timing light toward the timing marks. If the timing is correct, the timing light flash will coincide with the appearance of the timing mark at the check point. (When the timing marks are properly aligned, the number 1 cylinder is in firing position.)

    NOTE: The shop service manual will explain what the marks on the crank pulley mean. Typically, there is a center mark for top dead center and a number of marks for degrees before and after top dead center.

    If the timing is incorrect, proceed as follows:

    a. Loosen the clamp or lock screw on the distributor so that it may be turned;

    b. Move the distributor clockwise or counterclockwise until the timing mark is synchronized with the timing flash at the timing check point;

    c. Retighten the distributor clamp or lock screw.

8. Increase the engine speed through the specified timing stages, checking the degree of advance at each stage, and comparing this with the manufacturer's specifications.

9. Stop the engine and disconnect the timing light and tachometer.

10. Reconnect the vacuum line if it was disconnected.

    NOTE: Some late model vehicles have a bracket on the front of the engine for a magnetic pick-up. A magnetic pick-up is installed and connected to a special meter that provides a timing readout when the engine is running.

Date Completed _____ Instructor's Check _____

NAME _____ SECTION _____ DATE _____ SCORE _____

Chapter 31 IGNITION SYSTEM SERVICE
JOB SHEET 19

Replace a Distributor Cap

Before you begin: Read Chapter 31 in *Auto Mechanics*.

Student _____ Section _____ Date _____

Make of Car _____ Model _____ Year _____

Time Started _____ Time Finished _____ Total Time _____

Flat Rate Time _____

Special Tools, Equipment, Parts, and Materials

Distributor cap _____   _____

_____   _____

_____   _____

References

Manufacturer's Shop Manual _____

Repair Manual _____

Service Bulletin _____

Specifications

Look up the following specifications and record them in the spaces provided below.

Firing order _____ Rotor rotation: Clockwise _____ Counterclockwise _____

Label cylinder numbering pattern:

_____
Instructor's Check

Procedure

1. Determine the direction of rotor rotation and check whether it is clockwise _____ or counterclockwise _____ .

2. Crank the engine until the rotor is pointing to the firing position for the number 1 spark plug.

    Safety Caution: Make sure the coil primary wire is disconnected to prevent a shock when touching the secondary wires. (Check the shop service manual for correct method.)

3. Remove each of the secondary wires from the distributor cap.

4. Remove the cap by removing the spring clips or hold-down screws.

5. Compare the old cap to the replacement cap. If they are not exactly the same, check with your instructor.

6. Examine the spark plug wires. If the insulation is cracked or oil soaked, report the condition to your instructor before continuing.

7. Install the new distributor cap.

8. Install the spark plug wires in the distributor cap, starting with the number 1 wire at the location indicated by the rotor. Install the remaining wires in the correct firing order and in the direction from the number 1 wire that the rotor travels.

_____
Instructor's Check

NOTES

Date Completed _____ Instructor's Check _____

NAME _____ SECTION _____ DATE _____ SCORE _____

Chapter 31 IGNITION SYSTEM SERVICE
JOB SHEET 20

Replace Spark Plug Wires

Before you begin: Read Chapter 31 in *Auto Mechanics*.

Student _____ Section _____ Date _____

Make of Car _____ Model _____ Year _____

Time Started _____ Time Finished _____ Total Time _____

Flat Rate Time _____

Special Tools, Equipment, Parts, and Materials

Terminal crimping tool   Spark plug wire distributor terminals

Wire cutters   Spark plug wire connectors

Spark plug wires

_____   _____

_____   _____

References

Manufacturer's Shop Manual _____

Repair Manual _____

Service Bulletin _____

Specifications

Look up the following specifications and record them in the spaces provided below.

Firing order _____ Cylinder numbers _____

Rotor rotation: _____ Clockwise _____ Counterclockwise _____

Instructor's Check

Procedure

1. Note the direction (clockwise or counterclockwise) of rotor rotation.

   Safety Caution: Make sure the coil primary wire is disconnected to prevent a shock from a secondary wire.

2. Use masking tape to mark the number 1 spark plug cable position at the distributor.

3. Disconnect the spark plug wires from the spark plugs.

4. Disconnect the spark plug wires from the distributor cap.

5. Mark each wire as it is removed to identify it to a cylinder.

6. Match a new wire length to each of the wires that were removed and attach the terminals.

7. Wipe the distributor cap with a clean rag and inspect it for cracks. If the cap is cracked or the center contact in the cap is worn, the distributor cap should be replaced.

8. Install the distributor cap. Be sure that the cap positioning plug is in place on the distributor housing.

9. Install a new wire of the correct length in the number 1 spark plug position.

10. Install a new wire of the correct length at each of the other cylinder positions in the correct firing order.

11. Observe the correct rotor rotation.

12. Make sure each wire is routed correctly through any looms or brackets.

13. Start the engine and look for any evidence of missing or cross firing.

_____

Instructor's Check

NOTES

Date Completed _____ Instructor's Check _____

NAME_____ SECTION_____ DATE_____ SCORE_____

Chapter 32 MANUALLY OPERATED CLUTCH
ASSIGNMENT SHEET 26

Clutch Operation

Before you begin: Read Chapter 32 in *Auto Mechanics*. Explain how the clutch works on application.

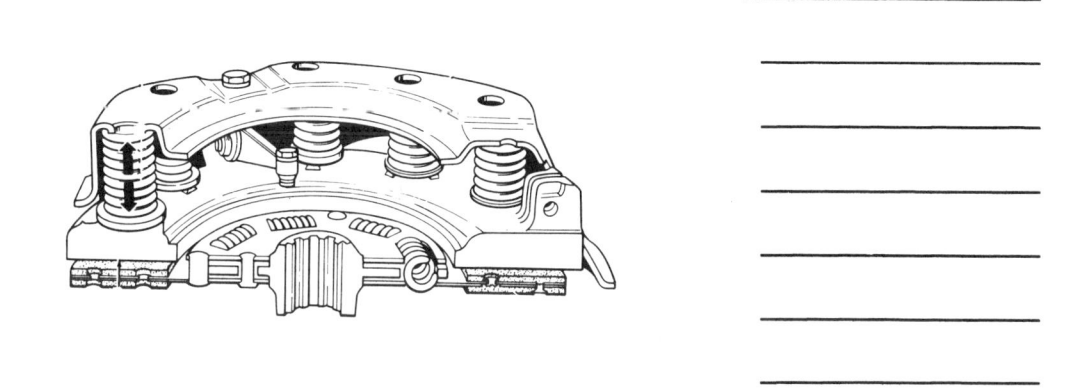

1._____
_____
_____
_____
_____
_____
_____
_____
_____

Use the spaces provided below to explain how the clutch works on release.

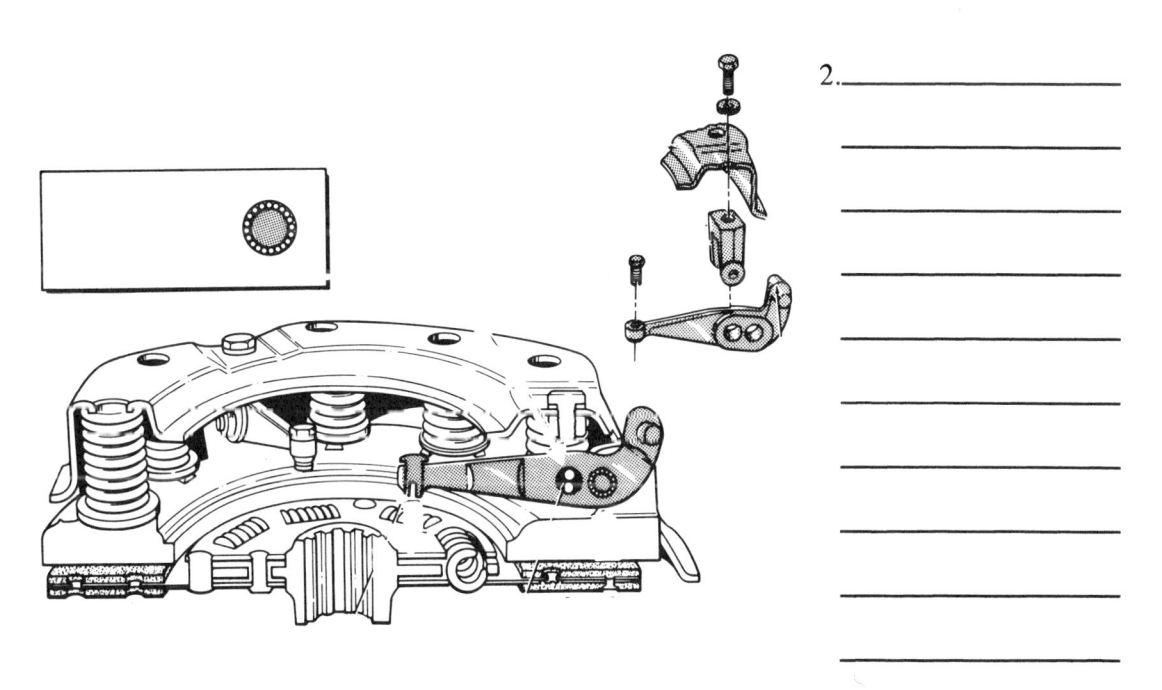

2._____
_____
_____
_____
_____
_____
_____
_____
_____
_____
_____
_____
_____

Clutch Parts Identification

Identify the parts of the clutch in the spaces provided below.

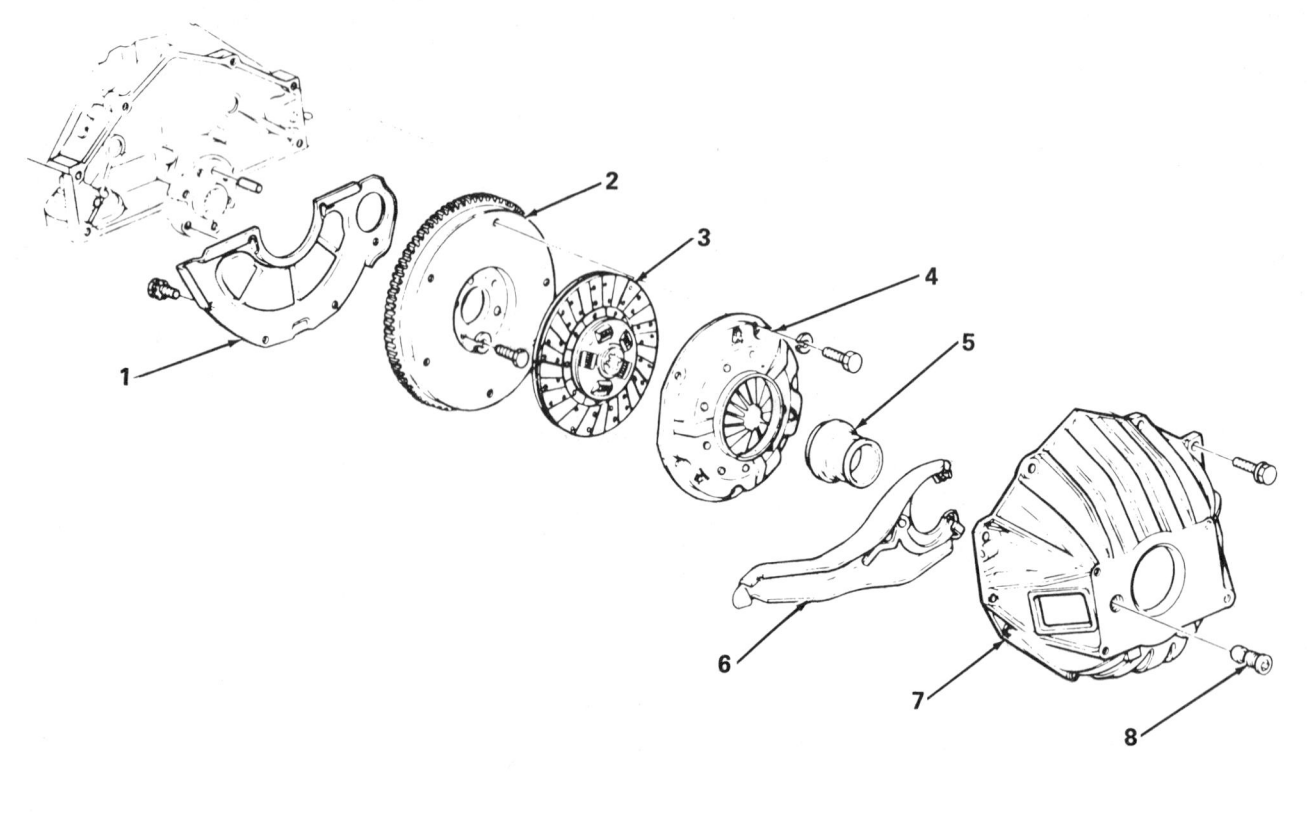

1. _____
2. _____
3. _____
4. _____
5. _____
6. _____
7. _____
8. _____

NAME _____ SECTION _____ DATE _____ SCORE _____

Chapter 32 MANUALLY OPERATED CLUTCH
ASSIGNMENT SHEET 27

Pressure Plate Parts Identification

Before you begin: Read Chapter 32 in *Auto Mechanics*. Identify the parts of the coil spring pressure plate assembly in the spaces provided below.

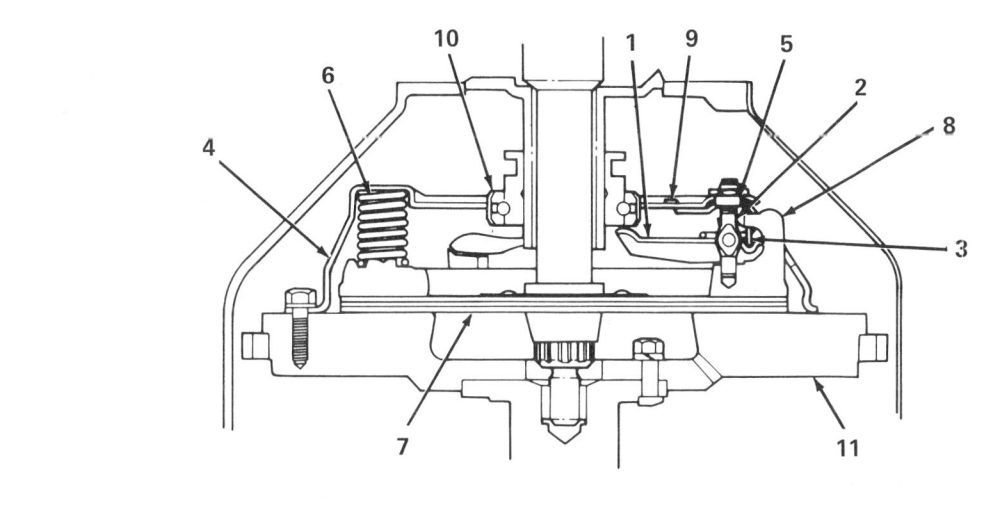

1. _____   5. _____   9. _____

2. _____   6. _____   10. _____

3. _____   7. _____   11. _____

4. _____   8. _____

Identify the parts of a diaphragm spring pressure plate assembly in the spaces provided below.

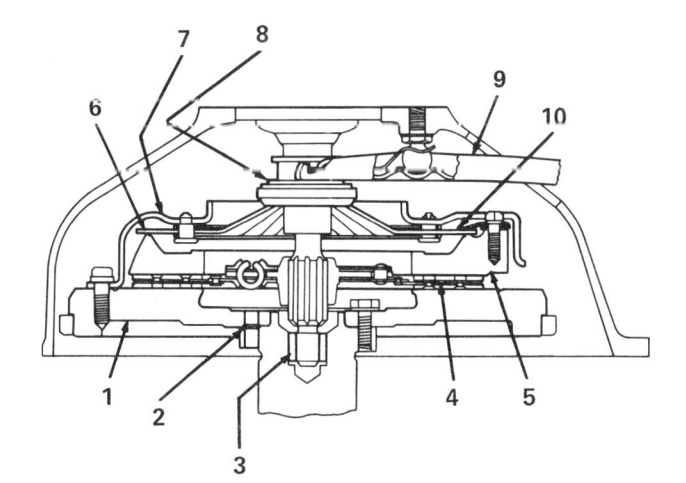

1. _____
2. _____
3. _____
4. _____
5. _____
6. _____
7. _____
8. _____
9. _____
10. _____

Clutch Linkage Parts Identification

Identify the parts of the hydraulic clutch linkage in the spaces provided below.

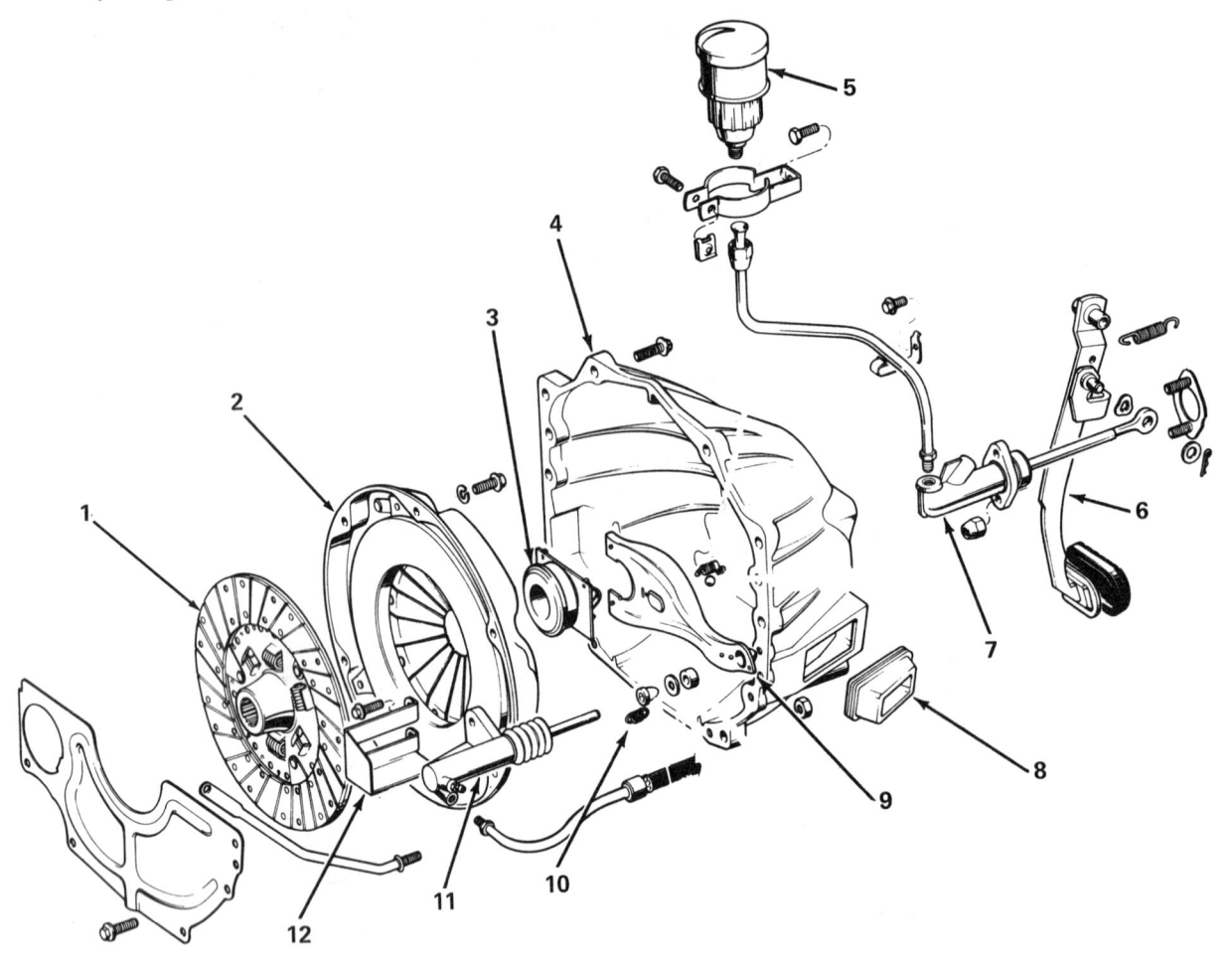

1. _____
2. _____
3. _____
4. _____
5. _____
6. _____
7. _____
8. _____
9. _____
10. _____
11. _____
12. _____

Review of New Terms

For each definition in Column 2, select the term in Column 1 that best matches its meaning. Write the identifying *letter* of the term in the Answer column.

Column 1	*Column 2*	*Answer*
A. Clutch linkage	1. A clutch that uses more than one disc.	1. _____
B. Clutch pedal	2. The rods and levers that allow the driver to operate the clutch.	2. _____
C. Multiple-plate clutch	3. A bearing operated by the clutch linkage used to disengage the clutch.	3. _____
D. Semi-centrifugal clutch	4. A clutch that uses centrifugal force during application.	4. _____
E. Release bearing	5. The part used by the driver to operate the clutch.	5. _____

NAME _____ SECTION _____ DATE _____ SCORE _____

Chapter 33 CLUTCH SERVICE
JOB SHEET 21

Clutch Adjustment

Before you begin: Read Chapter 33 in *Auto Mechanics*.

Student _____ Section _____ Date _____

Make of Car _____ Model _____ Year _____

Time Started _____ Time Finished _____ Total Time _____

Flat Rate Time _____

Special Tools, Equipment, Parts, and Materials

Tape rule

Vise-grip pliers

References

Manufacturer's Shop Manual _____

Repair Manual _____

Service Bulletin _____

Specifications

Look up the clutch adjustment specifications for the vehicle you are working on and record them in the space provided below.

Clutch pedal free-play _____

Instructor's Check

Procedure

1. Check the pedal free travel. A clutch pedal free play or free travel adjustment is necessary whenever the clutch does not disengage or engage properly, or when new clutch parts are installed. First measure and note the distance from the floor pan to the top of the pedal. Then depress the pedal slowly until the clutch release fingers contact the clutch release bearing.

2. Note the reading on the tape. The difference between the reading with the pedal in the depressed position and the reading with the pedal in the fully released position is the pedal free travel. If the free travel is not correct according to specifications, the clutch linkage will require adjustment.
Write in your freetravel measurement in the space provided. _____

_____
Instructor's Check

3. Locate the adjuster on the linkage. Usually the rod connected to the release fork is constructed in two threaded pieces so that it can be made longer or shorter.

4. The adjustment is made by loosening the jam nut and lengthening or shortening the rod as required. Some adjusters must be disconnected from the linkage before they can be adjusted.

   NOTE: Improper adjustment of the clutch pedal free travel is often one of the causes of clutch failure and can be a factor in some transmission failures.

5. Check the adjustment by measuring the free travel as explained earlier.

   NOTE: Preventive maintenance on the clutch consists of periodic lubrication of the clutch linkage and adjusting the clutch pedal free play. The clutch linkage should be lubricated each time the vehicle has a chassis lubrication. All the points of friction should be lubricated with engine oil. Some types of linkage with high-pressure grease fittings require lubrication with chassis grease.

_____
Instructor's Check

NOTES

Date Completed _____ Instructor's Check _____

NAME _____ SECTION _____ DATE _____ SCORE _____

Chapter 33 CLUTCH SERVICE
JOB SHEET 22

Remove and Replace a Clutch

Before you begin: Read Chapter 33 in *Auto Mechanics*.

Student _____ Section _____ Date _____

Make of Car _____ Model _____ Year _____

Time Started _____ Time Finished _____ Total Time _____

Flat Rate Time _____

Special Tools, Equipment, Parts, and Materials

Lift jack   _____

Stationary jacks (2)   _____

Center punch   _____

Clutch/disc centering tool   _____

Torque wrench   _____

References

Manufacturer's Shop Manual _____

Repair Manual _____

Service Bulletin _____

Specifications

Look up the torque specification for the clutch cover to flywheel bolts and write them in the space provided below.

Clutch cover to flywheel bolt torque _____

_____
Instructor's Check

Procedure

1. The procedure of removing a clutch varies with the type of car. On front-engine and rear drive vehicles, the transmission and drive shaft must be taken out before removing the clutch. On rear-engine and front drive vehicles, the engine must be removed to service the clutch.

    Safety Caution: Support the car with safety stands before doing work under the automobile.

2. After the transmission has been taken out, remove the clutch release bearing and sleeve assembly from the clutch release fork.

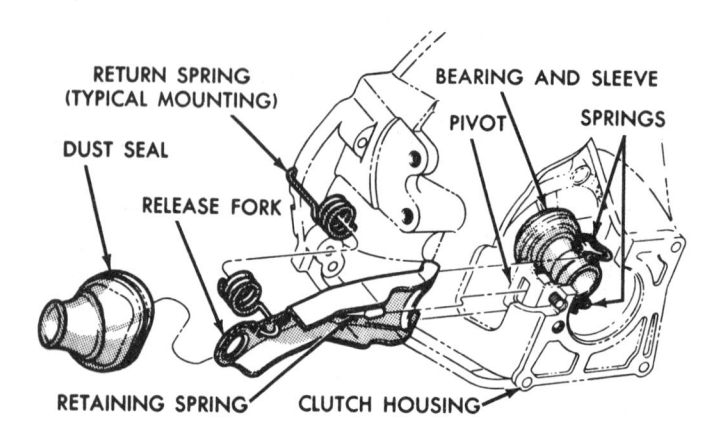

3. Mark the clutch cover and flywheel so that they will be installed in the same place.

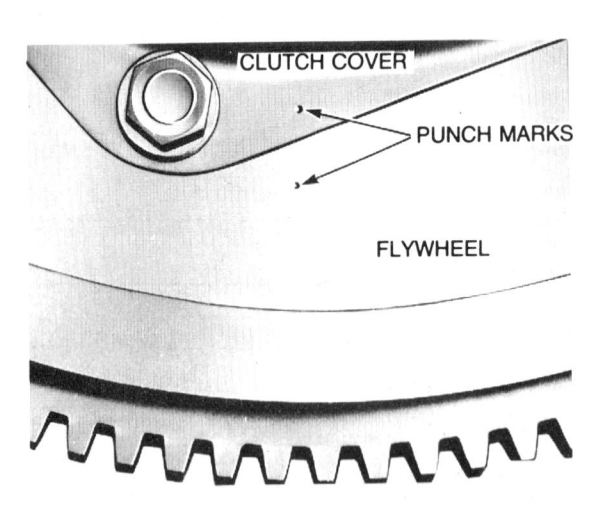

4. Loosen and back off each of the clutch cover attaching bolts, one or two turns at a time, to avoid bending the cover flange.

5. Remove the clutch assembly and disc from the clutch housing.

    NOTE: Handle the clutch and disc carefully to avoid contaminating the friction surface.

NAME _____ SECTION _____ DATE _____ SCORE _____

6. Lubricate the transmission input clutch shaft bushing in the end of the crankshaft with a small amount of grease. Place the lubricant in the radius in back of the bushing.

7. Clean the surfaces of flywheel and pressure plate thoroughly with fine sandpaper or crocus cloth and make certain that all oil and grease has been removed.

8. Hold the clutch disc, pressure plate, and cover in mounting position, with the springs on the disc damper facing away from the flywheel.

   NOTE: Do not touch the disc facing, as dirt or grease may result in clutch chatter.

9. Insert a clutch disc aligning arbor through the hub of the disc and into the bushing. If an arbor is not available, use a spare transmission input clutch shaft.

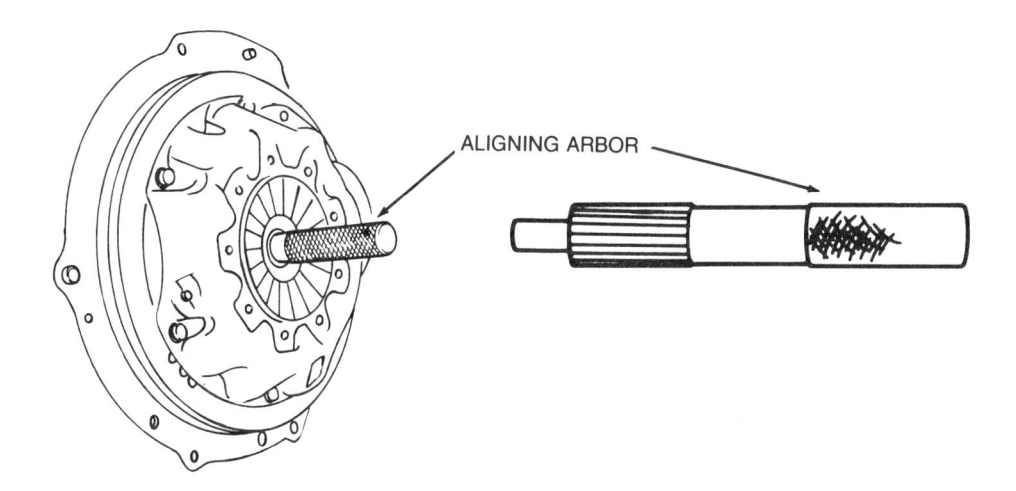

10. Install the clutch cover attaching bolts (after aligning the balance punch marks), but do not tighten them. To avoid bending the clutch cover, the bolts should be tightened a few turns at a time (alternately) until they are all snug.

11. Tighten bolts to specification with a torque wrench.

12. Reassemble the clutch fork and release bearing assembly. Lubricate these components as required by the manufacturer.

13. Install the transmission and drive shaft and adjust the clutch free travel.

NOTES

Date Completed _____ Instructor's Check _____

NAME _____ SECTION _____ DATE _____ SCORE _____

Chapter 34 MANUALLY OPERATED TRANSAXLE AND TRANSMISSION
ASSIGNMENT SHEET 28

Three-Speed Power Flow

Before you begin: Read Chapter 34 in *Auto Mechanics*. In the spaces at the right of the illustrations below, identify the gear the transmission is in and explain the power flow through the transmission.

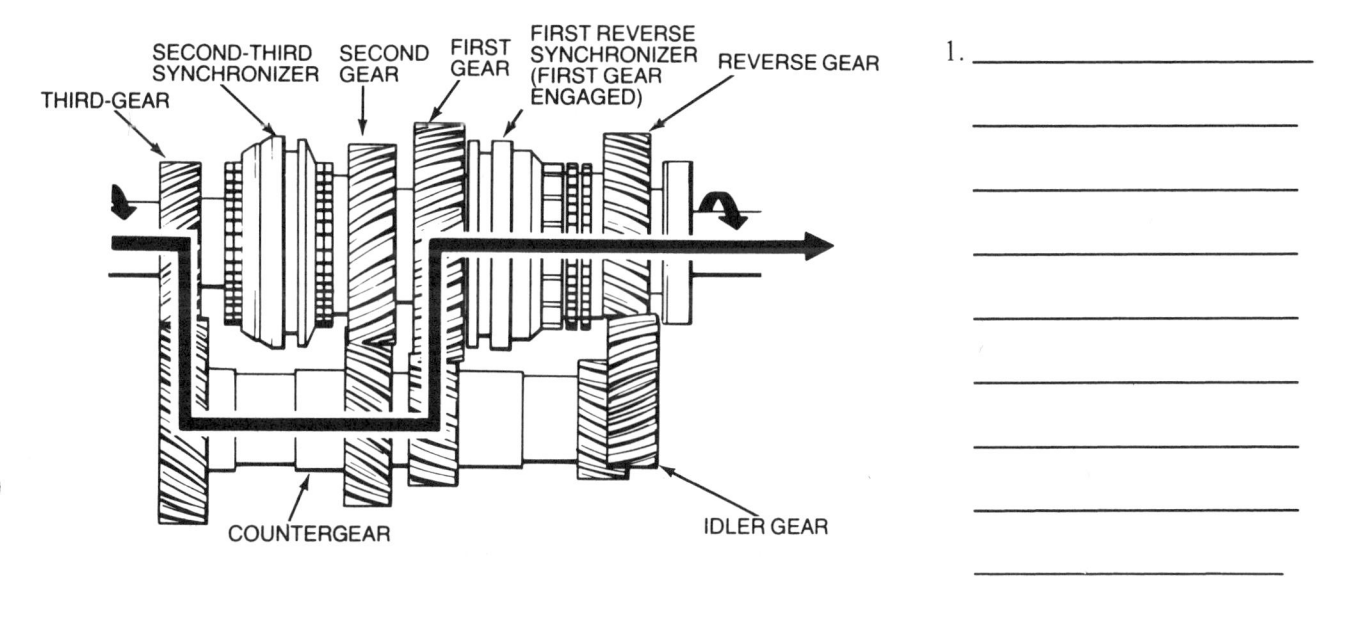

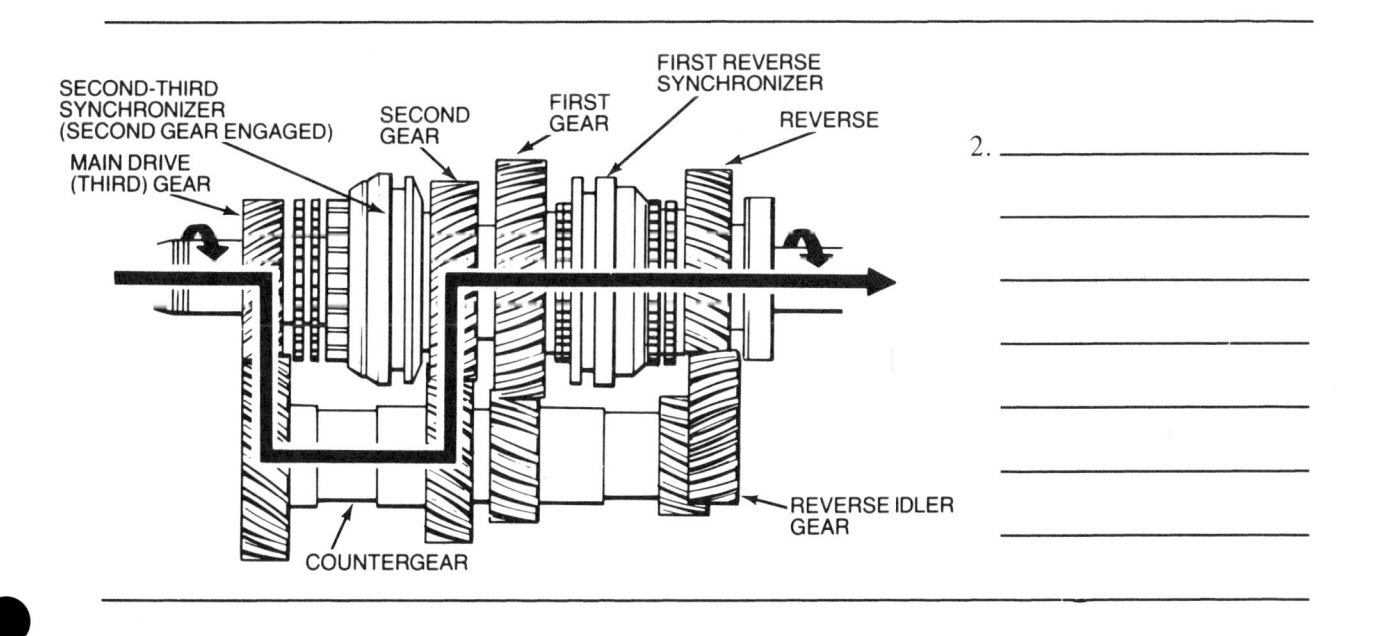

1. _____

2. _____

155

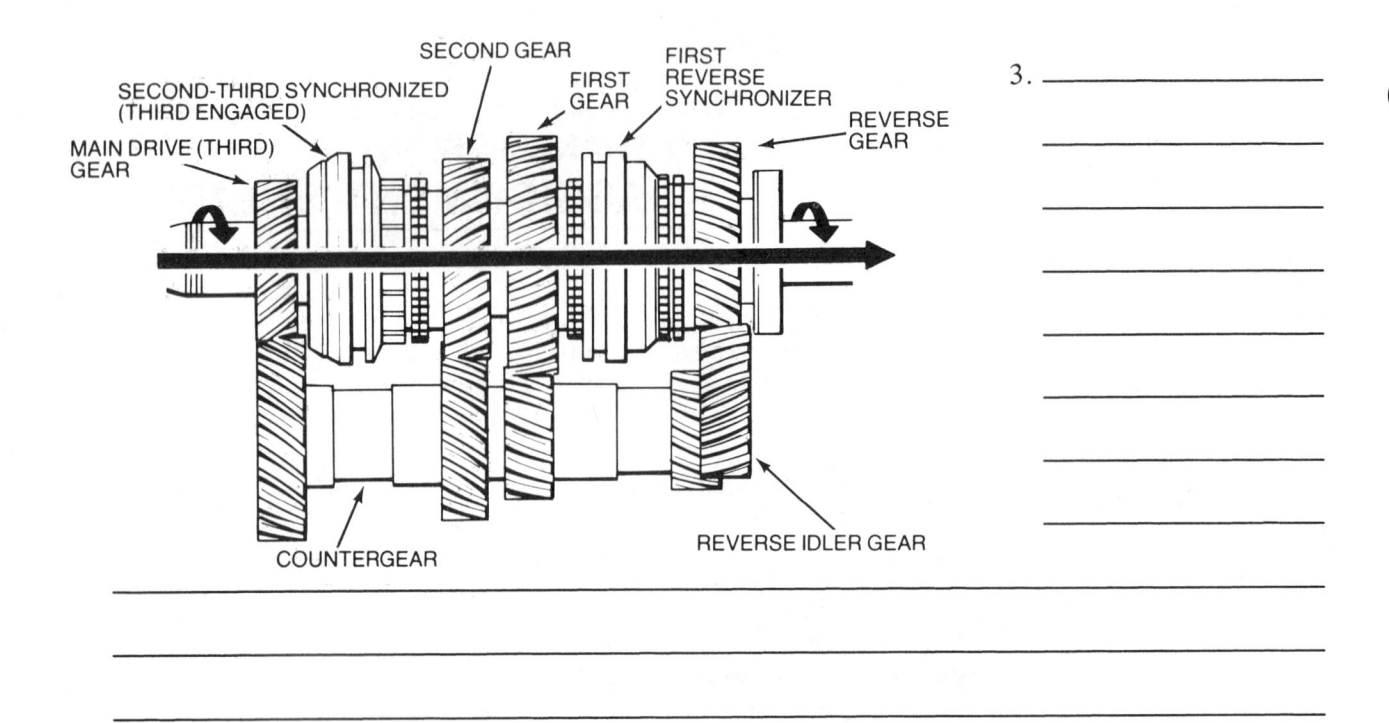

SECOND-THIRD SYNCHRONIZED (THIRD ENGAGED)
MAIN DRIVE (THIRD) GEAR
SECOND GEAR
FIRST GEAR
FIRST REVERSE SYNCHRONIZER
REVERSE GEAR
COUNTERGEAR
REVERSE IDLER GEAR

3. _____

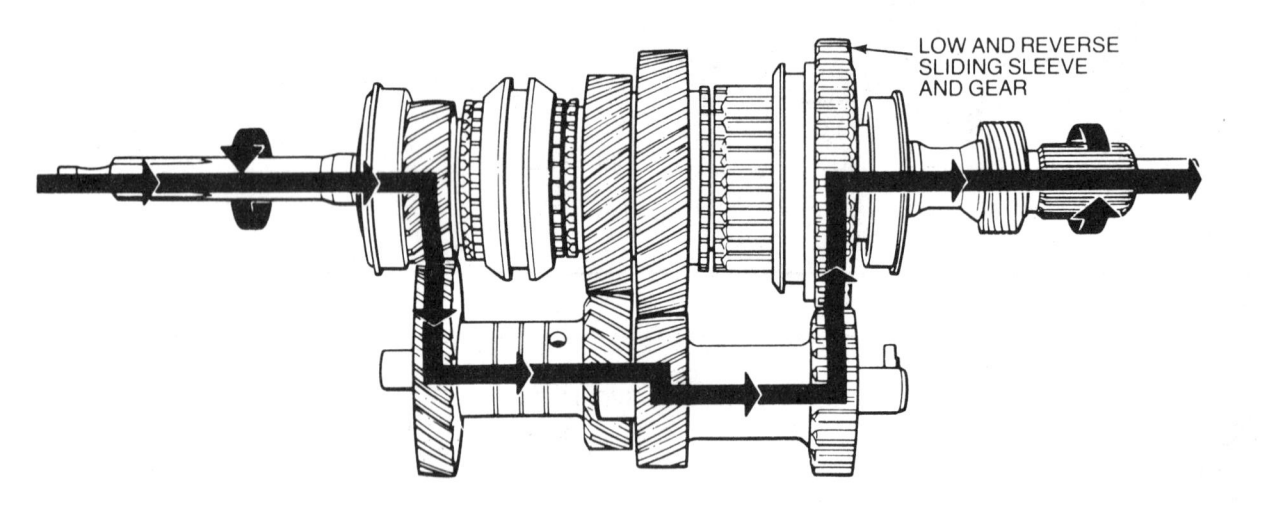

LOW AND REVERSE SLIDING SLEEVE AND GEAR

4. _____

NAME_____ SECTION_____ DATE_____ SCORE_____

Chapter 34 MANUALLY OPERATED TRANSAXLE AND TRANSMISSION
ASSIGNMENT SHEET 29

Four-Speed Transmission Parts Identification

Before you begin: Read Chapter 34 in *Auto Mechanics*. Identify the parts of a four-speed transmission in the spaces provided below.

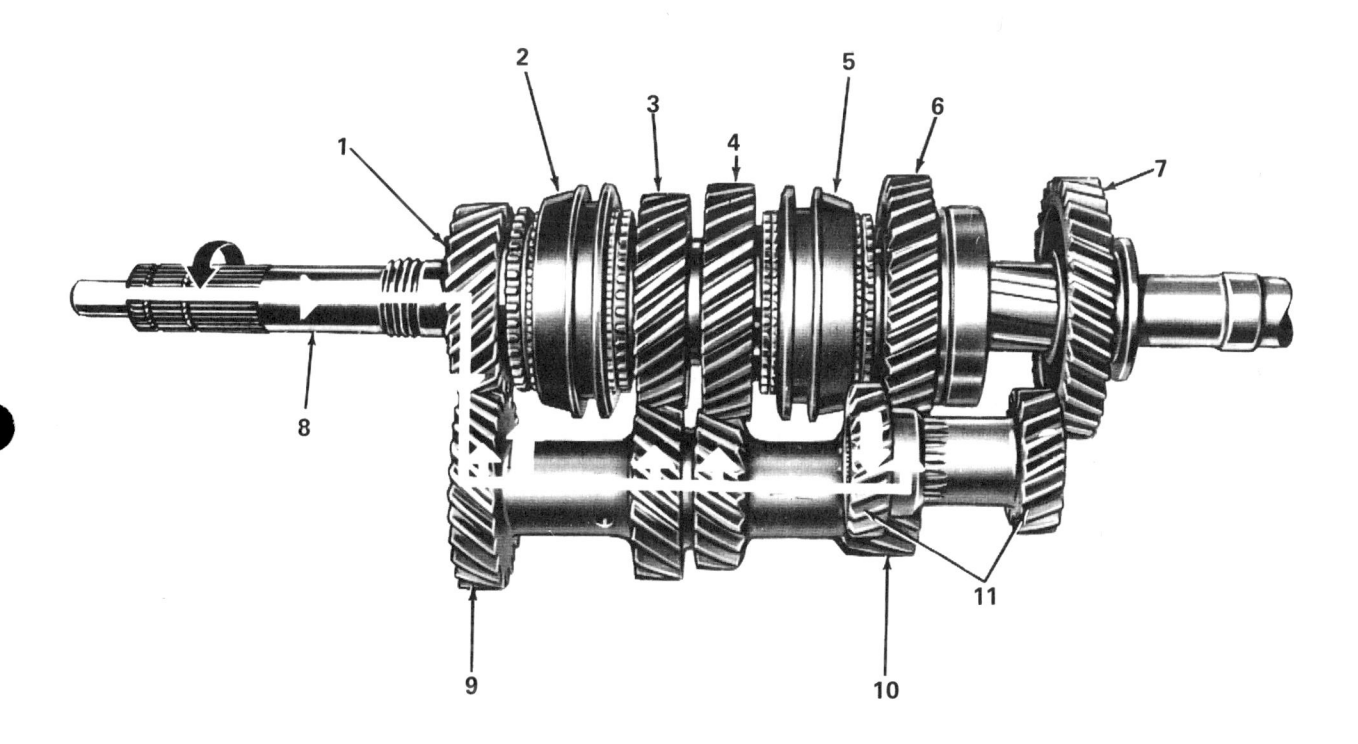

1. _____
2. _____
   _____
3. _____
4. _____
5. _____
6. _____

7. _____
8. _____
9. _____
   _____
10. _____
    _____
11. _____
    _____

157

Review of New Terms

For each definition in Column 2, select the term in Column 1 that best matches its meaning. Write the identifying *letter* of the term in the Answer column.

Column 1

A. Control linkage

B. Gear ratio

C. Overdrive transmissions

D. Synchronizer

E. Transaxle

Column 2

1. A transmission that provides a gear ratio higher than one to one.

2. An axle assembly and transmission combined into one housing.

3. The floor or steering column linkage used by the driver to select the transmission gears.

4. A device that makes the speed of gears and shafts the same so that they can be meshed without clashing.

5. The numerical relationship of the number of teeth on two gears in mesh with each other.

Answer

1. _____

2. _____

3. _____

4. _____

5. _____

NAME _____ SECTION _____ DATE _____ SCORE _____

Chapter 35 MANUAL TRANSMISSION AND TRANSAXLE SERVICE
ASSIGNMENT SHEET 23

Remove and Replace a Manual Transmission

Before you begin: Read Chapter 35 in *Auto Mechanics*.

Student _____ Section _____ Date _____

Make of Car _____ Model _____ Year _____

Time Started _____ Time Finished _____ Total Time _____

Flat Rate Time _____

Special Tools, Equipment, Parts, and Materials

Vise-grip pliers   Transmission guide studs (2)

Lift jack   Transmission jack

Stationary or "safety" jacks

_____   _____

_____   _____

References

Manufacturer's Shop Manual _____

Repair Manual _____

Service Bulletin _____

                                        _____
                                                Instructor's Check

Procedure

1. Remove shift rods from transmission levers. Drain the fluid from the transmission.

2. Disconnect the drive shaft at the rear universal joint. Mark both parts to reassemble in the same position.

3. Carefully pull the drive shaft yoke out of the transmission extension housing.

159

4. Disconnect the speedometer cable and backup light switch leads.

5. Raise the engine slightly with the support fixture or jack.

6. Disconnect the extension housing from the removable center cross member.

    Safety Caution: Support the transmission with a suitable jack and remove the center cross member.

7. Remove the transmission to the clutch housing bolts. Slide the transmission toward the rear until the clutch shaft clears the clutch disc before lowering the transmission.

8. Lower the transmission and remove it from under the vehicle.

9. Place a small amount of multipurpose lubricant around the inner end of the clutch shaft pilot bushing in the flywheel and on the clutch shaft release bearing sleeve area.

    NOTE: Do not lubricate the end of the clutch shaft, clutch disc splines, or clutch release levers.

10. With the transmission on a suitable jack, slide the assembly under the vehicle. Raise the transmission until the clutch shaft is centered in the clutch housing bore. Roll the transmission slowly forward until the clutch shaft enters the clutch disc.

11. Turn the clutch shaft until splines are aligned; then work the transmission forward until seated against the clutch housing.

    Safety Caution: Do not allow the transmission to hang after the pinion shaft has entered the clutch disc.

12. Install the transmission to the clutch housing bolts and tighten to specifications with a torque wrench.

13. Align cross member bolt holes with a pointed drift and install attaching bolts. Tighten to specifications.

14. Remove the engine support fixture.

15. Install the extension housing to the rear engine mount bolts.

16. Fasten the shift unit to the extension housing mounting plate.

17. Connect shift control rods to transmission levers and connect the speedometer cable.

18. Carefully guide the front universal joint yoke into the extension housing and onto mainshaft splines. Connect the drive shaft to rear axle pinion yoke aligning marks made at removal. Reconnect exhaust pipes (if removed).

Date Completed _____ Instructor's Check _____

NAME _____ SECTION _____ DATE _____ SCORE _____

Chapter 35 MANUAL TRANSMISSION AND TRANSAXLE SERVICE
ASSIGNMENT SHEET 24

Overhaul a Manual Transmission

Before you begin: Read Chapter 35 in *Auto Mechanics.*

Student _____ Section _____ Date _____

Make of Car _____ Model _____ Year _____

Time Started _____ Time Finished _____ Total Time _____

Flat Rate Time _____

Special Tools, Equipment, Parts, and Materials

Transmission spanner wrenches   Transmission gasket set

Drift punches   Transmission-gear pullers

Clutch-plate centering tool   _____

Plastic hammer   _____

_____   _____

_____   _____

References

Manufacturer's Shop Manual _____

Repair Manual _____

Service Bulletin _____

_____
Instructor's Check

Procedure

1. Disassembly procedures are different for different transmissions, but the following procedures for a three-speed are typical.

2. Remove the case cover attaching bolts and then the case cover and gasket. Remove bolts holding the clutch shaft bearing retainer to the front of the transmission case. Slide the retainer and gasket forward off the clutch shaft.

3. Pry the clutch shaft oil seal from the bearing retainer.

   NOTE: To avoid leakage around the new seal, do not nick or scratch the bore in which the seal is pressed or the surface on which the seal bottoms.

4. Tap the drive pinion forward carefully with a brass drift, to provide maximum disassembly clearance for mainshaft removal.

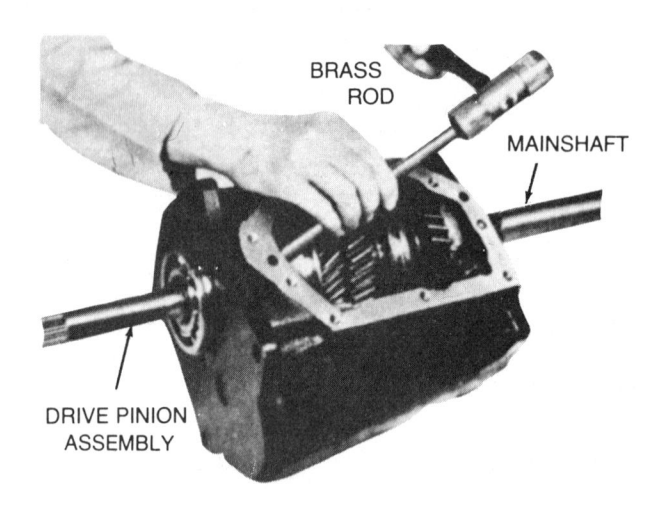

5. Remove the bolt and retainer holding the speedometer pinion adapter in the extension housing. Carefully work adapter and pinion out of the extension housing.

6. Remove bolts that attach the extension housing to the rear of the transmission case. Tap it with a plastic hammer to break the gasket seal and carefully guide the housing off the rear of the mainshaft.

7. An arbor tool may be used to push the reverse idler shaft and key out of the case. Remove the idler gear with the arbor in place to hold the rollers.

NAME _____ SECTION _____ DATE _____ SCORE _____

8. After removing the reverse idler gear and thrust washers, remove the mainshaft assembly through the rear of the case.

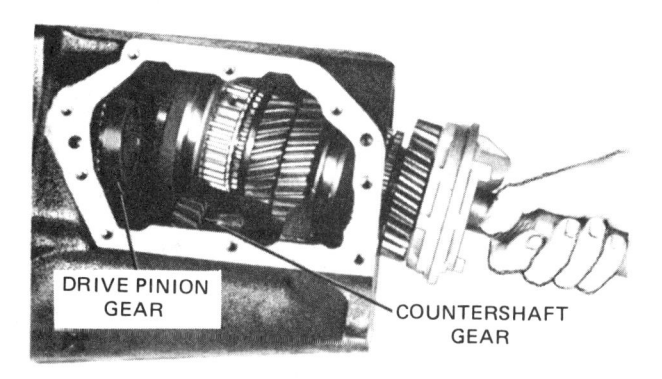

9. Tap the countershaft rearward with a mallet and arbor tool and remove the key. Continue to drive the countershaft out of the case, maintaining contact between shaft and arbor so that washers will not drop between them.

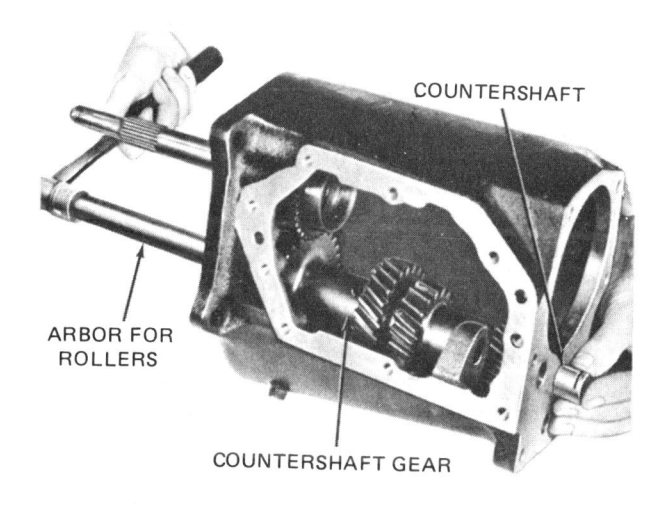

10. Lower the countershaft gear to the bottom of the case to permit removal of the main driver gear.

11. Remove the snap ring from the clutch shaft bearing outer race or cup.

12. Using a plastic hammer, drive the clutch shaft into the case and remove it through the rear.

13. Lift countershaft gear and arbor assembly out through the rear of the case.

14. Remove the snap ring that retains the second-third synchronizer clutch gear from the front end of the mainshaft. Slide the second-third synchronizer assembly off the end of the mainshaft along with the second gear synchronizer ring.

15. Remove second gear from the mainshaft.

16. Spread the snap ring in the mainshaft bearing retainer to disengage it from the bearing groove and slide the retainer off the bearing race. Remove the snap ring holding the bearing to the mainshaft.

17. Set up parts in a press to force the bearing off the mainshaft. Supporting the front side of reverse gear allows the press to push the bearing off the shaft as pressure is applied to the shaft.

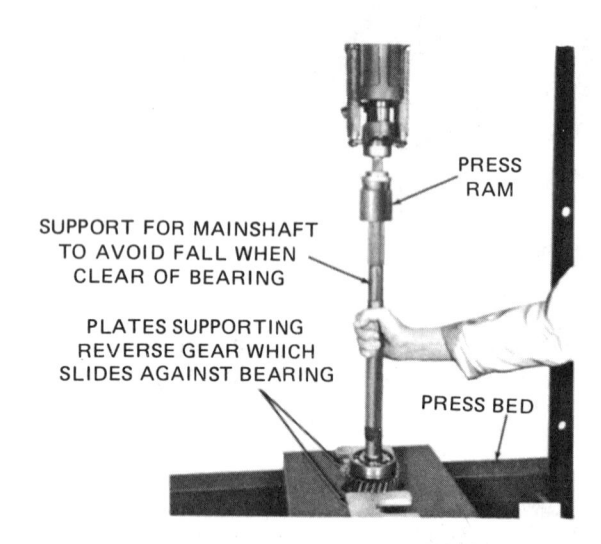

18. Clean the transmission case thoroughly with a suitable solvent, and allow it to dry.

19. Wash ball bearings with a clean solvent and allow them to dry.

20. Inspect gear teeth on synchronizer clutch gears and synchronizer rings. If there is evidence of chipping or excessively worn teeth, install new parts at reassembly.

21. Inspect teeth on the clutch shaft gear. If excessively worn, broken or chipped, a new clutch shaft should be installed. If the oil seal contact area on the clutch shaft is pitted, rusted, or scratched, a new shaft is recommended for best seal life.

22. Test the interlock sleeve and pin for free movement in the bore of the shift housing. Examine the detent balls for signs of pitting. If lever detents show signs of too much wear, install a new part. Inspect shift forks for wear on the shanks and pads.

23. Inspect mainshaft gear and bearing mating surfaces. If gear contact surfaces show signs of pitting or are worn too much, install a new mainshaft.

24. Inspect snap ring grooves for burred edges. Remove the burrs with a fine file or crocus cloth. Inspect synchronizer clutch gear splines on the shaft for burrs. Replace worn parts with new ones as required.

25. The reassembly procedure is the reverse of the disassembly procedure. When the transmission has been assembled and filled with lubricant, it may be installed on the vehicle.

Date Completed _____   Instructor's Check _____

NAME _____ SECTION _____ DATE _____ SCORE _____

Chapter 36 THE AUTOMATIC TRANSMISSION AND TRANSAXLE
ASSIGNMENT SHEET 30

Automatic Transmission and Transaxle Parts Identification

Before you begin: Read Chapter 36 in *Auto Mechanics*. Identify the parts of the torque converter by writing the names in the spaces provided.

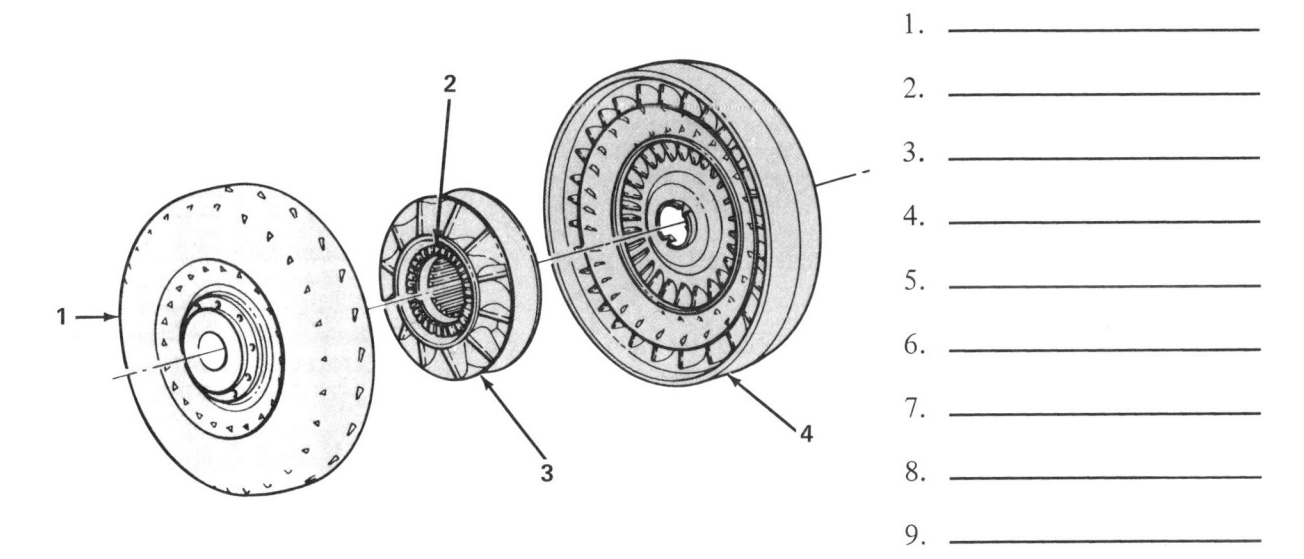

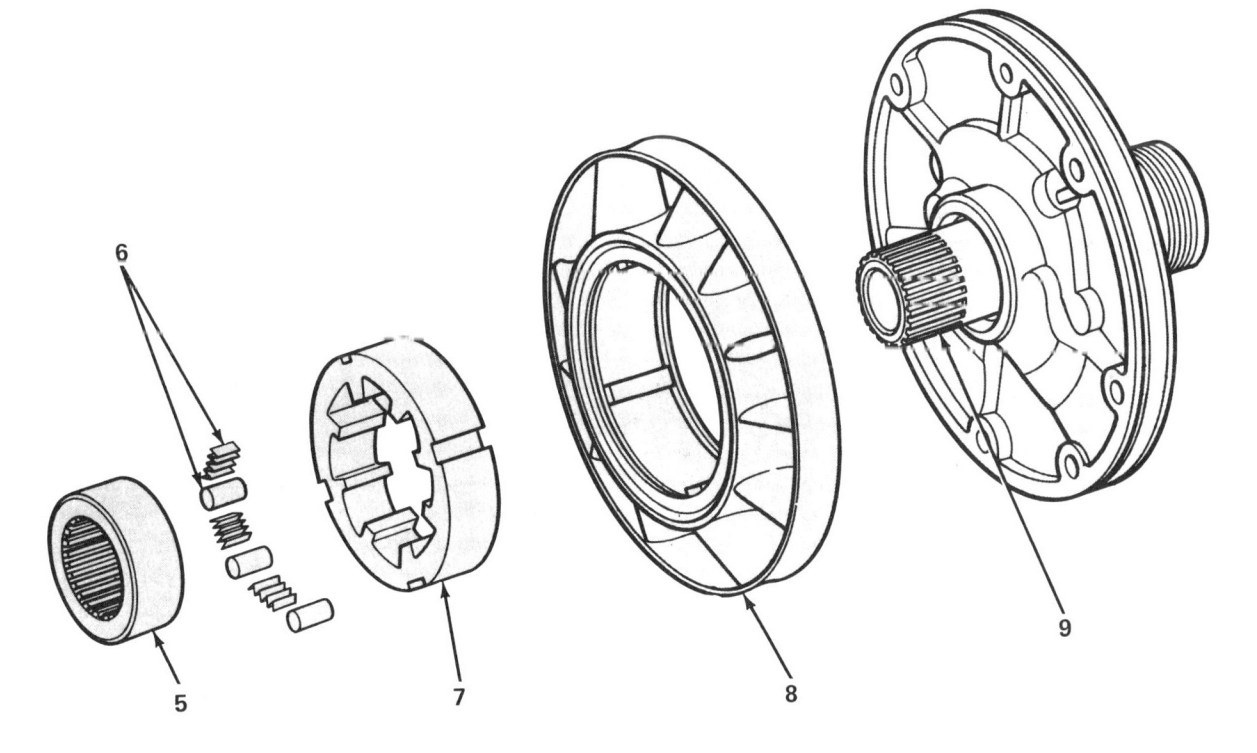

1. _____
2. _____
3. _____
4. _____
5. _____
6. _____
7. _____
8. _____
9. _____

165

Identify the parts of the lockup torque converter by writing the names in the spaces provided.

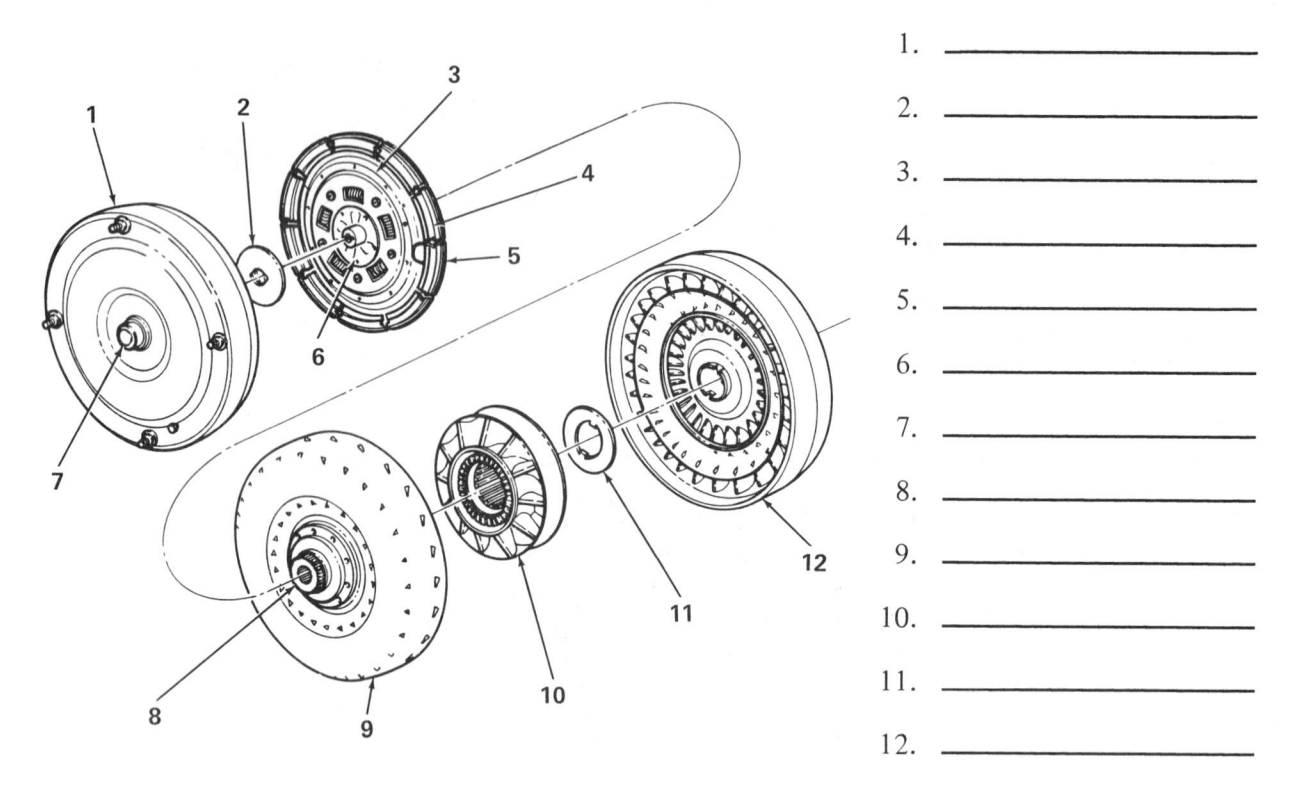

1. _____
2. _____
3. _____
4. _____
5. _____
6. _____
7. _____
8. _____
9. _____
10. _____
11. _____
12. _____

Identify the parts of the planetary gear set in the spaces provided below.

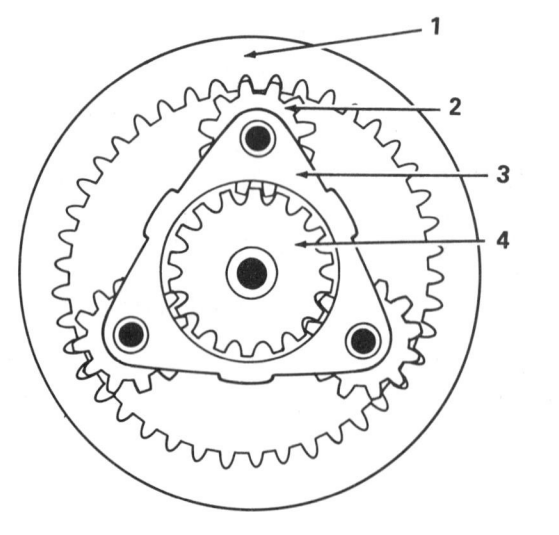

1. _____

2. _____

3. _____

4. _____

166

NAME _____ SECTION _____ DATE _____ SCORE _____

Simpson Planetary Parts Identification

Identify the parts of a Simpson planetary set in the spaces provided below.

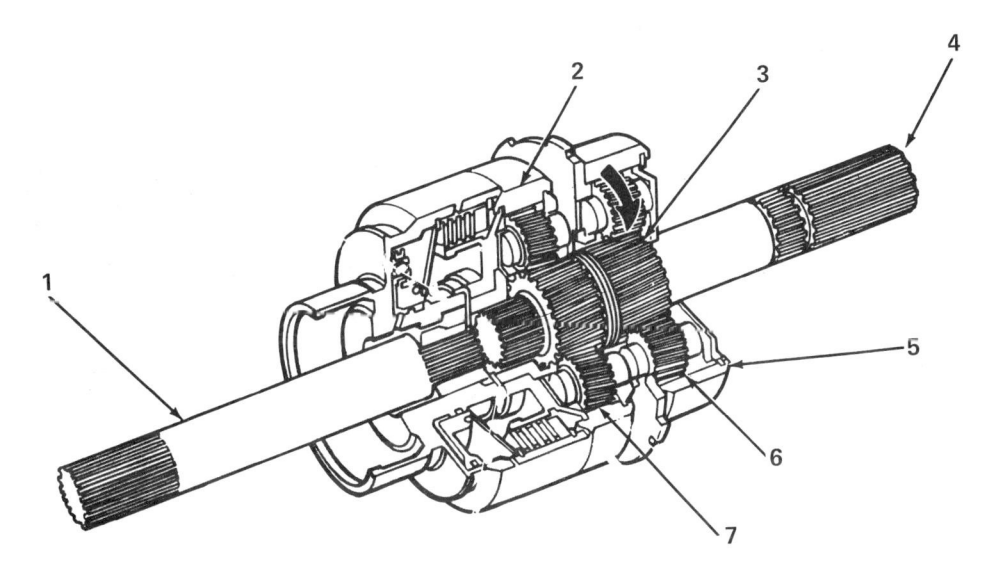

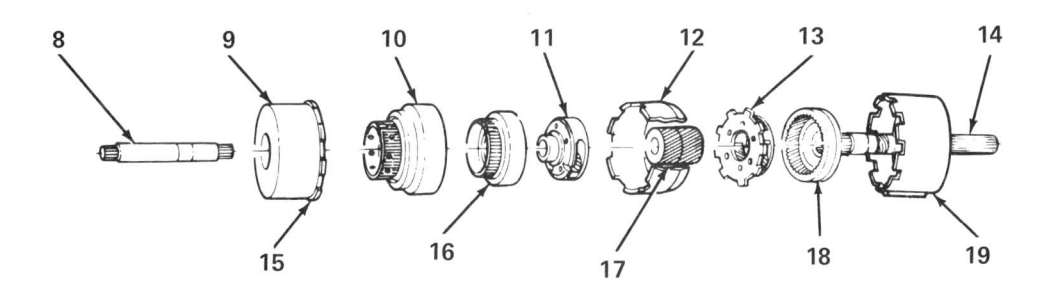

1. _____
2. _____
3. _____
4. _____
5. _____
6. _____
7. _____
8. _____
9. _____
10. _____
11. _____
12. _____
13. _____
14. _____
15. _____
16. _____
17. _____
18. _____
19. _____

167

Identify the parts of the Ravenaux planetary gear system by writing the names in the spaces provided.

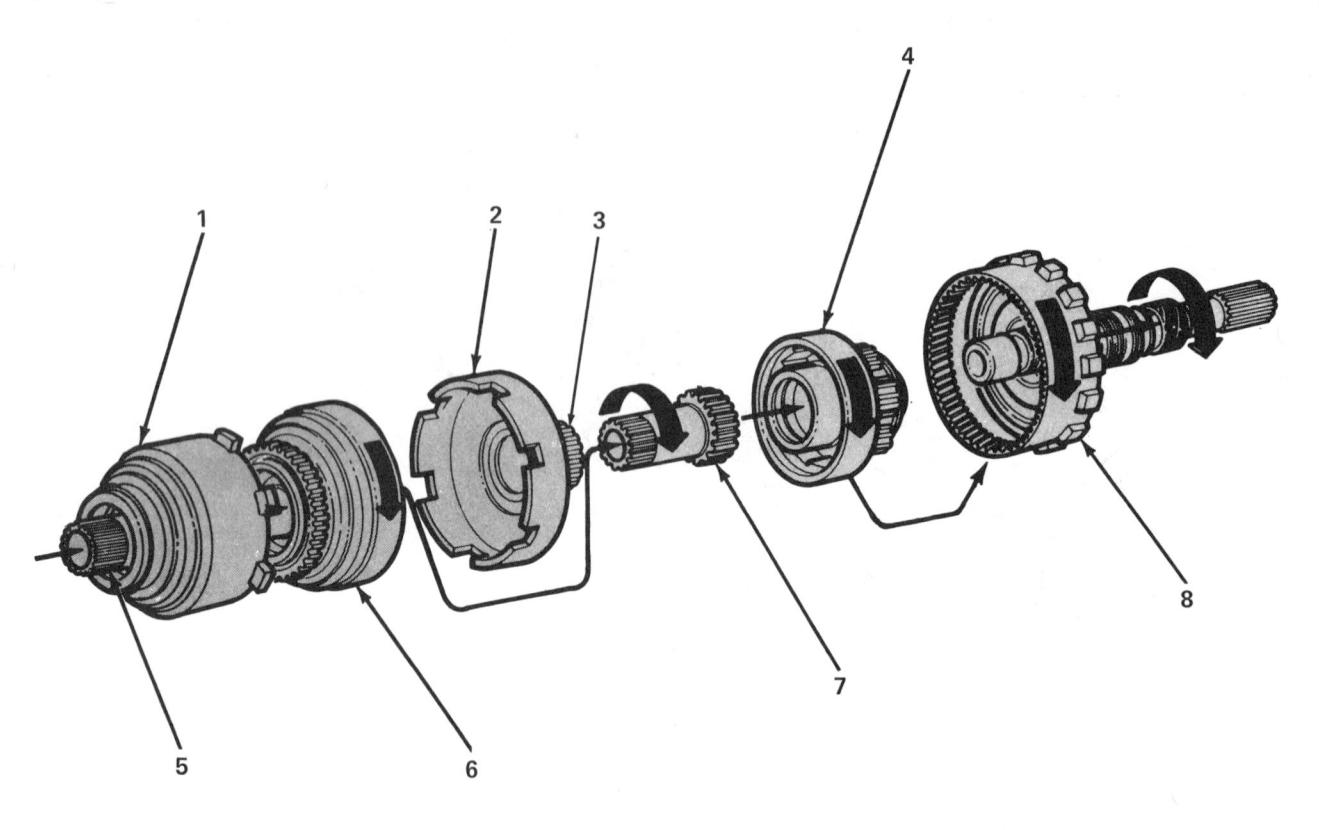

1. _____   5. _____

2. _____   6. _____

3. _____   7. _____

4. _____   8. _____

NAME _____ SECTION _____ DATE _____ SCORE _____

Chapter 36 THE AUTOMATIC TRANSMISSION AND TRANSAXLE
ASSIGNMENT SHEET 31

Band and Clutch Parts Identification

Before you begin: Read Chapter 36 in *Auto Mechanics*. Identify the parts of a band and linkage in the spaces provided below.

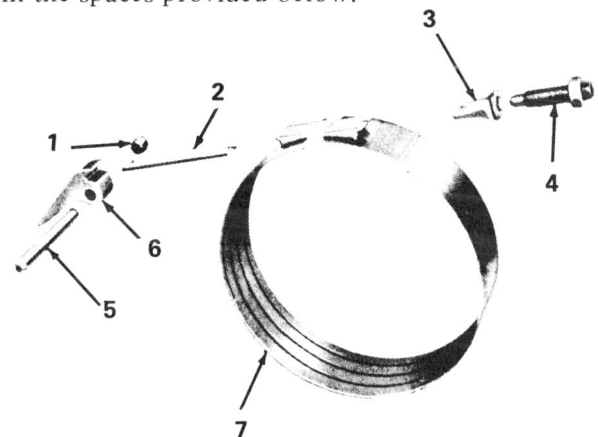

1. _____
2. _____
3. _____
4. _____
5. _____
6. _____
7. _____

Identify the parts of a multiple-disc clutch assembly in the spaces provided below.

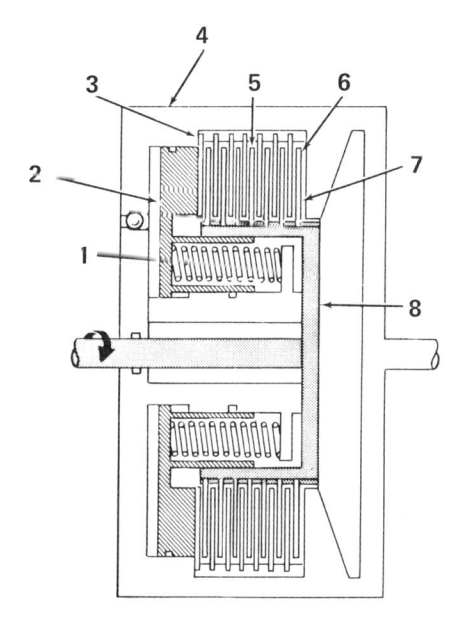

1. _____
2. _____
3. _____
4. _____
5. _____
6. _____
7. _____
8. _____

Identify the parts of the crescent pump by writing the names in the spaces provided.

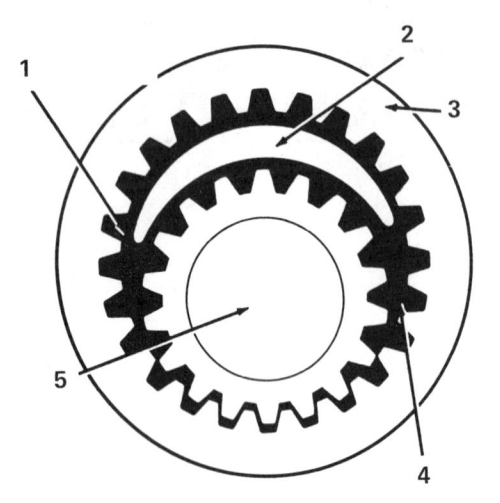

1. _____
2. _____
3. _____
4. _____
5. _____

Identify the parts of the hydraulic control system by writing the names in the spaces provided.

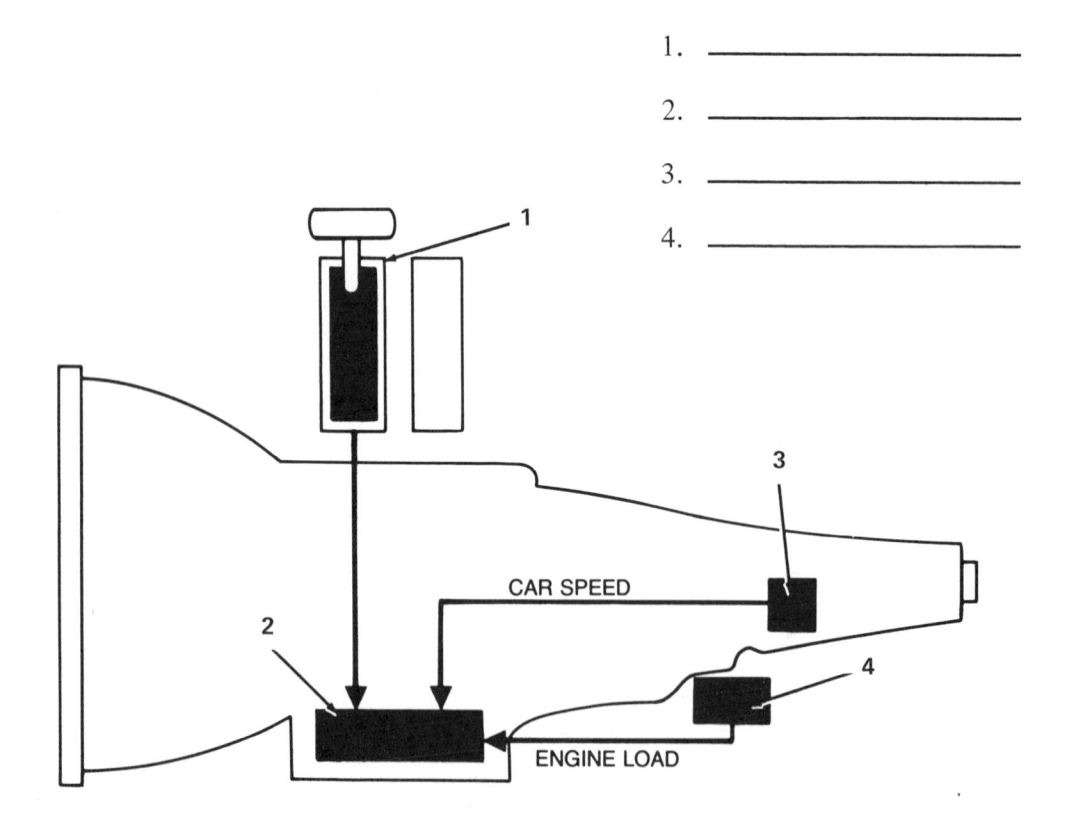

1. _____
2. _____
3. _____
4. _____

CAR SPEED

ENGINE LOAD

NAME _____ SECTION _____ DATE _____ SCORE _____

Identify the parts of the one way clutch in the spaces provided below.

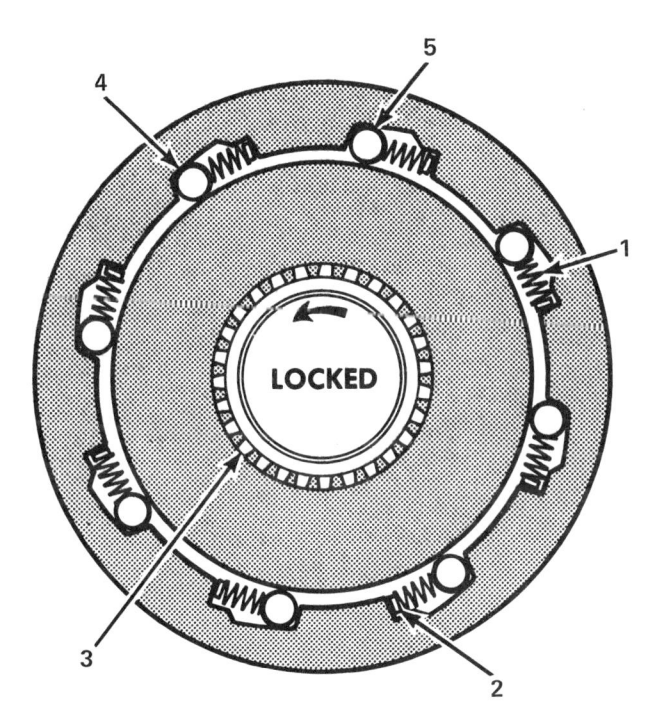

1. _____
2. _____
3. _____
4. _____
5. _____

Identify the parts of a modulator in the spaces provided below.

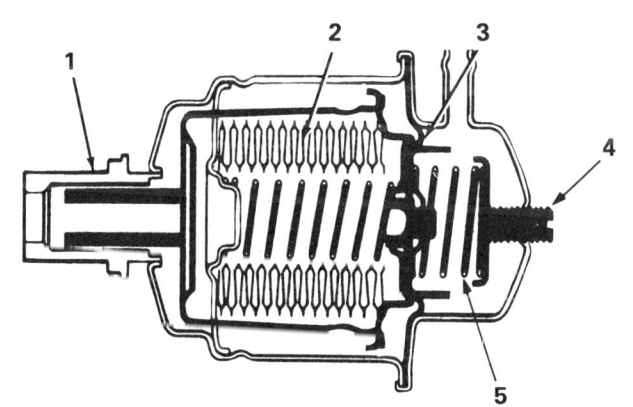

1. _____
2. _____
3. _____
4. _____
5. _____

171

Review of New Terms

For each definition in Column 2, select the term in Column 1 that best matches its meaning. Write the identifying *letter* of the term in the Answer column.

Column 1

A. Band
B. Governor
C. Hydraulic control valves
D. Modulator
E. Planetary gearbox
F. Planetary carrier
G. Planets
H. Ring gear
I. Stator
J. Sun gear

Column 2

1. The system of valves that senses driving conditions and automatically shifts the transmission.
2. The part of a planetary gearbox that supports the planet gears.
3. A vacuum canister mounted to the outside of the transmission that senses engine load.
4. One of the main parts of a torque converter used to redirect fluid back at the pump.
5. The part of the planetary gear system that meshes with the ring and sun gear.
6. A planetary holding unit wrapped around a drum to stop its rotation.
7. One of the main parts of a planetary gear system with external teeth used to mesh with the planets.
8. The system of gears used in an automatic transmission: a sun gear, planet gears, a carrier, and a ring gear.
9. The part of the planetary gear system with internal teeth used to mesh with the planets.
10. A device on the output shaft of the transmission used to sense vehicle speed.

Answer

1. _____
2. _____
3. _____
4. _____
5. _____
6. _____
7. _____
8. _____
9. _____
10. _____

NAME _____ SECTION _____ DATE _____ SCORE _____

Chapter 37 AUTOMATIC TRANSMISSION AND TRANSAXLE SERVICE
JOB SHEET 25

Drain and Refill Automatic Transmission and Transaxle Fluid

Before you begin: Read Chapter 37 in *Auto Mechanics*.

Student _____ Section _____ Date _____

Make of Car _____ Model _____ Year _____

Time Started _____ Time Finished _____ Total Time _____

Flat Rate Time _____

Special Tools, Equipment, Parts, and Materials

Transmission funnel   _____

Fluid pan gasket   _____

Filter (if required)   _____

New fluid   _____

_____   _____

References

Manufacturer's Shop Manual _____

Repair Manual _____

Service Bulletin _____

Specifications

Look up the following specifications and record them in the spaces provided below.

Fluid type _____

Fluid capacity (with torque converter) _____

Fluid capacity (without torque converter) _____

_____
Instructor's Check

Procedure

1. Jack or hoist the vehicle off the ground.

2. Inspect the fluid pan for the drain plug.

    NOTE: Most late model vehicles DO NOT have a drain plug, so the pan must be removed for a fluid change.

3. If the pan has a drain plug, remove it and allow the fluid to drain. Then remove the pan.

4. On units without a drain plug, remove the pan to drain the fluid.

5. Remove the flywheel inspection plate.

6. Rotate the engine and check for the drain plug on converter or fluid coupling. Many late model converters do not have plugs and cannot be drained.

7. If the converter can be drained, it may have two plugs, one for a vent and one for a drain. Remove both plugs and drain the converter. Replace the plugs.

8. Remove the filter or filter screen.

9. Clean or replace the filter as specified by the manufacturer.

10. Clean the fluid pan.

11. Install the pan with a new gasket, using a torque wrench to tighten cap screws.

12. Lower the vehicle.

13. Check fluid capacity of the transmission in the owner's manual. If the converter was drained, add only a portion of the fluid to the transmission.

    NOTE: Under or overfilling of fluid will cause the transmission to slip and damage the clutches.

14. Start the engine and allow time for warmup.

15. Check the fluid level.

16. Add additional fluid as required to bring the unit to the correct level.

NOTES

Date Completed _____ Instructor's Check _____

NAME _____ SECTION _____ DATE _____ SCORE _____

Chapter 37 AUTOMATIC TRANSMISSION AND TRANSAXLE SERVICE
JOB SHEET 26

Automatic Transmission and Transaxle Fluid Level Check

Before you begin: Read Chapter 37 in *Auto Mechanics*.

Student _____ Section _____ Date _____

Make of Car _____ Model _____ Year _____

Time Started _____ Time Finished _____ Total Time _____

Flat Rate Time _____

Special Tools, Equipment, Parts, and Materials

Fluid _____

Fluid funnel _____

_____ _____

_____ _____

References

Manufacturer's Shop Manual _____

Repair Manual _____

Service Bulletin _____

Specifications

Look up the following specifications and record them in the spaces provided below.

Fluid level checking quadrant range _____

Type of fluid _____

Instructor's Check

Procedure

1. Drive the vehicle onto a level floor.

2. Set the emergency brake firmly.

3. Start the engine and let it idle.

4. Move the shift quadrant lever through each of the operating ranges and then position it in the correct mode for checking the fluid level.

5. Remove the transmission dipstick and wipe it clean.

6. Push the dipstick back into position firmly.

7. Remove the dipstick and read the level. Dipsticks have two marks, one for *full* and one for *low* or *add*. The low mark on many dipsticks represents a pint.

    NOTE: There is, however, no standard marking system for dipsticks. Check the vehicle owner's manual for proper interpretation.

8. Add the proper amount of automatic transmission fluid.

    NOTE: Use of the wrong type of fluid can cause internal damage to the transmission.

9. Replace dipstick.

_____
Instructor's Check

NOTES

Date Completed _____ Instructor's Check _____

NAME _____ SECTION _____ DATE _____ SCORE _____

Chapter 37 AUTOMATIC TRANSMISSION AND TRANSAXLE SERVICE
JOB SHEET 27

Remove and Replace an Automatic Transmission

Before you begin: Read Chapter 37 in *Auto Mechanics*.

Student _____ Section _____ Date _____

Make of Car _____ Model _____ Year _____

Time Started _____ Time Finished _____ Total Time _____

Flat Rate Time _____

Special Tools, Equipment, Parts, and Materials

Lift jack   Transmission funnel

Stationary jacks (4)   Transmission jack

_____   _____

_____   _____

_____   _____

References

Manufacturer's Shop Manual _____

Repair Manual _____

Service Bulletin _____

_____
Instructor's Check

Procedure

1. Raise the vehicle on a hoist or support it on jack stands.

    Safety Caution: Make sure all persons and objects are out of the way before raising or lowering an automobile.

2. Disconnect the manual shift and detent linkage.

3. Disconnect the vacuum modulator line.

NOTE: A good time to drain the fluid pan is while the vehicle is up on the jack stands.

4. Disconnect the drive shaft at the rear universal joint. Mark both parts so they may be reassembled in the same position. Carefully pull the drive shaft yoke out of the transmission extension housing.

5. Disconnect the speedometer cable, back-up light, and neutral start switch leads.

    NOTE: Some models have exhaust systems which will have to be partially removed for clearance.

    Safety Caution: If necessary, install a support or jack at the rear of the engine.

6. Raise the rear of the engine.

7. Remove the bolts that hold the extension housing to the center crossmember.

8. Support the transmission with a transmission jack.

    Safety Caution: Never try to lift a transmission without a jack. The weight could cause an injury.

9. Remove the center crossmember.

10. Remove the torque converter to flex plate bolts.

11. Slide the transmission to the rear until the torque converter is clear.

12. Lower the transmission.

13. Installing the transmission is essentially the reverse of the removal procedure.

14. The transmission must be refilled with transmission fluid.

15. After start up, the vehicle should be road tested to determine that it operates correctly. Adjustments to the control linkage may be required.

NOTES

Date Completed _____ Instructor's Check _____

NAME _____ SECTION _____ DATE _____ SCORE _____

Chapter 37 AUTOMATIC TRANSMISSION AND TRANSAXLE SERVICE
JOB SHEET 28

Overhaul an Automatic Transmission

Before you begin: Read Chapter 37 in *Auto Mechanics*.

Student _____ Section _____ Date _____

Make of Car _____ Model _____ Year _____

Time Started _____ Time Finished _____ Total Time _____

Flat Rate Time _____

Special Tools, Equipment, Parts, and Materials

Transmission fluid   Overhaul set for transmission involved

Clutch compressing tool   Slide hammer

Dial indicator   Lock-ring pliers

_____   Inch/pound torque wrench

_____   _____

_____   _____

References

Manufacturer's Shop Manual _____

Repair Manual _____

Service Bulletin _____

Specifications

Look up the following specifications and record them in the spaces provided below.

Input shaft end-play _____

Front pump bolt torque _____

Valve body to case bolt torque _____

Band adjustment specifications _____

_____
Instructor's Check

Procedure

1. Clean the entire outside of the transmission prior to disassembly with a steam cleaner.

    NOTE: All openings should be plugged to prevent the entrance of water into the transmission.

2. Remove the torque converter by simply pulling it off the stator reaction shaft.

    NOTE: The converter should be placed in a pan upside down to drain. The fluid that circulates through the transmission also circulates through the torque converter. If there is any evidence of contaminated fluid either in the transmission or in the drained fluid from the converter, the converter must be flushed.

3. Prior to disassembly, check the transmission for gear train end-play.

    NOTE: The end-play is measured with a dial indicator. This check indicates if the planet gears have too much play. This play is corrected by one or more selective thrust washers inside the transmission.

4. Turn the transmission upside down and remove the pan. The screen and valve body are detached by removing their hold down bolts.

    NOTE: Many transmissions have check balls under the valve body. Their position must be noted. Always save any gaskets found between the valve body halves or case. These must be matched up with the new gaskets.

5. Next, remove the front pump housing.

    NOTE: Some front pumps must be removed with a slide hammer or hammers. If so, there will be two threaded holes in the pump housing to connect the slide hammers.

6. With the front pump housing removed, the front clutches and planetary components are removed by pulling them through the front opening in the case. The rear planetary units are also taken out from the front, usually after the removal of snap rings on the output shaft. The extension housing must be removed to allow access to the governor distributor sleeve and output shaft.

7. The clutch pack assemblies are disassembled, using a clutch compressing tool. First, the outside snap ring is removed. The clutch piston is retained by a second snap ring.

    Safety Caution: This snap ring is under spring pressure and should be removed only with a compressing tool.

    The tool removes the spring pressure by pressing on the piston. The snap ring is then removed. As the tool is released, the retainer and springs may be removed. The piston may be removed by taping the unit on a piece of wood or by applying compressed air behind the piston.

    Safety Caution: Wear safety glasses when using an air hose.

NAME _____ SECTION _____ DATE _____ SCORE _____

8. All the metallic components of the transmission may be cleaned in a solvent tank. The valve in the valve body may or may not be removed for cleaning, depending upon how much contamination is evident in the transmission. If the valve body is disassembled, it must be handled carefully so that springs and valves are not mixed up.

9. After cleaning the transmission, parts should be inspected carefully for abnormal wear. Normally the replacement parts will be provided in an overhaul set. This set contains all servo and clutch seals, as well as all necessary gaskets. If the transmission has very high mileage or extensive wear, the clutch discs or shaft bushings may need replacement.

10. A new seal is installed on each of the clutch pistons. The new seal must be stretched around the piston. Be careful to install the seal in the correct direction. The piston and seal are lubricated with transmission fluid and then pushed into the clutch cylinder. The return spring(s) and retainer are then placed into position. This assembly must then be compressed with the clutch tool and the snap ring installed. The steel and friction discs may then be installed in the cylinder. The steel discs installed at either end of the clutch pack may be thicker than those in the middle.

   NOTE: It is good practice to tie the parts together on disassembly to aid in reassembly.

11. A new seal is installed on each of the servo pistons.

    NOTE: Some servos use a bonded seal requiring a new piston and seal to be replaced as a unit. The piston and seal are lubricated with transmission fluid and installed in the piston bore.

12. The output shaft, governor assembly, and extension housing are replaced on the rear of the case. The planetary components may then be installed through the front case opening. The clutch packs are then installed and the front pump bolted in place.

    NOTE: As with all the other bolts, a torque wrench must be used. After reassembly, recheck the end-play with a dial indicator.

13. Replace all the check balls in the case passages. Using the correct gaskets, mount the valve body in place on the case. Install the filter screen. Adjust the band or bands to the proper specifications. Check that all the linkage inside the transmission is properly connected.

14. Replace the pan and pan gasket.

15. Following the overhaul instructions, assemble the transmission. Adjust and check tolerances as directed. Be sure that binding does not exist in the power train or torque converter. Install new gaskets and seals.

16. When applicable, bench-check oil pressures according to the manufacturer's specifications.

17. Install the transmission assembly in the car and attach the shifting controls.

18. Adjust the shifting controls.

   NOTE: Pay specific attention to cars with linkage connected to the carburetor.

19. Fill the transmission according to the manufacturer's instructions.

20. Test oil pressures and band adjustments according to the manufacturer's instructions.

_____
Instructor's Check

NOTES

Date Completed _____ Instructor's Check _____

NAME _____ SECTION _____ DATE _____ SCORE _____

Chapter 38 DRIVE LINE ARRANGEMENTS
ASSIGNMENT SHEET 32

Drive Line Parts Identification

Before you begin: Read Chapter 38 in *Auto Mechanics.* Identify the parts of the front wheel drive shafts in the spaces provided below.

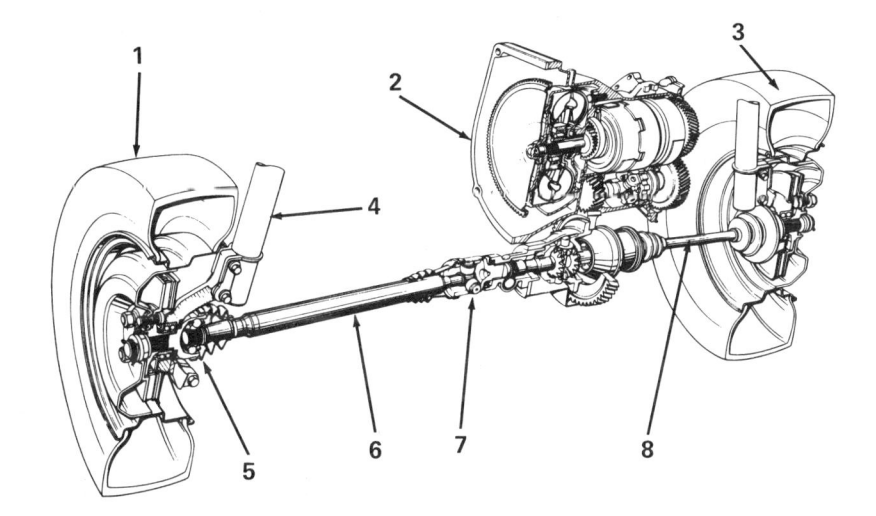

1. _____
2. _____
3. _____
4. _____
5. _____
6. _____
7. _____
8. _____

Identify the parts of the rear drive slip joint in the spaces provided below.

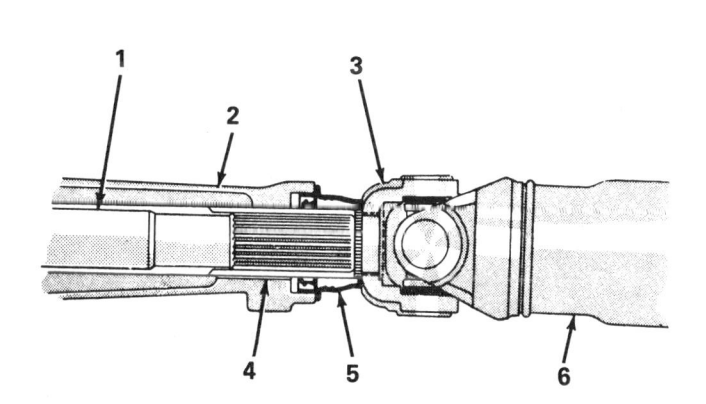

1. _____
2. _____
3. _____
4. _____
5. _____
6. _____

183

Identify the parts of the rear drive universal joint in the spaces provided below.

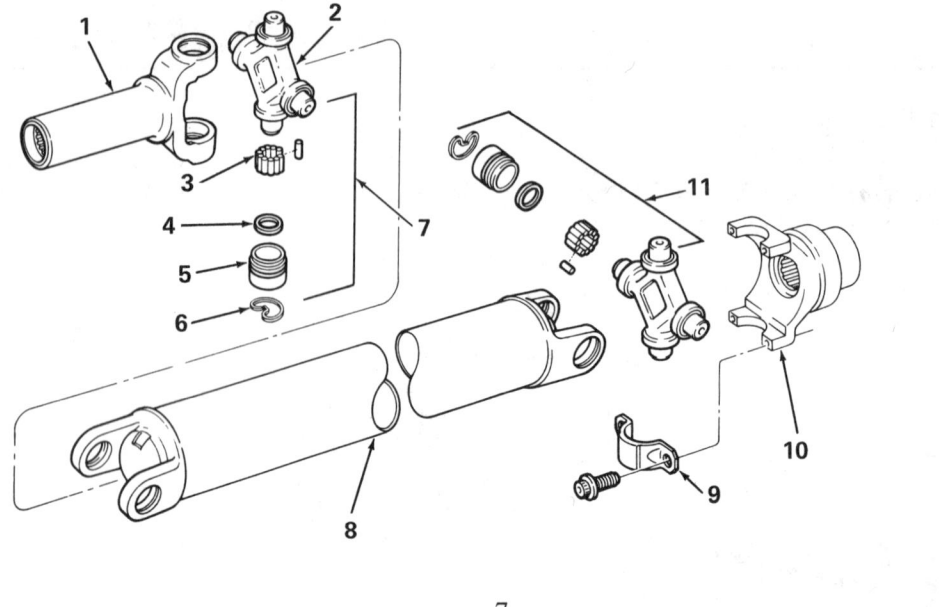

1. _____   7. _____
2. _____   8. _____
3. _____   9. _____
4. _____   10. _____
5. _____   11. _____
6. _____

Identify the parts of the constant velocity universal joint in the spaces provided below.

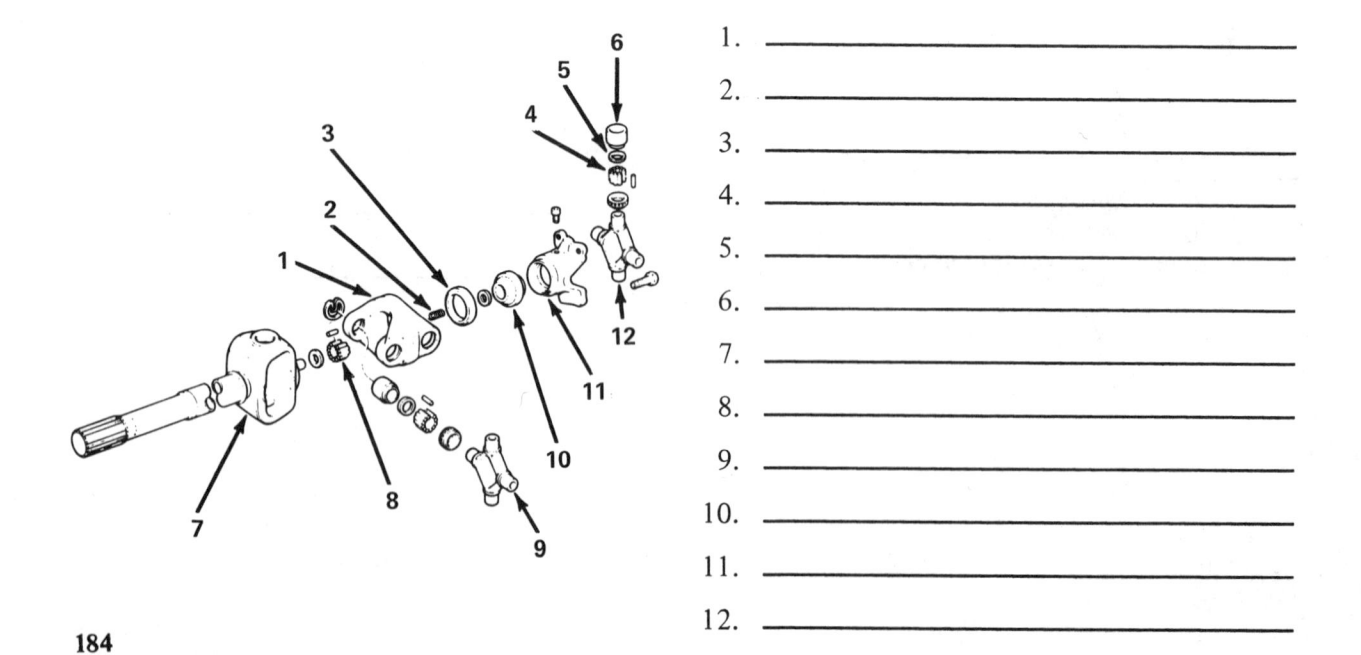

1. _____
2. _____
3. _____
4. _____
5. _____
6. _____
7. _____
8. _____
9. _____
10. _____
11. _____
12. _____

NAME_____ SECTION_____ DATE_____ SCORE_____

Review of New Terms

For each definition in Column 2, select the term in Column 1 that best matches its meaning. Write the identifying *letter* of the term in the Answer column.

Column 1

A. Inboard joint
B. Transfer case
C. Drive shaft
D. Drive line assembly
E. Universal joint
F. Part-time transfer case
G. Outboard joint
H. Full-time transfer case
I. Hotchkiss drive
J. Flexible joints

Column 2

1. The parts used to transfer engine power from the transmission to the rear axle assembly.
2. A large steel tube that transfers engine power from the transmission to the rear axle assembly.
3. Joints on a front-drive axle which allow the front wheels to turn and move up and down with the suspension.
4. A drive line assembly with two or three universal joints and an open drive shaft.
5. The inside joint on a front-drive axle which allows for front wheel up and down movement.
6. The outside joint on a front-drive axle which allows the front wheels to turn back and forth.
7. A transfer case that provides four-wheel drive under all road conditions.
8. A transfer case that allows the driver to select two- or four-wheel drive by shifting gears in the case.
9. A system of gears in a housing behind the transmission that directs power to a front and rear drive anxle.
10. The part of the drive line assembly that allows for a change in angle of the drive line as the vehicle goes over bumps.

Answer

1. _____
2. _____
3. _____
4. _____
5. _____
6. _____
7. _____
8. _____
9. _____
10. _____

NAME _____ SECTION _____ DATE _____ SCORE _____

Chapter 39 DRIVE LINE SERVICE
JOB SHEET 29

Rear Drive Line Inspection

Before you begin: Read Chapter 39 in *Auto Mechanics*.

Student _____ Section _____ Date _____

Make of Car _____ Model _____ Year _____

Time Started _____ Time Finished _____ Total Time _____

Flat Rate Time _____

Special Tools, Equipment, Parts, and Materials

Dial indicator   _____

_____   _____

_____   _____

References

Manufacturer's Shop Manual _____

Repair Manual _____

Service Bulletin _____

Specification

Look up the following specification and record it in the space provided below.

Drive Shaft Runout _____

_____
Instructor's Check

Procedure

1. Undercoating, mud, or any foreign material on one side of the drive shaft can throw it out of balance. A dent in the steel wall of the drive shaft can also cause it to vibrate. The drive shaft should be inspected visually for these problems.

2. Drive shaft vibrations may also be due to loose universal joint flange bolts or bent components in the universal joints. These parts should be inspected visually and replaced as necessary.

3. Runout or too much wobble of the drive shaft is measured with a dial indicator at both ends of the drive shaft, just forward or behind the balance weight(s).

4. Clean paint and any undercoating from the shaft in those areas.

5. Attach a dial indicator support to stud or C-clamp. Mount the dial indicator so the stylus is at a right angle to the shaft. To get an accurate reading, rotate the drive shaft by light downward hand pressure applied at the middle of the shaft. Runout greater than 0.010 inch is unacceptable. Replace the drive shaft if runout is excessive at the front end. Record the amount of runout you measure _____

6. If runout at the front is acceptable, measure runout at the rear. Attach the dial indicator support to the rear housing pinion boss. Mount the dial indicator so the stylus is at a right angle to the drive shaft. Rotate the shaft to measure runout. Record the amount of runout you measure _____

7. To get an accurate reading, rotate the drive shaft by light downward hand pressure applied at the middle of the shaft. Runout greater than 0.010 inch is unacceptable. If the reading is unacceptable, disconnect the shaft, rotate either the shaft or the rear yoke 180°, and reconnect the shaft. Measure the runout at the rear again. Record the amount of runout you measure _____

8. Road test the vehicle and check for vibration on deceleration.

_____
Instructor's Check

NOTES

Date Completed _____ Instructor's Check _____

NAME_____ SECTION_____ DATE_____ SCORE_____

Chapter 39 DRIVE LINE SERVICE
JOB SHEET 30

Removing and Replacing a Rear Drive Universal Joint

Before you begin: Read Chapter 39 in *Auto Mechanics*.

Student _____ Section_____ Date_____

Make of Car _____ Model _____ Year _____

Time Started _____ Time Finished _____ Total Time_____

Flat Rate Time _____

Special Tools, Equipment, Parts, and Materials

Grease

Universal joint kit

_____

_____

_____

_____

References

Manufacturer's Shop Manual _____

Repair Manual _____

Service Bulletin _____

_____
Instructor's Check

Procedure

1. Remove the drive shaft by unbolting the flange or strap attachment at the rear axle end. Withdraw the drive shaft front yoke from the transmission by moving the shaft rearward, passing it under the axle housing.

2. Before disassembling the universal joint, mark the yoke, cross, and bushings to help reassembly if inspection shows that parts are serviceable. Remove the four bushing retainers from the universal joint cross assembly.

3. Using a socket approximately the same diameter as the bushing, press one bushing and roller assembly out of the yoke by pressing the opposite bushing in.

4. Press out the remaining bushing and roller assembly by pressing on the end of the cross.

5. Remove the cross assembly from the yoke.

6. Clean all parts in a suitable solvent and allow them to dry. Examine bearing surfaces of the cross. They should be smooth and free from ripples and pits. If bearing surfaces or seal retainers are damaged, replace the cross assembly. Examine rollers in bushings. Rollers that have operated on a worn cross should be replaced. Rollers should be smooth so that they roll freely inside bushings.

7. Lubricate the bushing and roller assemblies with a recommended lubricant. Also fill reservoirs in the ends of the cross.

8. Place the cross in the drive shaft yoke, observing identification marks made at disassembly.

9. Install bushings and roller assemblies in the yoke, matching identifying marks. Press both bushing assemblies into the yoke while guiding the cross into bushings.

10. Correctly position bushings so retainers can be installed. Position the remaining two bushing assemblies on the cross. Install the retainer strap to hold bushings on the cross during installation of the shaft on the drive pinion flange. Lightly tap outer ends of bushings while rotating the cross to be sure cross and bushings operate freely.

_____
Instructor's Check

NOTES

Date Completed _____ Instructor's Check_____

NAME _____ SECTION _____ DATE _____ SCORE _____

Chapter 40 DIFFERENTIAL ASSEMBLY
ASSIGNMENT SHEET 33

Differential Power Flow

Before you begin: Read Chapter 40 in *Auto Mechanics*. Draw arrows on the illustration below to depict the power flow through the differential when the car is traveling straight ahead. Write a description of the power flow on the lines provided below.

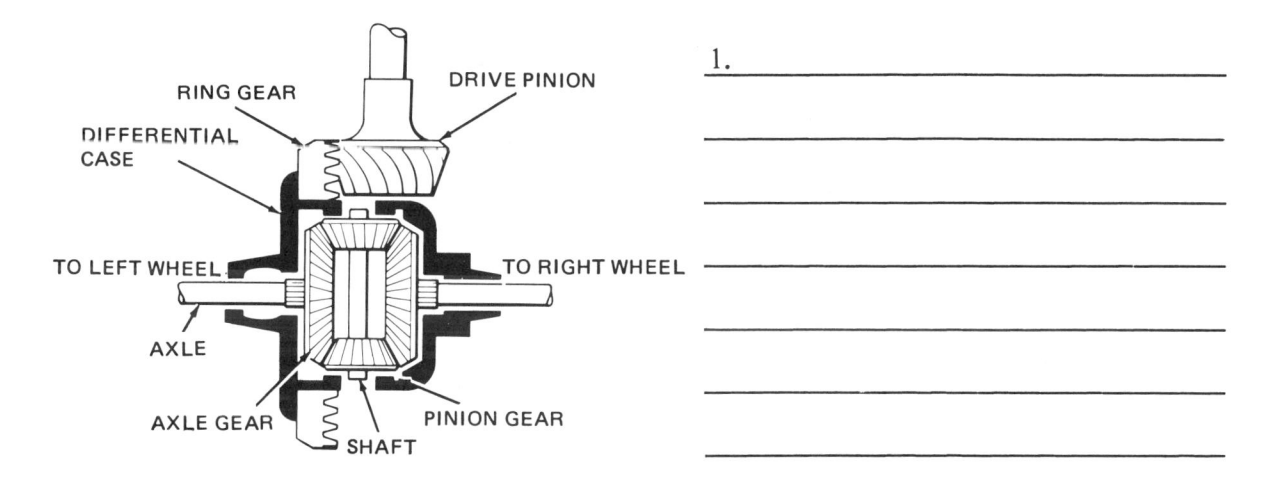

1. _____
_____
_____
_____
_____
_____
_____
_____

Draw arrows on the illustration below to depict the power flow through the differential when the car is making a left turn. Write a description of the power flow on the lines provided below.

2. _____
_____
_____
_____
_____
_____
_____
_____

191

Transaxle Parts Identification

Identify the transaxle parts in the spaces provided below.

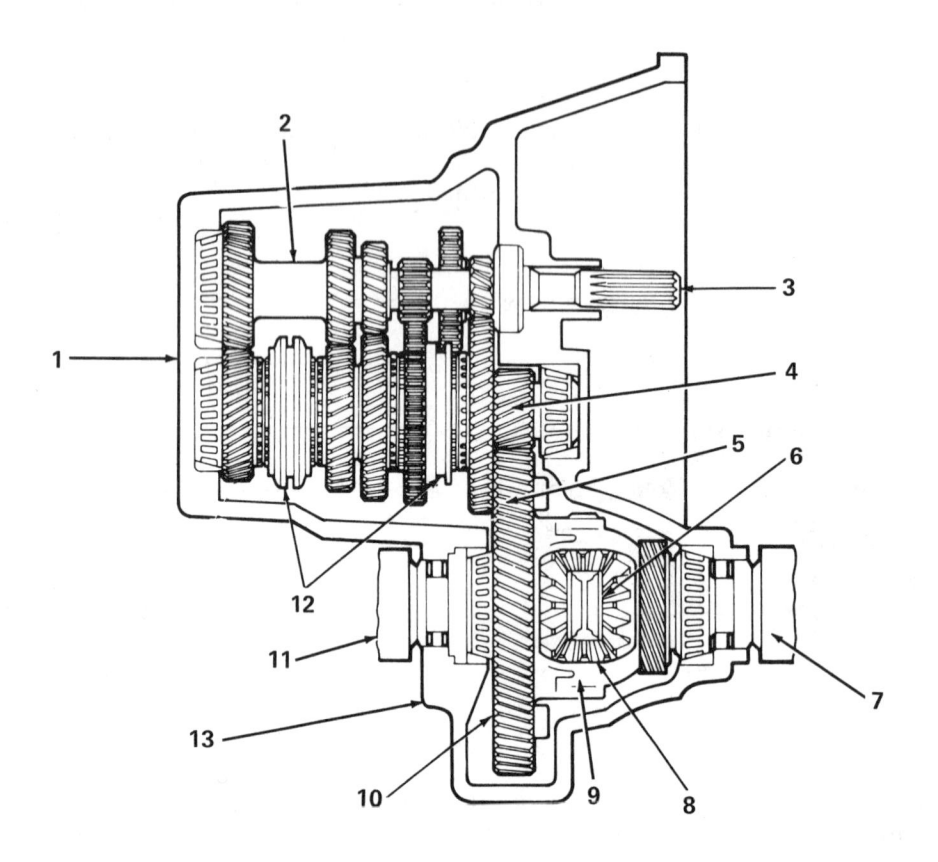

1. _____
2. _____
3. _____
4. _____
5. _____
6. _____
7. _____
8. _____
9. _____
10. _____
11. _____
12. _____
13. _____

NAME _____ SECTION _____ DATE _____ SCORE _____

Chapter 40 DIFFERENTIAL ASSEMBLY
ASSIGNMENT SHEET 34

Rear Drive Axle Parts Identification

Before you begin: Read Chapter 40 in *Auto Mechanics*. Identify the parts of the rear drive axle in the spaces provided below.

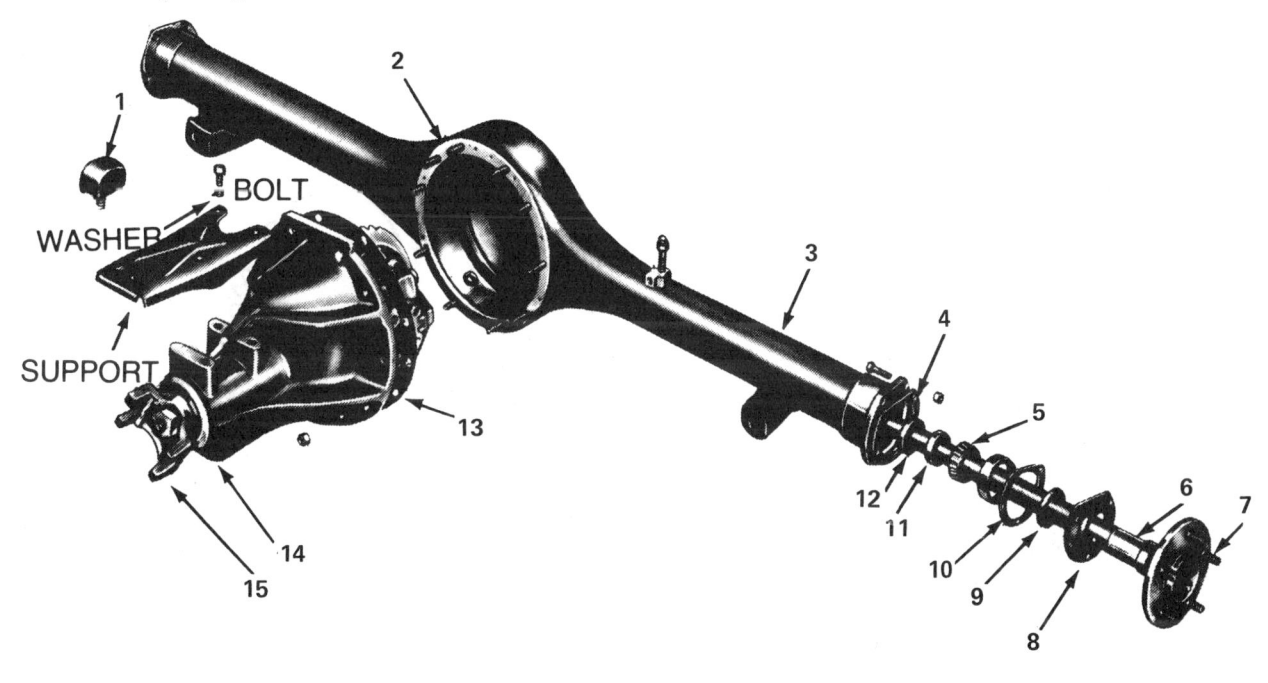

1. _____   6. _____   11. _____
2. _____   7. _____   12. _____
3. _____   8. _____   13. _____
4. _____   9. _____   14. _____
5. _____   10. _____ 15. _____

Limited Slip Differential Parts Identification

Identify the parts of a limited slip differential in the spaces provided below.

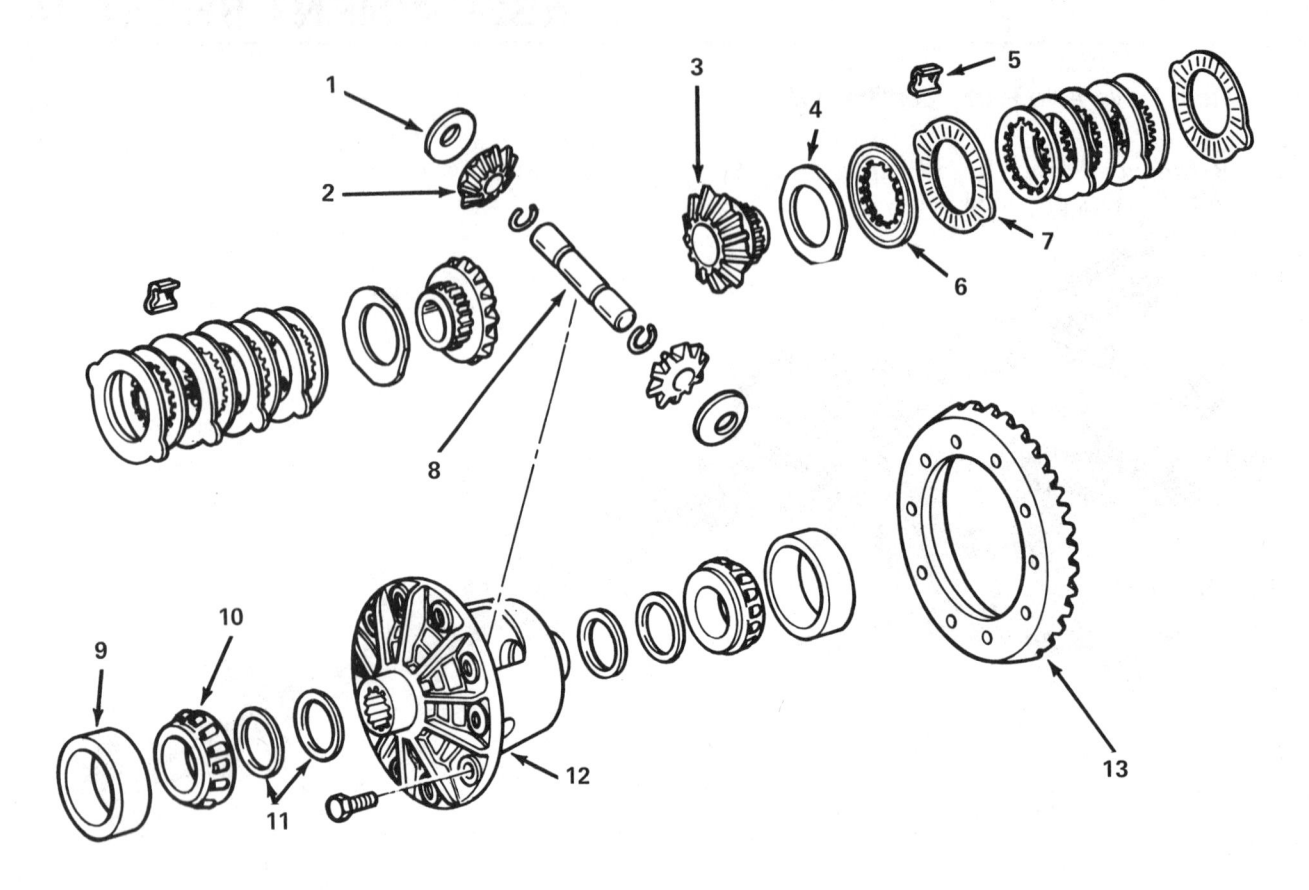

1. _____
2. _____
3. _____
4. _____
5. _____
6. _____
7. _____
8. _____
9. _____
10. _____
11. _____
12. _____
13. _____

Review of New Terms

For each definition in Column 2, select the term in Column 1 that best matches its meaning. Write the identifying *letter* of the term in the Answer column.

Column 1

A. Differential

B. Drive pinion

C. Hypoid gears

D. Rear axle ratio

E. Ring gear

Column 2

1. The numerical relationship between the drive pinion and the ring gear in the differential.

2. Drive pinion and ring gears whose shape allows them to mesh off center.

3. A system of gears in the rear axle assembly that allows the rear wheels to turn at different speeds when cornering.

4. The gear in the differential that meshes with the drive pinion gear.

5. A gear in the differential connected to the drive shaft.

Answer

1. _____

2. _____

3. _____

4. _____

5. _____

NAME _____ SECTION _____ DATE _____ SCORE _____

Chapter 41 DIFFERENTIAL ASSEMBLY SERVICE
JOB SHEET 31

Replace Rear Axle Bearing

Before you begin: Read Chapter 41 in *Auto Mechanics*.

Student _____ Section _____ Date _____

Make of Car _____ Model _____ Year _____

Time Started _____ Time Finished _____ Total Time _____

Flat Rate Time _____

Special Tools, Equipment, Parts, and Materials

Jack

Jack stands

Axle bearing and retainer

_____

_____

References

Manufacturer's Shop Manual _____

Repair Manual _____

Service Bulletin _____

Specifications

Look up the following specifications and record them in the spaces provided below.

Rear Axle Lubrication Type and Viscosity _____

Rear Axle Oil Capacity _____

_____

Instructor's Check

Procedure

1. Use a jack to raise the rear of the vehicle until the wheels are clear of the floor.

    Safety Caution: Support the vehicle with jack stands.

2. Remove the hub cap, lug nuts, and wheel from the side where the axle is to be removed.

3. Pull of the brake drum.

    NOTE: In some cases, it may be necessary to back off the rear brake adjustment.

4. Remove the axle retaining bolts from the backing plate.

    NOTE: Some rear axle assemblies use an axle lock inside the differential. On these units, a cover must be removed from the differential and a "C" or pin lock removed from the axle.

5. Withdraw the axle from the axle housing.

6. Use a chisel to cut off the bearing retainer.

    NOTE: Never use heat on an axle shaft or it may be weakened and fail.

7. Install the axle in an axle press attachment.

8. Press off the old bearing.

9. Press on the new bearing and retainer.

10. Install the axle in the axle housing.

11. Replace the axle retaining bolts and locks if used.

12. Install the brake drum.

13. Install the wheel, lug nuts, and hub cap.

14. Check the rear axle assembly lubricant level.

NOTES

Date Completed _____   Instructor's Check _____

NAME _____ SECTION _____ DATE _____ SCORE _____

Chapter 41 DIFFERENTIAL ASSEMBLY SERVICE
JOB SHEET 32

Troubleshoot a Rear Axle Assembly

Before you begin: Read Chapter 41 in *Auto Mechanics*.

Student _____ Section _____ Date _____

Make of Car _____ Model _____ Year _____

Time Started _____ Time Finished _____ Total Time _____

Flat Rate Time _____

Special Tools, Equipment, Parts, and Materials

Tire pressure gauge _____

_____ _____

_____ _____

References

Manufacturer's Shop Manual _____

Repair Manual _____

Service Bulletin _____

_____
Instructor's Check

Procedure

1. When troubleshooting a rear axle noise, first obtain from the automobile's driver a description of the noise and driving conditions when the noise occurred.

   NOTE: Noises caused by the engine, heater, transmission, tires, wheel bearings, exhaust system, and drive shaft, or the action of wind on the body, grille, travel rack, and air deflectors may be incorrectly diagnosed as axle noises. The automobile must be thoroughly checked and road tested in order to isolate the cause of the problem.

2. With the automobile stopped and the transmission in neutral, run the engine at different speeds. If there is noise during this test, it is caused by the engine, exhaust system, clutch, transmission, or engine-driven accessories.

199

3. Prior to road testing, check tire pressure and rear axle lubricant level. Some types of tire tread, tread wear, or tread patterns may cause noises. Drive the automobile on different road surfaces. If the noise changes with changes in the road surface, the tires may be the cause.

4. Road test the automobile.

   Safety Caution: Obtain permission from your instructor before road testing the automobile.

5. Noise caused by worn, loose, or damaged wheel bearings may be confused with axle noise. Wheel bearing noise is usually more noticeable when coasting at lower vehicle speeds. Applying the brakes gently will usually change wheel bearing noise. Another test is to turn the vehicle first left, then right. This side loads the bearings, causing the problem bearing to become noisy.

6. Drive the automobile long enough to bring the axle to operating temperature. Then drive at different speeds and in all transmission gear ranges. Rear axle noises are usually related to speed rather than engine rpm or transmission gears. Rear axle noises may be classified into two types: Gear noise and bearing noise. Gear noise is identified as a whine or high-pitched resonating sound that is louder at certain speeds.

7. Axle bearing noise is usually constant, and its pitch is directly related to vehicle speed. Since the drive pinion turns faster than the drive gear, the drive pinion bearing noises will be higher pitched than the differential bearing noises. Drive pinion bearings are usually heard at low speeds (20 to 30 mph).

8. Differential bearing noise is lower in pitch because of bearings turn at the same speed as the wheels when the automobile is driven straight ahead. Differential bearing noise will not change when the vehicle is turned left or right or when the brakes are gently applied.

9. Too much drive gear and drive pinion clearance will also result in a clunk noise. Gear noise can be caused by an incorrect drive gear and drive pinion adjustment. If the drive line clunks on first engaging the transmission, differential side gears in the differential case bores may be loose.

10. A knocking or clucking noise heard at low speed when coasting may be caused by a loose-fitting differential side gear in the differential case bore. Applying the brakes lightly will usually reduce the sound.

11. In the spaces provided below, describe the problem.

_____
_____
_____
_____
_____
_____
_____
_____

Date Completed _____ Instructor's Check _____

NAME _____ SECTION _____ DATE _____ SCORE _____

Chapter 41 DIFFERENTIAL ASSEMBLY SERVICE
JOB SHEET 33

Disassembly and Inspection of a Rear Drive Differential

Before you begin: Read Chapter 41 in *Auto Mechanics.*

Student _____ Section _____ Date _____

Make of Car _____ Model _____ Year _____

Time Started _____ Time Finished _____ Total Time _____

Flat Rate Time _____

Special Tools, Equipment, Parts, and Materials

Housing spreader   Spanner wrench

Carrier cover gasket

_____   _____

_____   _____

References

Manufacturer's Shop Manual _____

Repair Manual _____

Service Bulletin _____

_____
Instructor's Check

Procedure

1. Remove the differential carrier assembly from the rear axle housing. This is done by first removing both rear axles from the carrier assembly. The axles are often retained by a collar behind the axle flanges which must be removed prior to removing the axles.

2. Remove the drive shaft.

3. Drain the fluid from the housing.

4. On most units, the carrier assembly is bolted into the center of the housing. Remove the bolts and lift out the carrier assembly.

5. On some units, the carrier is held by the tension of the housing and bearing caps on the carrier bearing. Use a spreading tool to spring open the housing and remove the carrier assembly after the bolts have been removed.

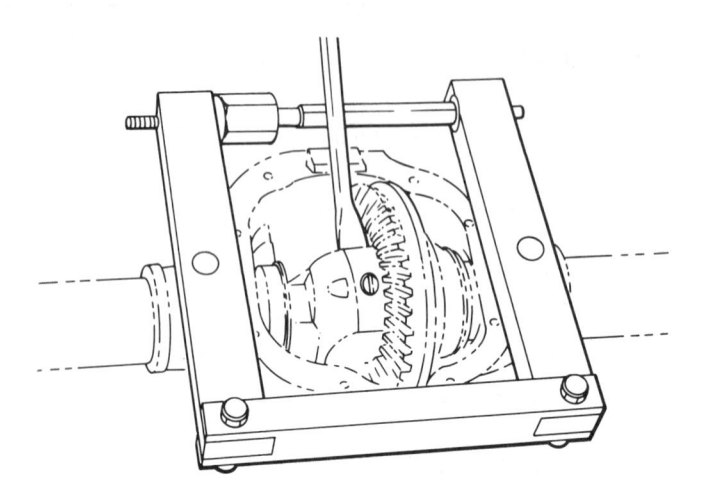

NOTE: Carrier bearing caps should always be marked with punch marks for proper replacement.

6. The carrier assembly is disassembled according to the manufacturer's service instructions. After disassembly, clean the parts with solvent.

7. Differential bearings and front and rear pinion bearing cone and cup assemblies should be smooth, with no broken or dented surfaces on rollers or roller contact surfaces.

8. Check the bearing roller retainer cages for distortion or cracks.

NAME_____ SECTION_____ DATE_____ SCORE_____

9. Check the ring gear and drive pinion teeth for a uniform contact pattern, showing smooth and unbroken surfaces without too much wear.

10. Machined surfaces of the pinion stem (at points of contact with either rear pinion bearing contact journal or rear pinion bearing mounting shim surface) should be smooth.

11. Replace parts which are not in good condition.

_____
Instructor's Check

NOTES

Date Completed _____ Instructor's Check _____

NAME_____ SECTION_____ DATE_____ SCORE_____

Chapter 41 DIFFERENTIAL ASSEMBLY SERVICE
JOB SHEET 34

Adjustment and Reassembly of a Differential

Before you begin: Read Chapter 41 in *Auto Mechanics*.

Student _____ Section _____ Date _____

Make of Car _____ Model _____ Year _____

Time Started _____ Time Finished _____ Total Time_____

Flat Rate Time _____

Special Tools, Equipment, Parts, and Materials

Inch-pound torque wrench   Dial indicator

Foot-pound torque wrench   Red or white lead

Spanner wrench

_____   _____

_____   _____

References

Manufacturer's Shop Manual _____

Repair Manual _____

Service Bulletin _____

Specifications

Look up the following specifications and record them in the spaces provided.

Pinion bearing preload _____

Ring and pinion backlash _____

Pinion depth _____

_____

Instructor's Check

Procedure

NOTE: Follow the procedure on Job Sheet 33 for disassembly and inspection of a differential.

1. To attain the correct meshing of the ring and pinion gears, several adjustments of the differential assembly are necessary.

    NOTE: Pinion depth is the position of the drive pinion gear in relation to the ring gear. The pinion may be moved in or out in relation to the ring gear by placing shims between the housing and pinion. Adding or subtracting shims moves the pinion back and forth. Markings on the ring and pinion show that they are a matched set and indicate the proper pinion depth.

2. The next adjustment is pinion bearing preload. For exactly the proper mesh, the pinion gear must be held to zero end play.

    NOTE: Zero end play, in a shaft mounted on two opposed tapered roller bearings, means zero clearance between the cone and rollers and between the rollers and cups in both bearings. If there is any clearance at the rollers, the pinion shaft will walk back and forth as the direction of thrust changes. A walking pinion shaft means that the pinion and ring gear are walking in and out of proper mesh.

3. To get zero end play, force the bearing cones against the rollers and the rollers against their cups by tightening the pinion shaft nut. As the pinion shaft nut is tightened, the pinion shaft flange, the oil slinger, the front bearing spacer, and the rear bearing cone are forced closer together.

4. In most rear axles, the bearing spacer is collapsible so that at a specified torque on the pinion nut, the spacer is squeezed to a shorter length. As the spacer gets shorter, the bearing cones are pulled closer together, pressing the bearing rollers against their cups. As the pinion shaft nut is tightened beyond the point of zero clearance at the roller bearings, the pinion shaft is stretched. This stretch in the pinion shaft tends to keep the bearing rollers seated under all operating conditions.

5. Adjust drive pinion preload by tightening the nut on the yoke end of the drive pinion to specifications with a foot-pound or newton-metre torque wrench. Then measure the preload by the amount of torque in inch-pounds required to keep the pinion rotating.

6. Mount the carrier assembly into the case. The carrier assembly, along with the ring gear, can be positioned from side to side by means of adjusters on each side of the carrier bearings.

    NOTE: Leave the bearing caps which mount over the carrier bearings untightened so the adjusters may be used to move the ring gear.

7. Position the ring gear as far into the pinion as possible to remove the play or backlash between the two gears. Position the ring gear away from the pinion to increase the backlash.

8. Measure and adjust backlash to specifications with a dial indicator mounted on the housing and set to measure the backlash on the ring gear.

9. When the backlash is set, tighten the side adjuster and bearing caps to specifications.

NAME _____ SECTION _____ DATE _____ SCORE _____

10. Observe the gear tooth contact patterns as a final check to determine if pinion depth and backlash adjustment have brought the ring and pinion into proper mesh.

   NOTE: Gear tooth pattern may be observed by coating the ring and pinion gear with a thin film of red or white lead. Rotating the pinion gear through one complete revolution will leave a distinct contact pattern on the ring gear.

   NOTE: Charts showing acceptable and unacceptable patterns are provided by the manufacturer. Backlash or pinion depth may have to be readjusted to achieve the correct tooth pattern.

11. After a check shows the correct tooth pattern and final adjustments are finished, the differential assembly may be reassembled into the rear axle housing. As the unit is reassembled, coat parts with gear lubricant.

12. Install axle side gears and pinion gears in the carrier.

13. Torque all the bolts to specified limits.

_____
Instructor's Check

NOTES

Date Completed _____ Instructor's Check _____

NAME _____ SECTION _____ DATE _____ SCORE _____

Chapter 42 THE SUSPENSION SYSTEM
ASSIGNMENT SHEET 35

Front Suspension Part Identification

Before you begin: Read Chapter 42 in *Auto Mechanics*. Identify the parts of the short long arm suspension in the spaces provided below.

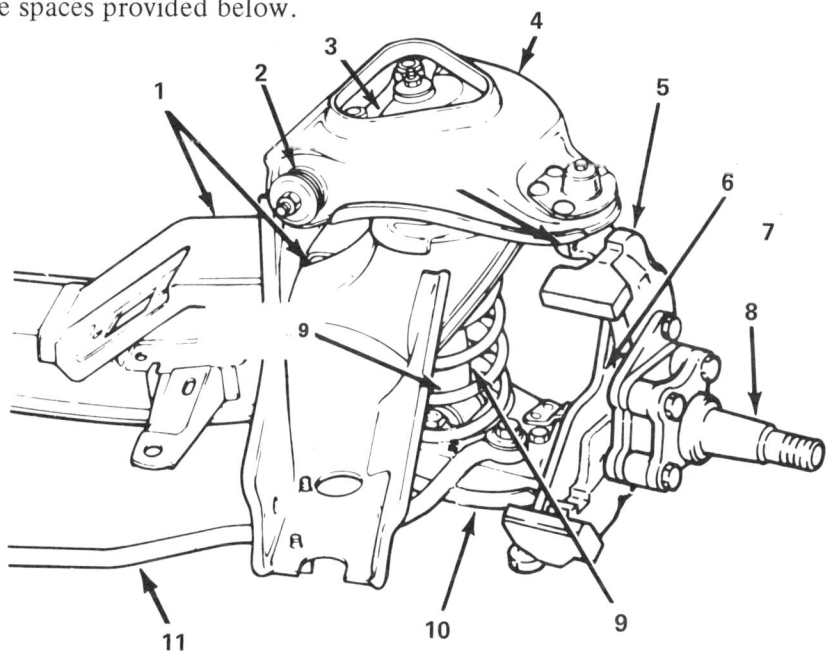

1. _____

2. _____

3. _____

4. _____

5. _____

6. _____

7. _____

8. _____

9. _____

10. _____

11. _____

209

In the spaces provided below, identify the parts of the MacPherson strut suspension.

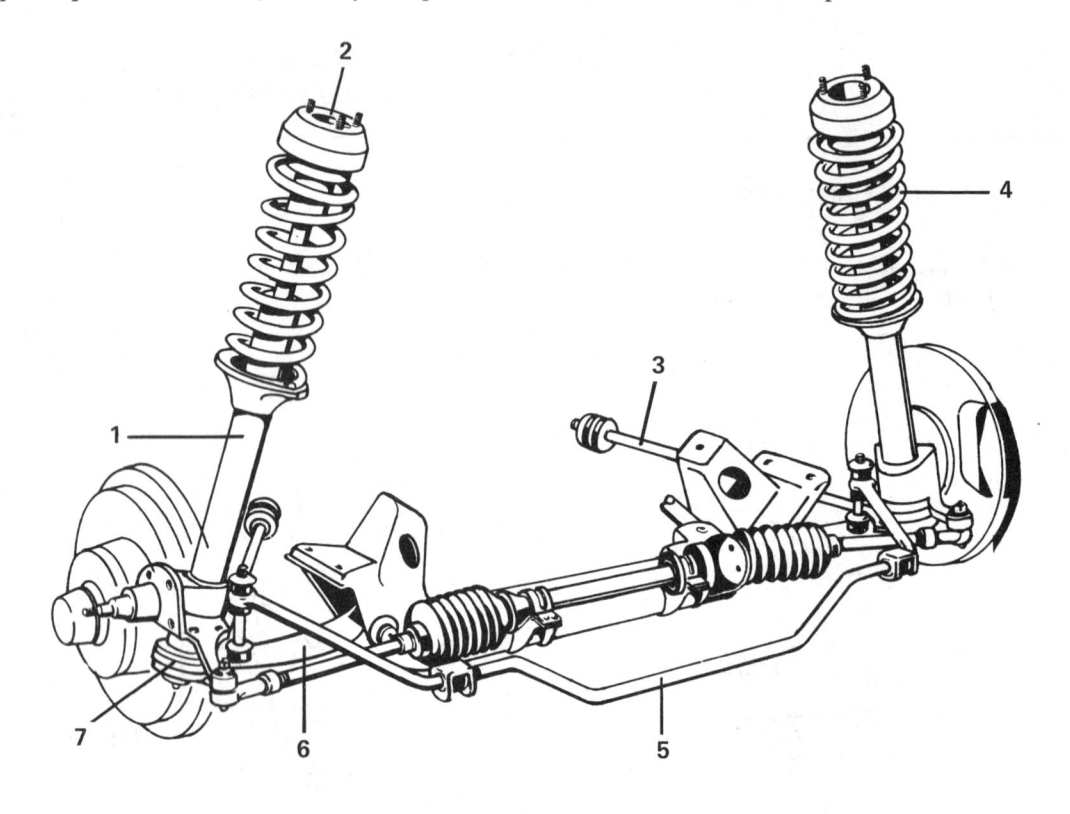

1. _____   5. _____
2. _____   6. _____
3. _____   7. _____
4. _____

NAME _____ SECTION _____ DATE _____ SCORE _____

Shock Absorber Part Identification

Identify the parts of the shock absorber in the spaces provided below.

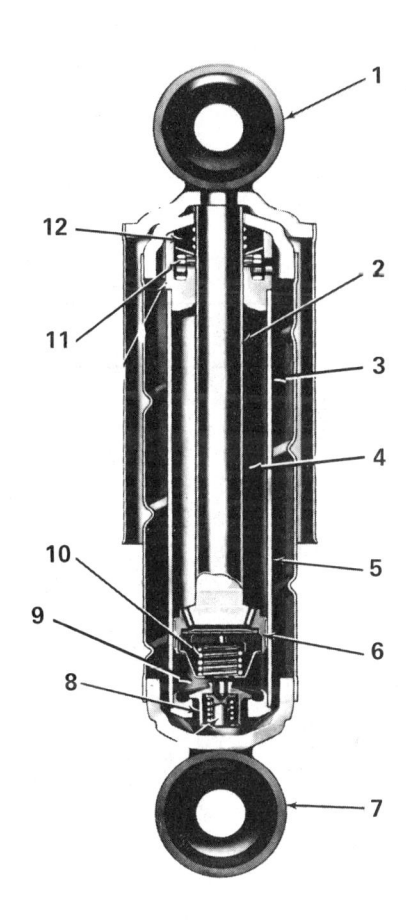

1. _____
2. _____
3. _____
4. _____
5. _____
6. _____
7. _____
8. _____
9. _____
10. _____
11. _____
12. _____

Front Wheel Bearings

Identify the parts of the front wheel bearing assembly mounted on a spindle in the spaces provided below.

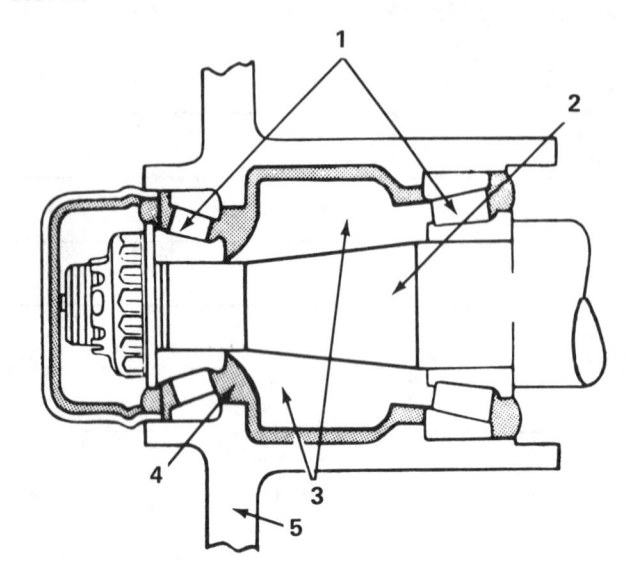

1. _____
2. _____
3. _____
4. _____
5. _____

Identify the parts of the front wheel bearing assembly with disc brakes in the spaces provided below.

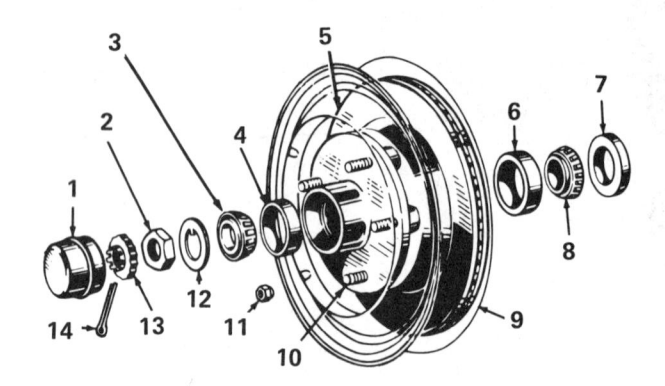

1. _____
2. _____
3. _____
4. _____
5. _____
6. _____
7. _____
8. _____
9. _____
10. _____
11. _____
12. _____
13. _____
14. _____

NAME _____ SECTION _____ DATE _____ SCORE _____

Chapter 42 THE SUSPENSION SYSTEM
ASSIGNMENT SHEET 36

Rear Suspension Systems

Before you begin: Read Chapter 42 in *Auto Mechanics*. Identify the suspension system shown below and describe its operation in the space provided.

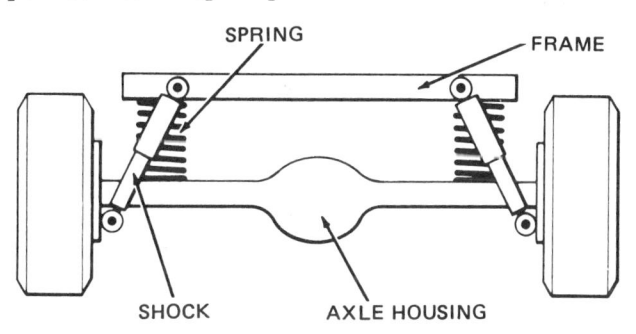

1. _____

Identify the suspension system shown below and describe its operation in the spaces provided.

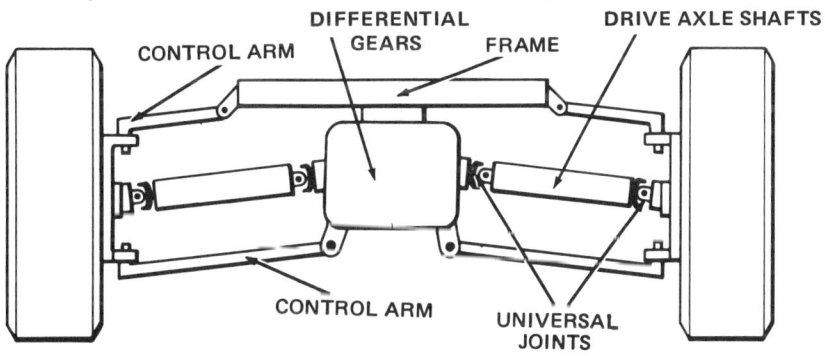

2. _____

Identify the parts of the trailing arm independent suspension system in the spaces provided.

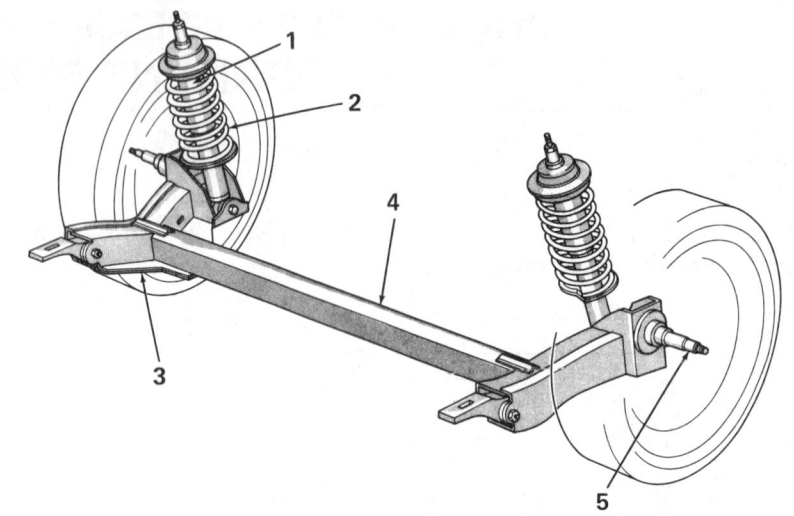

1. _____
2. _____
3. _____
4. _____
5. _____

Review of New Terms

For each definition in Column 2, select the term in Column 1 that best matches its meaning. Write the identifying *letter* of the term in the Answer column.

Column 1

A. Independent front suspension
B. Jounce bumper
C. Load leveling system
D. MacPherson strut system
E. Rigid rear suspension
F. Shock absorber
G. Short long arm suspension
H. Stabilizer bar
I. Torsion bar

Column 2

1. A suspension system in which a long and short control arm are used to support the wheel.
2. A suspension system in which each front wheel is suspended apart from the other.
3. A suspension system in which both rear wheels are attached to a rigid rear axle housing.
4. A bar used to reduce body motion.
5. A rubber part used to absorbe shock during full suspension system movement.
6. A bar that twists at a controlled rate to act as a spring in a suspension system.
7. A hydraulic device to control spring operation.
8. A suspension system that combines the upper control arm, spring, and shock absorber into one strut.
9. A system used to make horizontal a vehicle that is heavily loaded.

Answer

1. _____
2. _____
3. _____
4. _____
5. _____
6. _____
7. _____
8. _____
9. _____

NAME _____ SECTION _____ DATE _____ SCORE _____

Chapter 43 SUSPENSION SYSTEM SERVICE
JOB SHEET 35

Repacking Front Wheel Bearings

Before you begin: Read Chapter 43 in *Auto Mechanics*.

Student _____ Section _____ Date _____

Make of Car _____ Model _____ Year _____

Time Started _____ Time Finished _____ Total Time _____

Flat Rate Time _____

Special Tools, Equipment, Parts, and Materials

Wheel-bearing packer   Safety or stationary jack

Grease-retainer seating tool   Wheel-bearing grease retainers

Lift jack   Torque wrench

_____   _____

_____   _____

_____   _____

References

Manufacturer's Shop Manual _____

Repair Manual _____

Service Bulletin _____

Specifications

Look up the following specifications and record them in the spaces provided below.

Spindle Nut Torque _____

Wheel Bearing Grease Type _____

_____
Instructor's Check

Procedure

1. Raise the vehicle so the front wheels are free of the floor.

    Safety Caution: Support the car with safety stands before doing work under the automobile or removing wheels.

2. Remove the wheel cover, grease cap, cotter pin, nut lock, and bearing adjustment nut.

3. Remove the thrust washer and outer bearing cone.

4. If the vehicle has drum brakes, slide the wheel hub and drum assembly off the spindle.

5. If the vehicle has disc brakes, remove bolts that attach the disc brake caliper assembly to the steering knuckle. Slowly slide the caliper assembly up and away from the brake disc and support the caliper assembly on the steering knuckle arm.

    NOTE: Do not let the caliper assembly hang by the brake hose, or the brake hose may be damaged.

6. Drive out the inner grease seal and remove the inner bearing from the hub. Clean the hub and drum assembly and the bearings in kerosene, mineral spirits, or other similar cleaning fluids.

    NOTE: Do not dry the bearings by air spinning.

7. Examine bearing cups for pitting or other damage. If cups or races are damaged, remove them from the hub with a soft steel drift positioned in the slots in the hub.

    NOTE: Bearing cup areas in the hub should be smooth. Scored or raised metal could keep the cups from seating against the shoulders in the hub. The bearing cones and rollers should have smooth, unbroken surfaces without any pits. The ends of the rollers and both cone flanges should also be smooth and free from chipping or other damage.

8. Force the recommended lubricant between bearing cone rollers by hand or repack with a suitable bearing packer. Install the inner cone and a new seal, with the lip of the seal facing inward. Position the seal flush with the end of the hub. The seal flange may be damaged if a seal driving tool is not used.

9. Clean the spindle and apply a light coating of wheel bearing lubricant over the polished surfaces

10. Install the wheel, tire, and drum assembly on the spindle.

11. Install the outer bearing cone, thrust washer, and adjusting nut.

12. Adjust the bearing by tightening the adjustment nut on the spindle to seat the grease seal and the bearings. Then back it off. Use a torque wrench to tighten the nut to specifications. Then back off the nut to a "just loose" position.

NAME _____ SECTION _____ DATE _____ SCORE _____

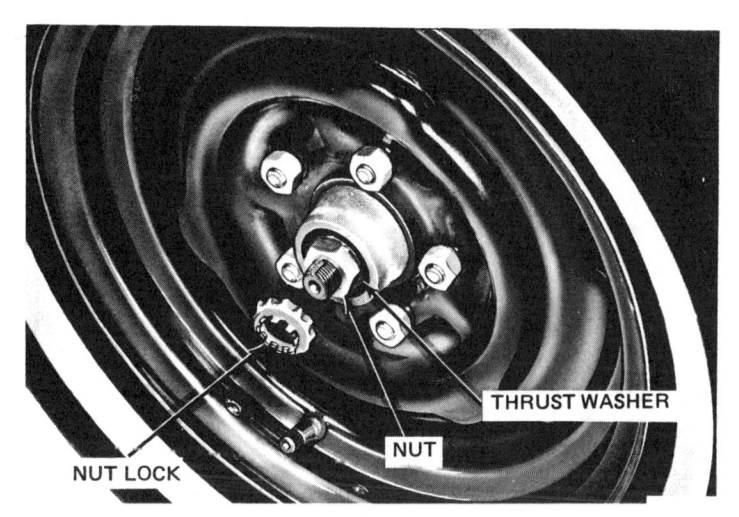

[Image: wheel hub with labels THRUST WASHER, NUT, NUT LOCK]

NOTE: Tapered roller bearings used on most vehicles have a lightly loose feel when properly adjusted. Tapered roller bearings must never be preloaded. The steady thrust on roller ends which comes from preloading can damage them.

13. Install the nut lock and/or cotter key.

14. Install the grease cap and hub cap.

15. Lower the vehicle.

_____
Instructor's Check

NOTES

Date Completed _____ Instructor's Check _____

NAME _____ SECTION _____ DATE _____ SCORE _____

Chapter 43 SUSPENSION SYSTEM SERVICE
JOB SHEET 36

Replacing a Coil Spring

Before you begin: Read Chapter 43 in *Auto Mechanics*.

Student _____ Section _____ Date _____

Make of Car _____ Model _____ Year _____

Flat Rate Time _____

Special Tools, Equipment, Parts, and Materials

Hoist or jack   Ball joint tool

Spring compressor   Replacement coil springs

_____   _____

_____   _____

_____   _____

References

Manufacturer's Shop Manual _____

Repair Manual _____

Service Bulletin _____

_____
Instructor's Check

Procedure

1. Raise the vehicle on a hoist and remove the front wheels and brake assemblies to get to the suspension components.

    Safety Caution: Make sure all persons and objects are out of the way before raising or lowering an automobile.

2. Remove the shock absorber and stabilizer bar (if used).

3. Before the ball joint nuts can be removed, the coil spring must be contained with a spring compressor tool.

   Safety Caution: The coil spring between the two control arms is under tremendous pressure. When the control arms are disconnected, the spring could fly out, causing extensive damage or injury.

4. With the spring compressed, the lower ball joint may be removed. The ball joint is held in the steering knuckle assembly by a tapered stud with a nut and cotter key. Remove the cotter key and nut. Since the stud is tapered, it must be pressed out of the steering knuckle with a special ball joint tool, called a taper breaker.

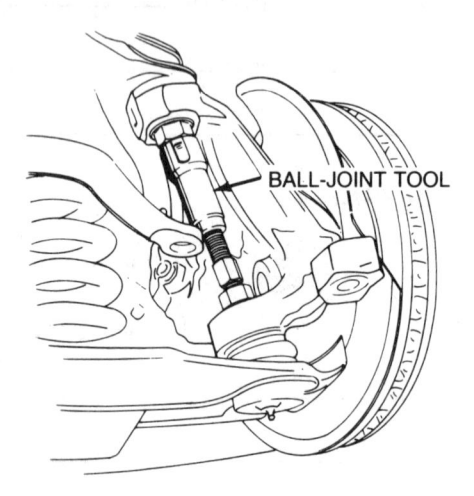

5. Remove the old spring and install another.

   NOTE: Coil springs should always be replaced in pairs, either in front or rear. This ensures that alignment angles and spring action will be correct.

6. Reassembly of the control arms, spring, and ball joints almost follows the steps of disassembly in reverse.

7. Mount the control arms to the frame.

8. Mount the spring into position with a compressor in place.

9. Attach the ball joints to the steering knuckle with nuts and cotter keys.

10. Torque all nuts and bolts to specifications.

11. Remove the spring compressor and replace the shock absorber.

12. Replace the brake and wheel assembly.

13. Lower the vehicle.

Date Completed _____   Instructor's Check _____

NAME _____ SECTION _____ DATE _____ SCORE _____

Chapter 43 SUSPENSION SYSTEM SERVICE
JOB SHEET 37

Replacing a Ball Joint

Before you begin: Read Chapter 43 in *Auto Mechanics*.

Student _____ Section _____ Date _____

Make of Car _____ Model _____ Year _____

Time Started _____ Time Finished _____ Total Time _____

Special Tools, Equipment, Parts, and Materials

Special ball-joint tools as recommended by manufacturer

Spring compressor tool

Ball joint

_____

Instructor's Check

References

Manufacturer's Shop Manual _____

Repair Manual _____

Service Bulletin _____

Procedure

1. Raise the front of the vehicle on a hoist or jack and support it on jack stands.

2. Remove the front brake assemblies.

3. Remove the shock absorbers and stabilizer bar if used.

   Safety Caution: The coil spring must be contained with a spring compressor tool. The coil spring between the two control arms is under tremendous pressure. When the control arms are disconnected, the spring could fly out, causing extensive damage or injury.

4. With the spring compressed, the ball joint or joints may be removed. The ball joint is held in the steering knuckle assembly by a tapered stud with a nut and cotter key.

5. Remove the cotter key and nut. Since the stud is tapered, it must be pressed out of the steering knuckle with a special ball joint tool, called a taper breaker.

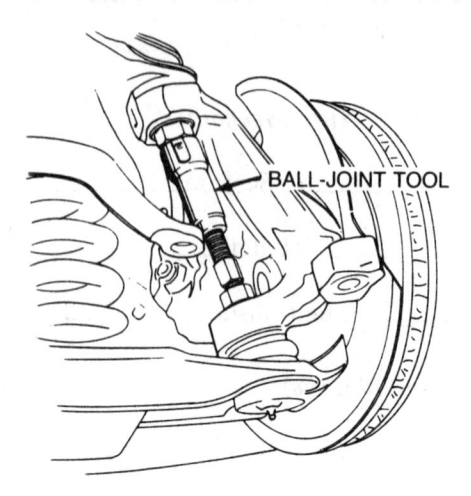

6. Next, remove the ball joint from the control arm. If the ball joints are riveted to the control arm, rivet heads must be ground or chiseled off. Replacement ball joints usually are held with bolts. Remove the worn ball joint and install a new one.

7. Reassembly of the control arms, **spring**, and ball joints is about the reverse of disassembly.

8. Mount the control arms to the frame.

9. Mount the spring into position with a compressor in place.

10. Attach the ball joints to the steering knuckle with nuts and cotter keys.

11. Torque all nuts and bolts to specifications.

12. Remove the spring compressor and replace the shock absorber.

13. Replace the brake and wheel assembly.

14. Lower the vehicle.

Date Completed _____ Instructor's Check _____

NAME _____ SECTION _____ DATE _____ SCORE _____

Chapter 43 SUSPENSION SYSTEM SERVICE
JOB SHEET 38

Replacing a Control Arm Bushing

Before you begin: Read Chapter 43 in *Auto Mechanics*.

Student _____ Section _____ Date _____

Make of Car _____ Model _____ Year _____

Time Started _____ Time Finished _____ Total Time _____

Flat Rate Time _____

Special Tools, Equipment, Parts, and Materials

Spring compressor   Ball joint tool

Control arm bushings   _____

_____   _____

_____

References

Manufacturer's Shop Manual _____

Repair Manual _____

Service Bulletin _____

_____
Instructor's Check

Procedure

1. Raise the vehicle on a hoist or jack and support it with safety stands.

2. Remove the front brake assembly

3. Remove the shock absorbers and stabilizer bar if used.

Safety Caution: The coil spring must be contained with a spring compressor tool. The coil spring between the two control arms is under tremendous pressure. When the control arms are disconnected, the spring could fly out, causing extensive damage or injury.

4. With the spring compressed, the ball joint or joints may be removed. The ball joint is held in the steering knuckle assembly by a tapered stud with a nut and cotter key. Remove the cotter key and nut. Since the stud is tapered, it must be pressed out of the steering knuckle with a special ball joint tool.

5. Inspect the bushings that support the control arms to the frame.

   NOTE: Worn or loose bushings must be replaced.

6. After the control arm is disconnected at the ball joint end, remove it by disconnecting it from the frame.

7. The control arm may be mounted to the frame by pivot bolts or by lock nuts on a cross shaft. Remove these bolts or nuts to remove the control arm.

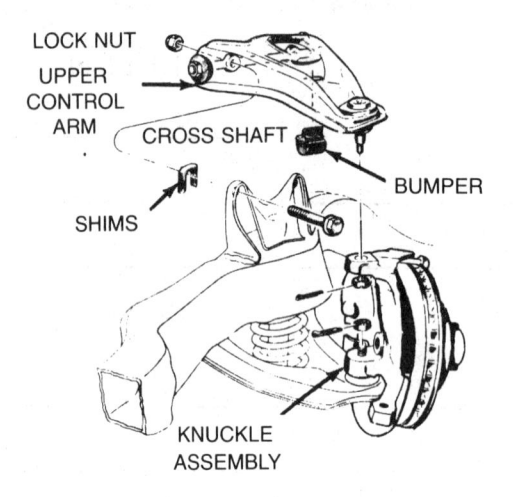

8. When the control arm is removed, the bushing assembly can be replaced. The bushing is generally held in the control arm with a press fit. Special tools are available to remove and replace the bushing.

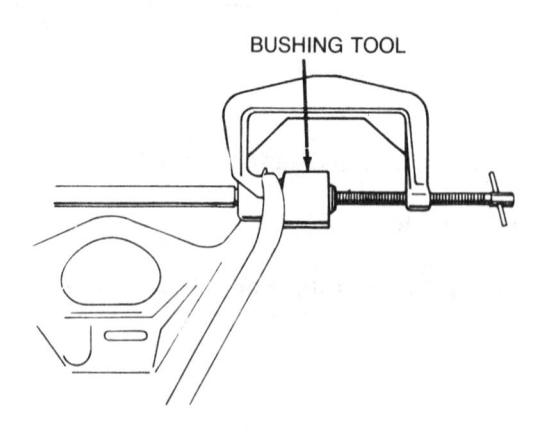

NAME_____ SECTION_____ DATE_____ SCORE_____

9. Reassembly of the control arms, spring, and ball joints is the reverse of disassembly.

10. Mount the control arms to the frame.

11. Mount the spring into position with a compressor in place.

12. Attach the ball joints to the steering knuckle with nuts and cotter keys.

13. Torque all nuts and bolts to specifications.

14. Remove the spring compressor and replace the shock absorber.

15. Replace the brake and wheel assembly.

16. Lower the vehicle.

_____
Instructor's Check

NOTES

Date Completed _____ Instructor's Check _____

NAME _____ SECTION _____ DATE _____ SCORE _____

Chapter 44 STEERING AND WHEEL ALIGNMENT
ASSIGNMENT SHEET 37

Steering Parts Identification

Before you begin: Read Chapter 44 in *Auto Mechanics*. Identify the parts of the steering gear in the spaces provided below.

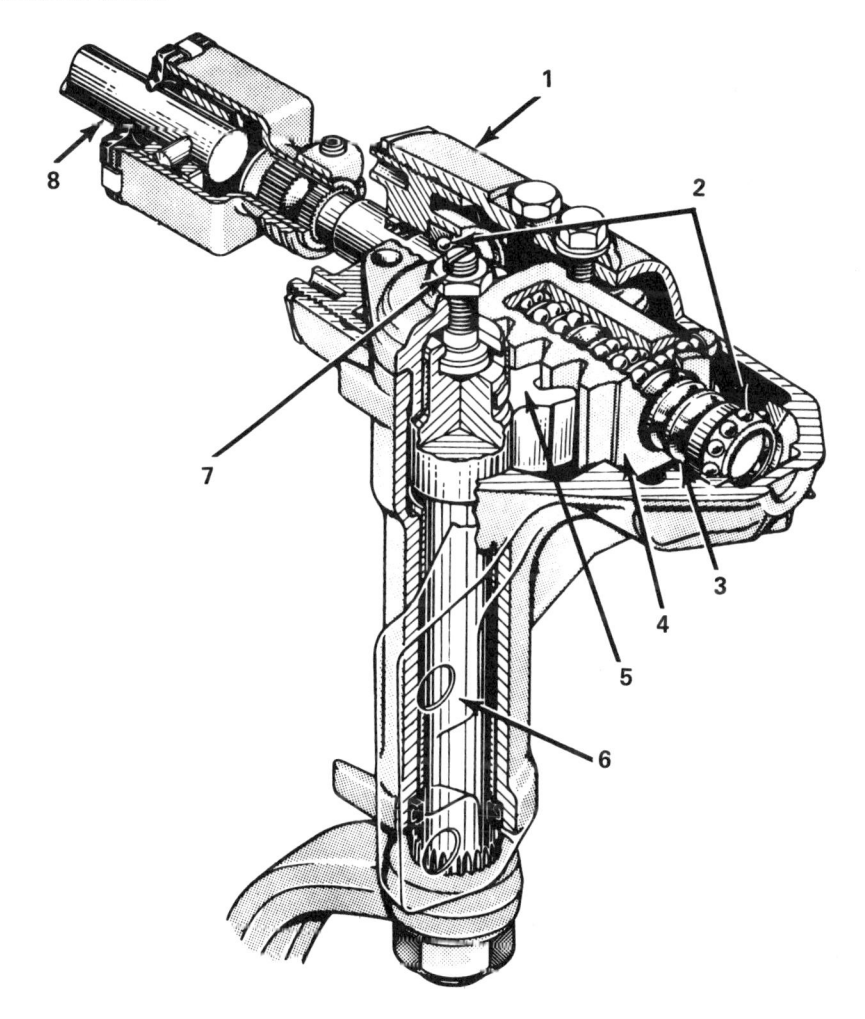

1. _____ 5. _____

   _____ 6. _____

2. _____   _____

3. _____ 7. _____

4. _____ 8. _____

227

Identify the parts of the steering gear in the spaces provided below.

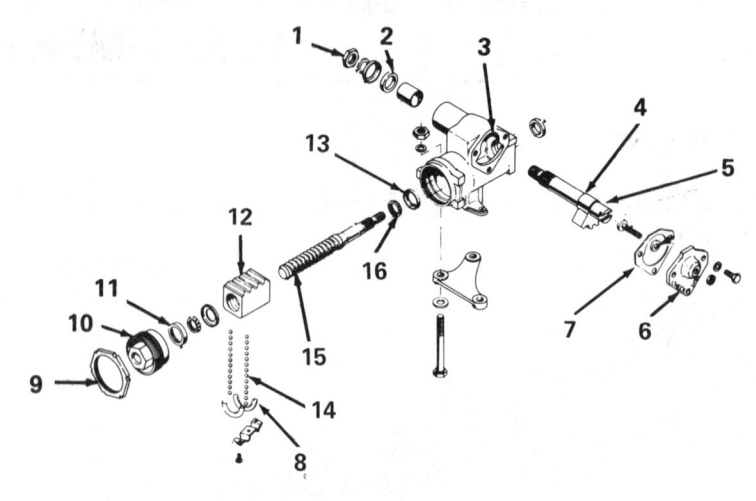

1. _____
   _____
2. _____
3. _____
4. _____
5. _____
   _____
6. _____
7. _____
8. _____
9. _____

10. _____
    _____
11. _____
    _____
12. _____
13. _____
14. _____
15. _____
16. _____

NAME _____ SECTION _____ DATE _____ SCORE _____

Chapter 44 STEERING AND WHEEL ALIGNMENT
ASSIGNMENT SHEET 38

Steering Parts Identification

Before you begin: Read Chapter 44 in *Auto Mechanics*. Identify the parts of the steering linkage in the spaces provided below:

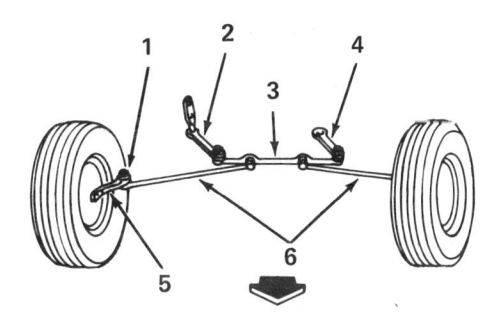

1. _____   4. _____

2. _____   5. _____

3. _____   6. _____

Identify the parts of the rack and pinion power steering in the spaces provided below.

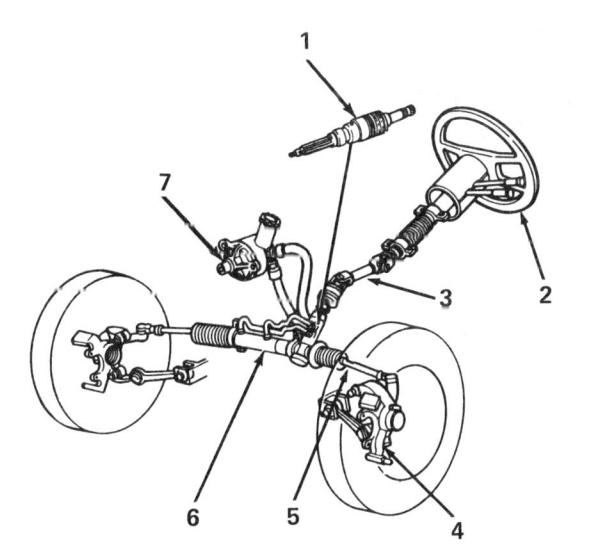

1. _____
2. _____
3. _____
4. _____
5. _____
6. _____
7. _____

229

Review of New Terms

For each definition in Column 2, select the term in Column 1 that best matches its meaning. Write the identifying *letter* of the term in the Answer column.

Column 1

A. Camber
B. Caster
C. Rack and Pinion steering
D. Steering axis inclination
E. Steering column
F. Steering linkage
G. Toe-in
H. Turning radius
I. Variable ratio steering
J. Wheel alignment

Column 2

1. A type of steering that uses a toothed rack connected to the wheels and a pinion gear connected to the steering wheel.
2. The part that connects the steering gears to the front wheels.
3. The inward or outward tilt of the top of a vehicle's tires.
4. A steering gear that provides a different ratio during different parts of a turn.
5. The backward or forward tilt of the centerline of the ball joints.
6. The housing that supports the steering shaft.
7. The relative angles of the two front wheels during a turn.
8. An angle formed by the centerline of the ball joints and the verticle centerline.
9. The position of the front wheels in relation to the suspension.
10. The condition in which the wheels are closer together at the front edge than at the rear edge.

Answer

1. _____
2. _____
3. _____
4. _____
5. _____
6. _____
7. _____
8. _____
9. _____
10. _____

NAME _____ SECTION _____ DATE _____ SCORE _____

Chapter 45 STEERING AND WHEEL ALIGNMENT SERVICE
JOB SHEET 39

Adjusting a Steering Gear

Before you begin: Read Chapter 45 in *Auto Mechanics*.

Student _____ Section _____ Date _____

Make of Car _____ Model _____ Year _____

Time Started _____ Time Finished _____ Total Time _____

Flat Rate Time _____

Special Tools, Equipment, Parts, and Materials

Pitman arm puller _____

Spring scale _____

Torque wrench _____

References

Manufacturer's Shop Manual _____

Repair Manual _____

Service Bulletin _____

Specifications

Look up the following specifications and record them in the spaces provided below.

Spring pull _____ Steering wheel nut preload _____

Instructor's Check

Procedure

1. Raise the vehicle on a hoist or jack and support it with jack stands.

2. Disconnect the steering linkage from the pitman arm.

3. Check the lubricant level in the steering box.

4. Place the steering wheel in the exact middle of travel by counting turns.

5. Attach the spring scale to the steering wheel or an inch-pound (centimetre-kilogram) torque wrench on the nut as specified by manufacturer.

6. If the spring scale or preload reading is correct, the unit requires no adjustment.

7. If the spring scale or preload reading is incorrect, loosen the worm shaft bearing adjustment.

8. Loosen the cross shaft adjustment.

9. Tighten the worm shaft adjuster to the required preload.

10. Tighten the cross shaft adjuster to the proper preload.

11. Recheck the preload at the wheel.

12. Turn the steering wheel lock to the lock position and check for binding.

13. Replace the steering linkage to the pitman arm.

14. Lower the vehicle.

_____
Instructor's Check

NOTES

Date Completed _____ Instructor's Check _____

NAME _____ SECTION _____ DATE _____ SCORE _____

Chapter 45 STEERING AND WHEEL ALIGNMENT SERVICE
JOB SHEET 40

Replacing Tie Rod Ends

Before you begin: Read Chapter 45 in *Auto Mechanics*.

Student _____ Section _____ Date _____

Make of Car _____ Model _____ Year _____

Time Started _____ Time Finished _____ Total Time _____

Flat Rate Time _____

Special Tools, Equipment, Parts, and Materials

Tie-rod end removing tool

Vise-grip or pipe wrench

Toe-in gauge or tram

Center punch and hammer

Steel tape or yardstick

_____

_____

_____

References

Manufacturer's Shop Manual _____

Repair Manual _____

Service Bulletin _____

Specification

Look up the following specification and record it in the space provided below.

Toe-in _____

_____

Instructor's OK

Procedure

1. Raise the vehicle on a hoist or jack and support it with jack stands.

2. Use a wire brush to clean the area around the tie rod end to be replaced.

3. Loosen and remove the clamp bolt on the tie rod end.

4. Remove the cotter key and nut from the tie rod stud.

5. Use a ball peen hammer to strike the steering knuckle where the tie rod stud fits.

    NOTE: Never use heat on suspension parts. This may weaken them and cause them to fail.

6. If the hammer fails to loosen the stud, install a tie rod puller over the stud. Pull the stud out of the steering knuckle.

7. Remove the tie rod end from the tie rod by unthreading it. Note the number of threads or turns needed to remove it.

8. Install the new end into the tie rod. Thread it in the same number of threads or turns.

9. Install the tie rod in the steering knuckle. Install a new nut and cotter key.

10. Check that the toe-in is adjusted to specifications. Readjust as necessary. See Job Sheet 42, Adjusting Toe-in, for instructions.

11. Lower the vehicle.

_____
Instructor's Check

NOTES

Date Completed _____ Instructor's Check _____

NAME _____ SECTION _____ DATE _____ SCORE _____

Chapter 45 STEERING AND WHEEL ALIGNMENT SERVICE
JOB SHEET 41

Adjusting Camber and Caster

Before you begin: Read Chapter 45 in *Auto Mechanics*.

Student _____ Section _____ Date _____

Make of Car _____ Model _____ Year _____

Time Started _____ Time Finished _____ Total Time _____

Flat Rate Time _____

Special Tools, Equipment, Parts, and Materials

Wheel alignment equipment   _____

Camber caster shims   _____

_____   _____

_____   _____

References

Manufacturer's Shop Manual _____

Repair Manual _____

Service Bulletin _____

Specifications

Look up the following specifications and record them in the spaces provided below.

Camber _____ Caster _____

_____
Instructor's Check

235

Procedure

1. Raise the vehicle on a hoist or lift it with a jack and support it with jack stands.

2. Check the tire pressure, suspension system wear, wheel runout, wheel bearing adjustment, and spring heights.

3. Position the vehicle on the alignment rack.

4. Attach alignment equipment following equipment manufacturer's directions. Write in the measurements in the spaces provided: Camber _____ Caster _____

5. Compare wheel alignment angles to manufacturer's specifications.

    NOTE: Camber, caster, and toe-in are the only alignment factors that are adjustable. If steering axis inclination or turning radius are incorrect, suspension components must be replaced.

6. Adjust camber and caster by moving the suspension control arms.

    NOTE: The most common system uses shims between the top control arm and the frame. Shims may be added, subtracted, or transferred to change the readings as follows:

    a. *Camber:* Change shims at both the front and rear of the shaft. Adding the same number of shims at both front and rear of the support shaft will decrease positive camber.

    b. *Caster:* Transfer shims, front to rear or rear to front. The transfer of a shim to the front bolt from the rear bolt will decrease positive caster.

7. To adjust for camber and caster, loosen the upper control arm shaft to frame nuts, add or subtract shims are required, and retighten nuts. Camber and caster can be adjusted in one operation.

8. Toe-in must be checked after changing camber or caster.

9. Some systems use an eccentric mount for the control arm. A bolt is loosened and an eccentric turned to change the position of the control arm.

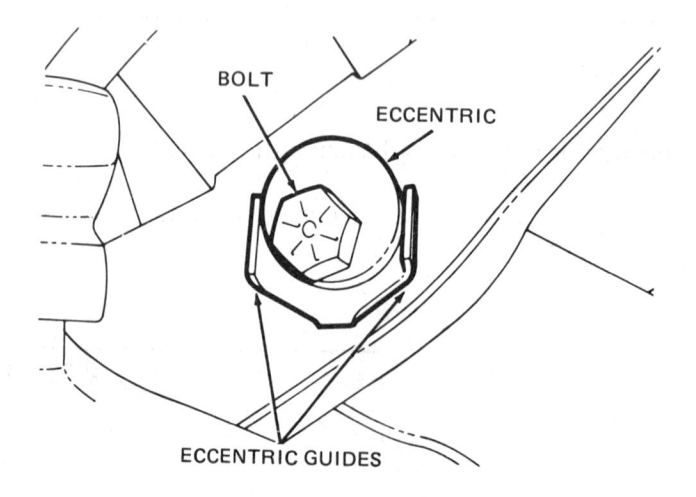

10. Lower vehicle.

Date Completed _____ Instructor's Check _____

NAME _____ SECTION _____ DATE _____ SCORE _____

Chapter 45 STEERING AND WHEEL ALIGNMENT SERVICE
JOB SHEET 42

Adjusting Toe-In

Before you begin: Read Chapter 45 in *Auto Mechanics*.

Student _____ Section _____ Date _____

Make of Car _____ Model _____ Year _____

Time Started _____ Time Finished _____ Total Time _____

Flat Rate Time _____

Special Tools, Equipment, Parts, and Materials

Wheel alignment equipment   _____

Toe-in adjustment wrench   _____

References

Manufacturer's Shop Manual _____

Repair Manual _____

Service Bulletin _____

Specifications

Look up the following specification and record it in the space provided below.

Toe-in _____

_____

Instructor's Check

Procedure

1. Raise the vehicle on a hoist or support it on a jack and install jack stands.

2. Check tire pressure, tie rod end condition, suspension part condition, wheel bearing adjustment, and spring heights.

3. Drive the vehicle on an alignment rack.

4. Use the equipment manufacturer's directions to measure toe-in. Write the measurement in the space provided: Toe _____

5. Compare toe-in measured to specifications.

6. If an adjustment is required, loosen clamps on tie rod ends.

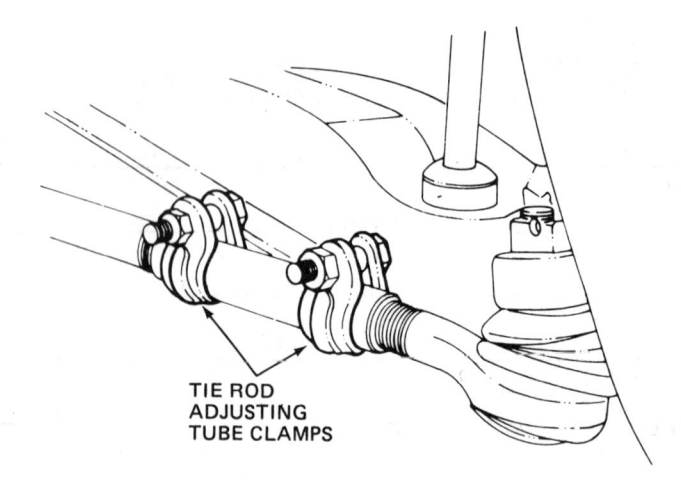

TIE ROD ADJUSTING TUBE CLAMPS

7. Adjust each tie rod equally in or out until gauge reads correct specification.

8. Recheck camber and caster measurement. Change as required.

9. Tighten tie rod end clamps.

10. Recheck toe-in. Adjust if necessary.

11. Remove jack stands and lower the vehicle.

   Safety Caution: Make sure all persons and objects are out of the way before lowering or raising an automobile.

NOTES

Date Completed _____ Instructor's Check _____

NAME _____ SECTION _____ DATE _____ SCORE _____

Chapter 46 THE BRAKE SYSTEM
ASSIGNMENT SHEET 39

Master Cylinder Parts Identification

Before you begin: Read Chapter 46 and Chapter 47 in *Auto Mechanics*. Identify the parts of the master cylinder in the spaces provided below.

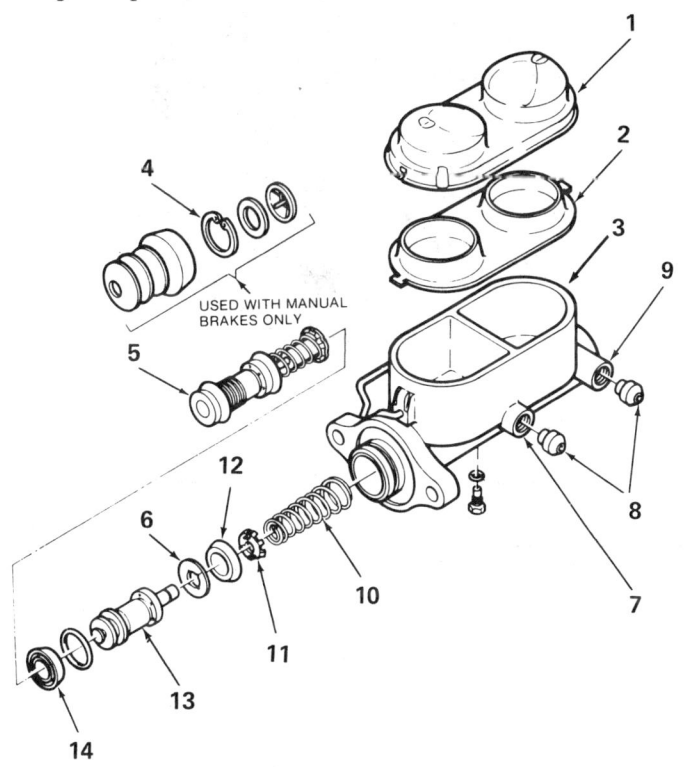

1. _____
2. _____
3. _____
4. _____
5. _____
6. _____
7. _____
8. _____
9. _____
10. _____
11. _____
12. _____
13. _____
14. _____

Drum Brake System Parts Identification

Identify the parts of the drum brake assembly in the spaces provided below.

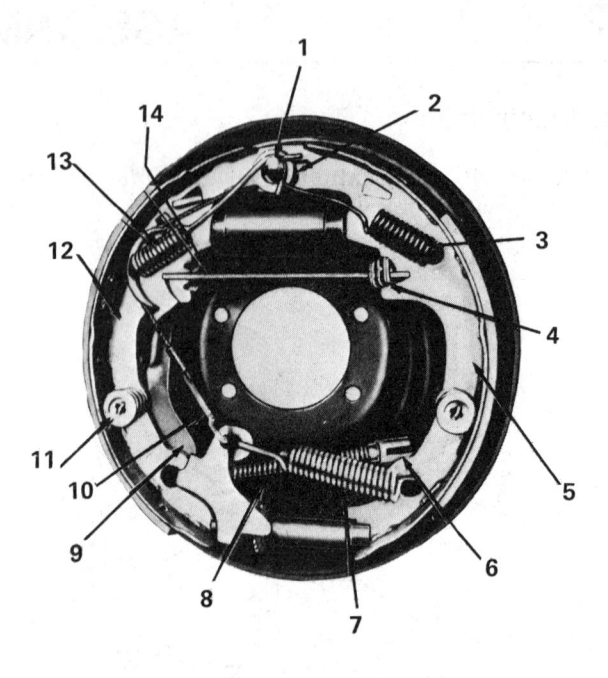

1. _____

2. _____
   _____

3. _____
   _____

4. _____

5. _____

6. _____
   _____

7. _____
   _____

8. _____
   _____

9. _____
   _____

10. _____

11. _____
    _____

12. _____

13. _____
    _____

14. _____

NAME _____ SECTION _____ DATE _____ SCORE _____

Chapter 46 THE BRAKE SYSTEM
ASSIGNMENT SHEET 40

Disc Brake System Components

Before you begin: Read Chapter 46 in *Auto Mechanics*. Identify the parts of the disc brake unit by writing the names in the spaces provided.

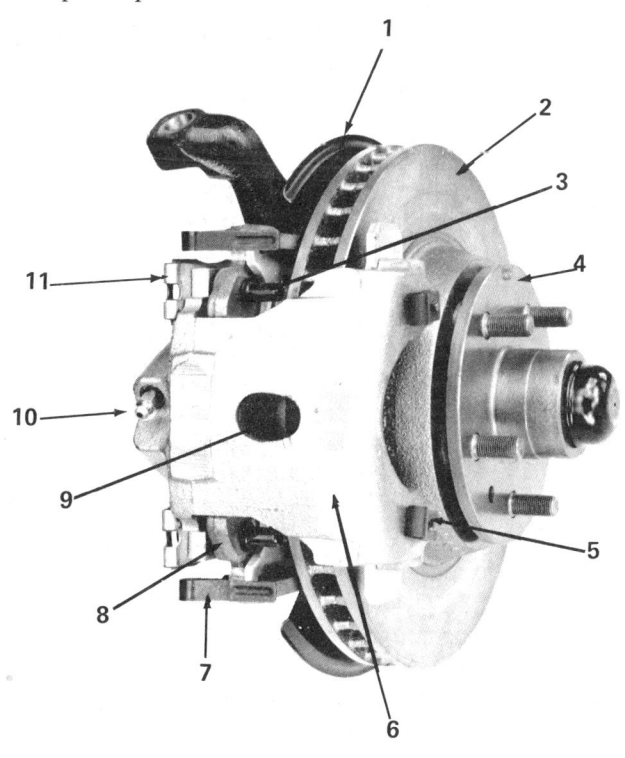

1. _____   7. _____
2. _____   8. _____
3. _____   9. _____
4. _____   10. _____
5. _____   11. _____
6. _____

241

Review of New Terms

For each definition in Column 2, select the term in Column 1 that best matches its meaning. Write the identifying *letter* of the term in the Answer column.

Column 1

A. Antiskid system
B. Caliper
C. Coefficient of friction
D. Disc brakes
E. Metering valve
F. Pascal's Law
G. Proportioning valve
H. Rotor
I. Self-adjusters
J. Self-energized brakes

Column 2

1. A housing for the hydraulic components of a disc brake system.
2. A cable-operated device used to adjust brake shoes automatically.
3. A valve that delays pressure build-up to the front brakes.
4. A system designed to prevent the wheels from locking or skidding during heavy braking.
5. A valve used to maintain the correct proportion of pressure between the front disc and rear drum brakes.
6. Brakes that use a wedging action of the brake shoes to help apply the brakes.
7. An index of the frictional characteristics of a material.
8. A principle of hydraulics that states that pressure at any point in a confined liquid is the same in every direction and applies equal force on equal areas.
9. A system that uses a rotor attached to the wheel and a caliper with brake pads to stop the wheel.
10. The part of the disc brake system that turns or rotates with the wheels.

Answer

1. _____
2. _____
3. _____
4. _____
5. _____
6. _____
7. _____
8. _____
9. _____
10. _____

NAME _____ SECTION _____ DATE _____ SCORE _____

Chapter 47 BRAKE SYSTEM SERVICE
JOB SHEET 43

Adjusting Brakes

Before you begin: Read Chapter 47 in *Auto Mechanics*.

Student _____ Section _____ Date _____

Make of Car _____ Model _____ Year _____

Time Started _____ Time Finished _____ Total Time _____

Flat Rate Time _____

Special Tools, Equipment, Parts, and Materials

Lift jack

Stationary jack

Brake adjusting tool

_____

References

Manufacturer's Shop Manual _____

Repair Manual _____

Service Bulletin _____

Instructor's Check

Procedure

1. Lift the vehicle on a hoist or jack and support with jack stands.

2. Check the master cylinder fluid level.

3. Remove rubber plugs from backing plates.

   Safety Caution: Brake dust contains asbestos. Do not blow the dust in the air because it is dangerous to breathe.

4. Locate the star adjusting wheel.

5. Use a screwdriver or brake adjusting tool to turn the adjuster in a direction to expand the shoes against the drum.

6. Adjust the brakes in an outward direction until the wheel is difficult to turn.

7. Back the adjuster wheel off until the wheel turns freely but with a small amount of drag.

8. Adjust each of the other assemblies in the same way.

9. Lower the vehicle.

10. Test drive the vehicle and check brake operation.

    Safety Caution: Obtain permission from your instructor before test driving a vehicle.

_____
Instructor's Check

NOTES

Date Completed _____ Instructor's Check _____

NAME _____ SECTION _____ DATE _____ SCORE _____

Chapter 47 BRAKE SYSTEM SERVICE
JOB SHEET 44

Bleeding Brakes

Before you begin: Read Chapter 47 in *Auto Mechanics*.

Student _____ Section _____ Date _____

Make of Car _____ Model _____ Year _____

Time Started _____ Time Finished _____ Total Time _____

Flat Rate Time _____

Special Tools, Equipment, Parts, and Materials

Pressure bleeder tank and fittings _____ Brake fluid _____

Glass jar _____ Bleeder hose with fitting _____

_____ _____

_____ _____

_____ _____

References

Manufacturer's Shop Manual _____

Repair Manual _____

Service Bulletin _____

_____
Instructor's Check

Procedure

1. Fill the master cylinder reservoirs with clean brake fluid. Attach the pressure bleeder hose to the master cylinder reservoirs with a fitting or adapter.

   NOTE: A pressure bleeder with fittings and adapter that connects to the master cylinder fluid reservoirs is necessary to pressure bleed the brake hydraulic system. Be sure enough brake fluid is in the pressure bleeder tank to complete the bleeding operation. The tank should be charged with 20-30 pounds of air pressure [138-207 kPa].

2. Open the valve in the pressure bleeder hose to pressurize the brake hydraulic system.

3. Attach a bleeder drain to the right rear wheel cylinder bleed screw. Submerge the free end of the hose in a glass container partly filled with brake fluid.

4. Loosen the bleed screw. When fluid coming from the submerged end of the hose is free of air bubbles, close the bleed screw and remove the bleeder hose.

5. Repeat at left rear, right front, and left front wheel cylinders in that order.

6. If the hydraulic system being bled has a dual system master cylinder with two filler caps, connect the pressure bleeder to the front reservoir to bleed the rear wheels and to the rear reservoir to bleed the front wheels.

   NOTE: Vehicles with front disc brakes usually have a metering valve in the hydraulic line to the front disc brakes. With no hydraulic pressure applied, the stem of the metering valve is in the depressed position.

7. Hold the valve stem in the depressed position, when pressure bleeding calipers on vehicles with a metering valve. If tape is used to depress the stem, be sure to remove the tape after bleeding is completed.

   NOTE: Do not attempt to force the metering valve stem into the valve body. This may damage the valve.

   Safety Caution: Wipe up any spilled brake fluid. Test the operation of the brake pedal. Be sure that a firm pedal is attained before moving the automobile.

   _____
   Instructor's Check

NOTES

Date Completed _____ Instructor's Check _____

NAME _____ SECTION _____ DATE _____ SCORE _____

Chapter 47 BRAKE SYSTEM SERVICE
JOB SHEET 45

Inspecting Brakes

Before you begin: Read Chapter 47 in *Auto Mechanics*.

Student _____ Section _____ Date _____

Make of Car _____ Model _____ Year _____

Time Started _____ Time Finished _____ Total Time _____

Flat Rate Time _____

Special Tools, Equipment, Parts, and Materials

Brake fluid   _____

_____   _____

References

Manufacturer's Shop Manual _____

Repair Manual _____

Service Bulletin _____

_____
Instructor's Check

Procedure

1. Apply and release foot pressure several times (with the engine running for power brakes) and check for friction and noise. Pedal movement should be smooth with a fast return and no squeaks from pedal or brakes.

2. Apply heavy foot pressure (with the engine running for power brakes) and check for sponginess. Measure the pedal reserve. The pedal should feel firm, not springy. The brake pedal should be over 2 inches [50 mm] from the floor for manual and power brakes.

3. Check for hydraulic leaks. Hold light foot pressure (with the engine off for power brakes) for 15 seconds and check that there is no pedal movement. Repeat with heavy foot pressure. Repeat the whole check for power brakes with the engine running.

4. Apply and release light pedal pressure (with the engine running for power brakes) and check that stoplights go on and off.

5. Check that the master cylinder reservoir vent hole(s) in the cap or cover is clean and open. Check that fluid level is within 1/4 inch [6 mm] of reservoir top (both sides for dual units) and that the fluid is clean.

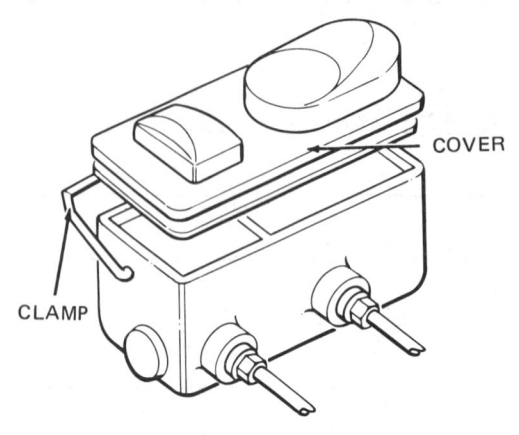

6. Add fluid, if necessary, by removing the clamp and lifting the cover. Use only the recommended fluid.

    Safety Caution: The use of the incorrect fluid or fluid with water in it can cause the brakes to fail.

7. Check for external hydraulic leaks. Look for dampness around the body, fittings and head nut, and hydraulic stoplight switch (if used). On manual brakes, flip back the dust boot and look for fluid.

8. Look under the hood and under the automobile on a hoist to check the hose, tubing, and connections for leaks. Check the backing plates and wheels for signs of brake fluid or grease leaks. Make sure tubing is free from dents or other damage. Check that the hose is flexible and free from cracks, cuts, or bulges.

9. With the parking brake released, check that all wheels spin freely without drag. With light pressure on the brake pedal, turn the wheels by hand. Check that there are no "free" and "tight" spots on any wheel and that all wheels have the same amount of drag.

10. Apply heavy pressure to the parking brake. The lever or pedal should move no more than 2/3 of full travel. Rear wheels should be locked. Release the parking brake and check that all wheels spin freely without drag.

11. Each time the drum brakes are adjusted, or at intervals recommended by the automobile manufacturer, pull the right front wheel and drum and inspect the lining for wear. If less than 1/16 inch [1.6 mm] of usable lining remains, the brakes should be relined. If the amount of lining left is questionable, pull the remaining drums and inspect these linings.

12. Disc brake lining may be inspected by removing the wheel and tire assembly.

13. Whenever the disc brake lining is worn to about the thickness of the metal shoe, all shoe and lining assemblies on both brakes should be replaced.

    Date Completed _____ Instructor's Check _____

NAME _____ SECTION _____ DATE _____ SCORE _____

Chapter 47 BRAKE SYSTEM SERVICE
JOB SHEET 46

Overhauling a Master Cylinder

Before you begin: Read Chapter 47 in *Auto Mechanics*.

Student _____ Section _____ Date _____

Make of Car _____ Model _____ Year _____

Time Started _____ Time Finished _____ Total Time _____

Flat Rate Time _____

Special Tools, Equipment, Parts, and Materials

Brake cylinder hone   Replacement master-cylinder parts

Electric drill, 1/4 inch   Pan and brush for clean parts

Brake fluid in squirt can   Alcohol

Crocus cloth   Dowel

References

Manufacturer's Shop Manual _____

Repair Manual _____

Service Bulletin _____

_____
Instructor's Check

Procedure

1. Disconnect the hydraulic lines, remove attaching bolts (or nuts), and remove the master cylinder from the automobile.

   NOTE: On some automobiles, the manual pushrod must be disconnected from the brake pedal to permit removal of the master cylinder.

2. Remove the reservoir cover and drain the fluid from both reservoirs.

3. Press the pushrod against the primary piston to compress the spring and remove the piston stop screw.

4. Remove the snap ring (if used) from the inside hub of the cylinder. Then remove primary and secondary piston assemblies.

5. Discard the primary piston assembly.

6. Remove the spring, spring retainer, washer, and cups from the secondary piston.

7. Clamp the master cylinder in a vise with side outlets up. Remove the outlet port tube seats if necessary with self-tapping screws supplied in the repair kit. Thread the self-tapping screws supplied in the repair kit. Thread the self-tapping screws into the tube seats, place a screwdriver tip under the screw head, and pry the screw upward.

8. Thoroughly clean the cylinder and polish the cylinder bore with crocus cloth or a brake hone. Do not use a hone that will result in oversize or a poor finish.

    Safety Caution: Never allow the hone to come out of the cylinder under power or the stones could fly out of the holder and cause injury.

9. If the cylinder bore is badly pitted, rusted, or scored, replace the cylinder. Check compensating and fluid inlet ports for burrs. Rinse all metal parts to be reused in clean alcohol and place on clean paper. Discard all old parts to be replaced.

10. Dip all rubber parts in clean brake fluid and place them in a clean pan or on clean paper. Assemble secondary cups and retainer on the secondary piston with cups back to back. From the opposite end of the secondary piston, assemble protector washer, primary cup (flat side next to washer), retainer, and piston return spring. Use the exploded view illustration as a guide to assembly.

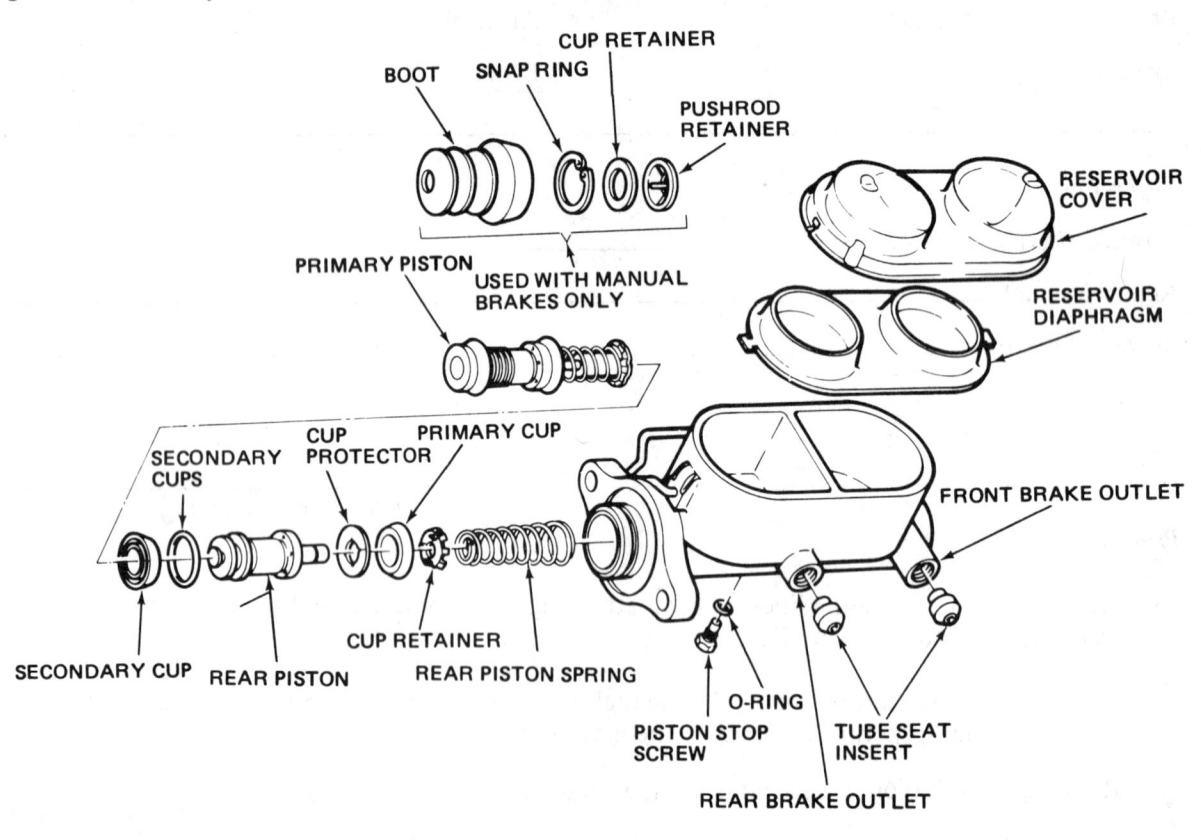

NAME _____ SECTION _____ DATE _____ SCORE _____

11. Coat the cylinder bore and cups of the secondary and primary pistons with clean brake fluid. Guide the secondary piston assembly (spring end first) into the cylinder bore, followed by the primary piston assembly. Press against the primary piston to compress the spring approximately 1/4 inch [6 mm] and install the piston stop screw.

12. Release the piston and tighten the stop screw. If the master cylinder includes a piston-retaining snap ring, rubber seal ring, dust guard, or pushrod, assemble these parts on the master cylinder.

13. Insert the end of the spring into the recess of the rubber check valve and assemble spring, check valve, and tube seat insert in both outlets. Thread the tube seat plug or tube nuts of the correct thread size into the cylinder to press the tube seat inserts into place.

14. Remove air from the cylinder by bleeding before installation on the vehicle. Support the cylinder assembly in a vise and fill reservoirs with the correct brake fluid.

15. Press the piston assembly inward slowly with a wooden dowel or pushrod. Allow the pistons to return under spring pressure. Repeat until air bubbles no longer appear.

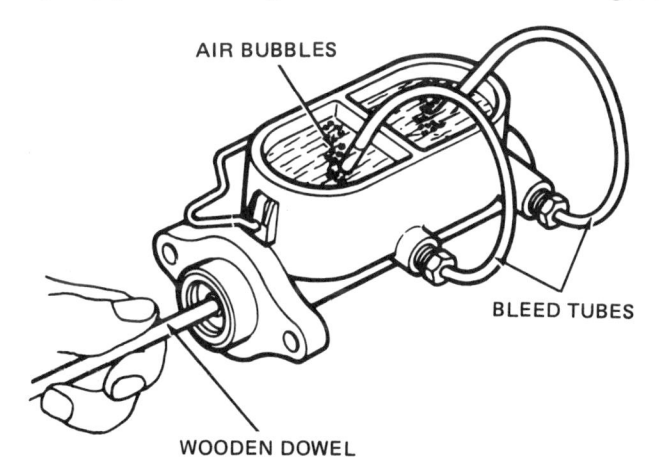

16. Install the cylinder on the vehicle. Remove the bleed tubes and connect the hydraulic lines. The entire system will require bleeding.

NOTES

Date Completed _____ Instructor's Check _____

251

NAME _____ SECTION _____ DATE _____ SCORE _____

Chapter 48 TIRES AND WHEELS
ASSIGNMENT SHEET 41

Tire Construction

Before you begin: Read Chapter 48 in *Auto Mechanics*. Identify the parts of the tire in the spaces provided below.

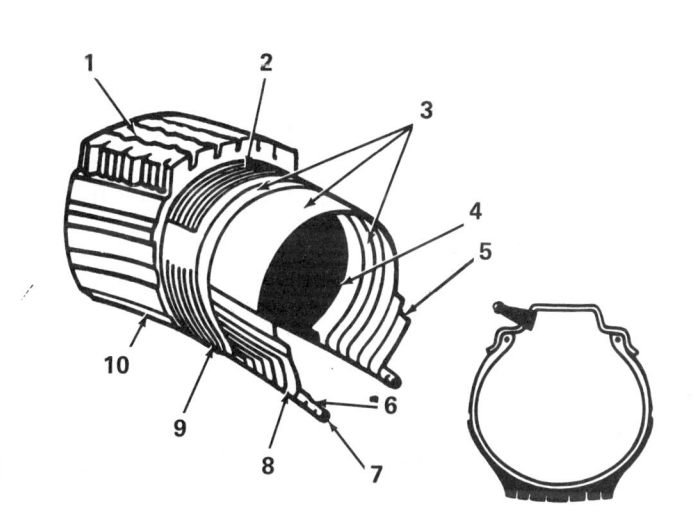

1. _____
2. _____
3. _____
4. _____
5. _____
6. _____
7. _____
8. _____
9. _____
10. _____

Tire Design

In the space provided identify the type of tire design shown in the illustrations below and describe the advantages of each.

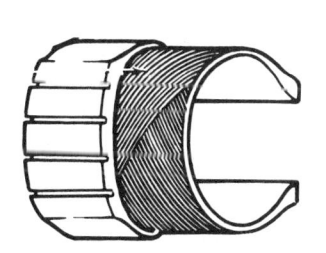

1. _____
_____
_____
_____
_____
_____

(Continued on next page)

253

2. _____

3. _____

Review of New Terms

For each definition in Column 2, select the term in Column 1 that best matches its meaning. Write the identifying *letter* of the term in the Answer column.

Column 1

A. Aspect ratio
B. Belted tire
C. Bias-ply tire
D. Cord
E. Dropped center rim
F. Load rating
G. Load range
H. Plies
I. Pneumatic tires
J. Quality gradings
K. Radial tire
L. Retread
M. Rim
N. Tubeless tire

Column 2

1. A tire in which the layers of cord lie at right angles.
2. A tire that has the air sealed between the rim and tire and does not use an inner tube.
3. A tire that is reinforced with a buildup of cord under the tread area.
4. The ratio of tire width to height.
5. Tires that are filled with air.
6. The material used to hold the rubber parts of the tire in position.
7. A used tire on which a new tread section is molded.
8. Layers of cord used when the tire is constructed.
9. A tire design in which the layers of cord have a criss-crossing pattern.
10. The metal wheel on which the tire is mounted.
11. A wheel with a lowered center that provides raised flanges to prevent the wheel from getting off the rim during driving.
12. A range of tire load ratings at a specific inflation pressure.
13. A letter on the sidewall which indicates the amount of load a tire can support.
14. A system of tire quality gradings based upon treadwear, traction and resistance to high temperature.

Answer

1. _____
2. _____
3. _____
4. _____
5. _____
6. _____
7. _____
8. _____
9. _____
10. _____
11. _____
12. _____
13. _____
14. _____

NAME _____ SECTION _____ DATE _____ SCORE _____

Chapter 49 TIRE AND WHEEL SERVICE
JOB SHEET 47

Measure Wheel Runout

Before you begin: Read Chapter 49 in *Auto Mechanics*.

Student _____ Section _____ Date _____

Make of Car _____ Model _____ Year _____

Time Started _____ Time Finished _____ Total Time _____

Flat Rate Time _____

Special Tools, Equipment, Parts, and Materials

Dial indicator or runout gauge   _____

_____   _____

_____   _____

References

Manufacturer's Shop Manual _____

Repair Manual _____

Service Bulletin _____

Specifications

Look up the following specifications and record them in the spaces provided.

Wheel radial runout _____ Wheel lateral runout _____

_____
Instructor's Check

Procedure

1. Lift wheels to be checked off the floor.

    Safety Caution: Place jack stands so that the car will not slip or fall.

2. Remove hubcaps.

3. Measure tire radial runout in the center of the tread face and lateral runout just above the buffing rib on the tire sidewall. Mark the high points of lateral and radial runout for future use. Record your measurement in the space provided. _____

   NOTE: To avoid false readings from temporary flat spots in the tires, check the tires as soon as possible after the vehicle has been driven at least ten miles. Make all measurements with the tires inflated to recommended load inflation pressures and front wheel bearings adjusted properly.

4. When total radial or lateral runout exceeds specified limits, check wheel runout to determine whether the wheel or tire is at fault.

5. Wheel radial runout should be measured just inside of the wheel cover retaining nibs.

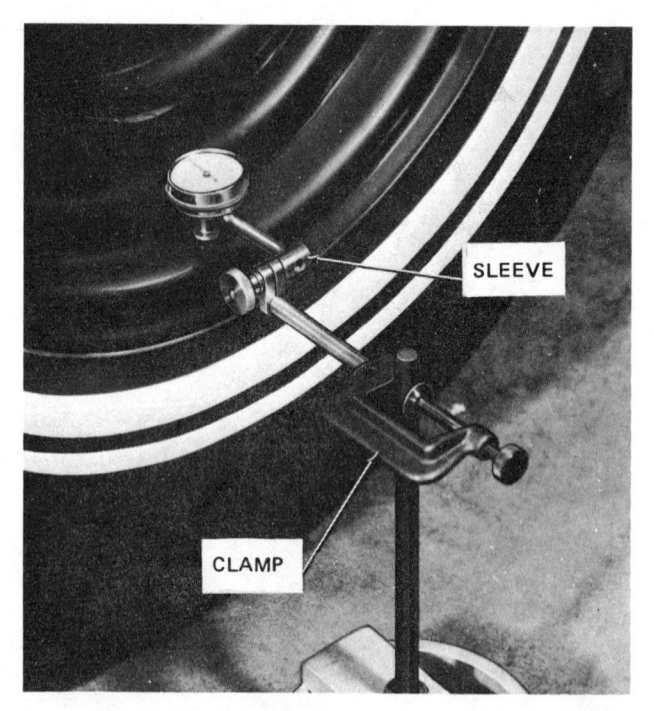

NAME _____ SECTION _____ DATE _____ SCORE _____

6. Wheel lateral runout should be measured on the bead flange, just inside of the curved lip.

   NOTE: Wheel radial runout should not be more than 0.035 inch [0.89 mm], and lateral runout should not be more than 0.045 inch [1.14 mm]. Record your measurement in the space provided. _____

7. Mark the high points of radial and lateral runout for possible future use.

   NOTE: Where either lateral or radial tire runout is higher than specifications but wheel runout is within specifications, it may be possible to reduce runout by placing the tire on the wheel so that the previously marked high points are 180° apart. In some cases, runout may be corrected only by replacing a tire or wheel.

8. Replace the hubcaps and lower the car.

_____
Instructor's Check

NOTES

Date Completed _____ Instructor's Check _____

NAME _____ SECTION _____ DATE _____ SCORE _____

Chapter 49 TIRE AND WHEEL SERVICE
JOB SHEET 48

Repair a Tire

Before you begin: Read Chapter 49 in *Auto Mechanics*.

Student _____ Section _____ Date _____

Make of Car _____ Model _____ Year _____

Time Started _____ Time Finished _____ Total Time _____

Flat Rate Time _____

Special Tools, Equipment, Parts, and Materials

Hot patch kit _____   _____

_____   _____

_____   _____

References

Manufacturer's Shop Manual _____

Repair Manual _____

Service Bulletin _____

_____
Instructor's Check

Procedure

1. When a tire loses all or most of its air pressure, it must be removed from the wheel for a complete inspection to determine what damage has occurred. Punctured tires should be removed from the wheel and permanently repaired from the inside. Examine the sidewall and tread for damage or wear. Nails or other sharp objects should be removed and the holes marked with chalk.

2. If a tank is available, the tire and rim should be submerged. Bubbles coming out of the tire will show where the leaks are.

    NOTE: Look for leaks particularly around the rim, at the valve, and along the tread. Carefully examine the bead and rim at any point where leakage is found.

3. If a tank is not available, apply a soapy solution to the tire and look for bubbles.

4. Check the tire for signs of swelling or blistering, especially in the shoulder area.

5. Remove the tire from the rim once your inspection is complete. Take care not to damage the bead or liner.

6. Once the tire is off the rim, examine its inside for signs of damage.

    NOTE: A ply separation near a puncture or other injury may not be easy to see, for the air will escape through the injury. Probing is the only way to detect separation.

    Safety Caution: Never repair a puncture in a tire with any of the following:

    a. Ply separation

    b. Chafed fabric injuries on tubeless tires

    c. Broken or damaged bead wires

    d. Flex breaks

    e. Loose cords or evidence of having been run flat

    f. Tread separation

    g. Wear below 1/16 inch [1.6 mm] depth in major grooves

    h. Cracks which go into the tire fabric

    i. Any open liner cut which shows exposed fabric

    j. Sidewall puncture

7. When a repairable tire problem is discovered, the tire must be taken off the rim. Follow manufacturer's instructions when using tier mounting equipment.

8. A hot patch kit to repair leaks in tires uses heat to vulcanize the patch to the tire. Scrape and buff the area around the leak and cover with a light coating of cement of the type specified for the patch being used.

9. Carefully remove the backing from the patch and center its base over the injury. Place the clamp over the patch and tighten. Finger tighten only; do not use a wrench or pliers.

10. Apply heat and allow to cool.

11. When cool, remove the clamp and remount the repaired tire on the rim.

12. Make a final check under water to determine that there are no leaks.

Date Completed _____ Instructor's Check _____

NAME _____ SECTION _____ DATE _____ SCORE _____

Chapter 50 HEATING AND AIR CONDITIONING SYSTEM
ASSIGNMENT SHEET 42

Heater System Components

Before you begin: Read Chapter 50 in *Auto Mechanics*. Identify the main components of the heating system in the spaces provided below.

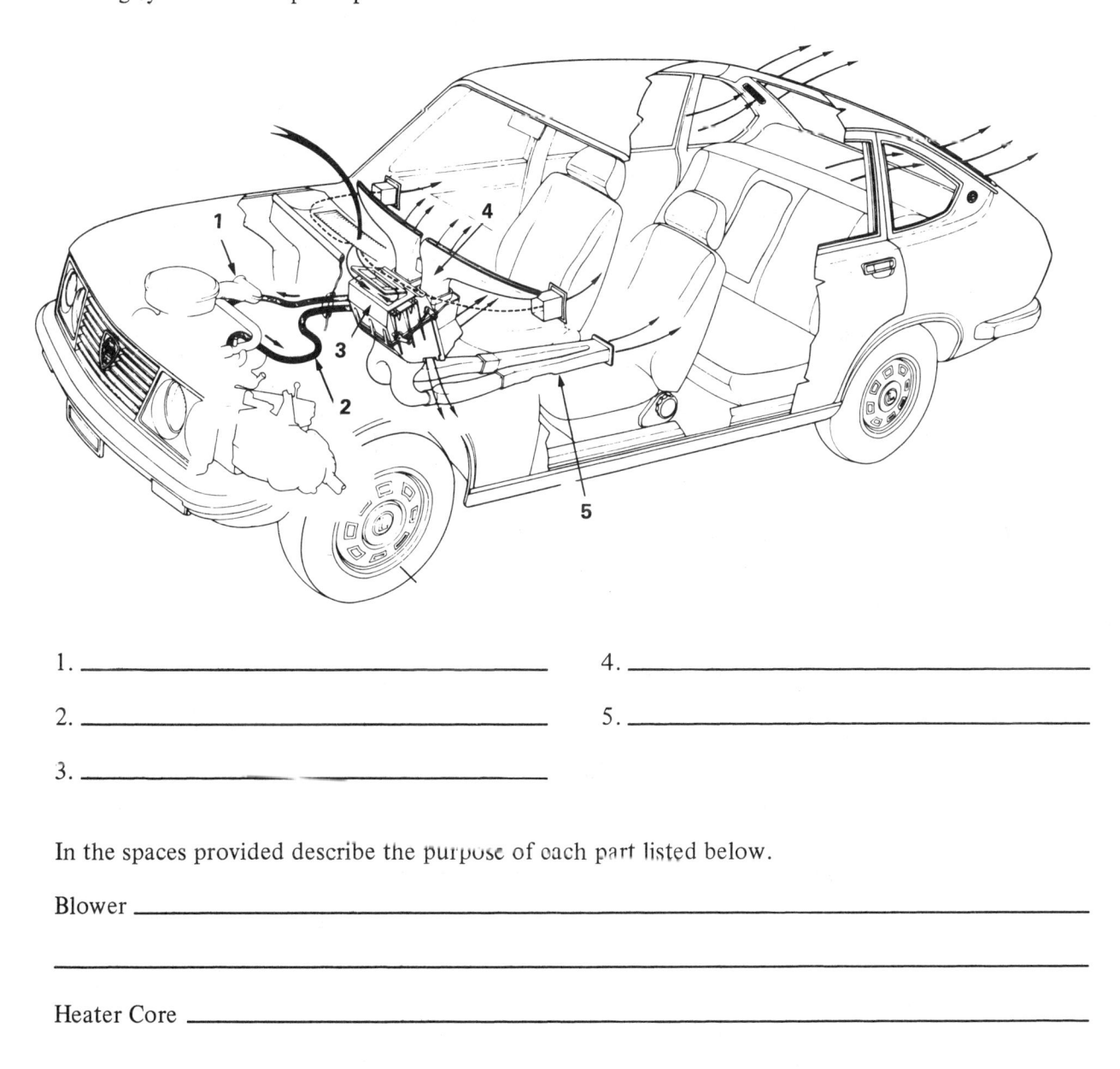

1. _____   4. _____

2. _____   5. _____

3. _____

In the spaces provided describe the purpose of each part listed below.

Blower _____

_____

Heater Core _____

_____

(Continued on next page)

Heater Hoses _____
_____

Vents _____
_____

Air Conditioning Components

Identify the parts of an air conditioning system in the spaces provided below.

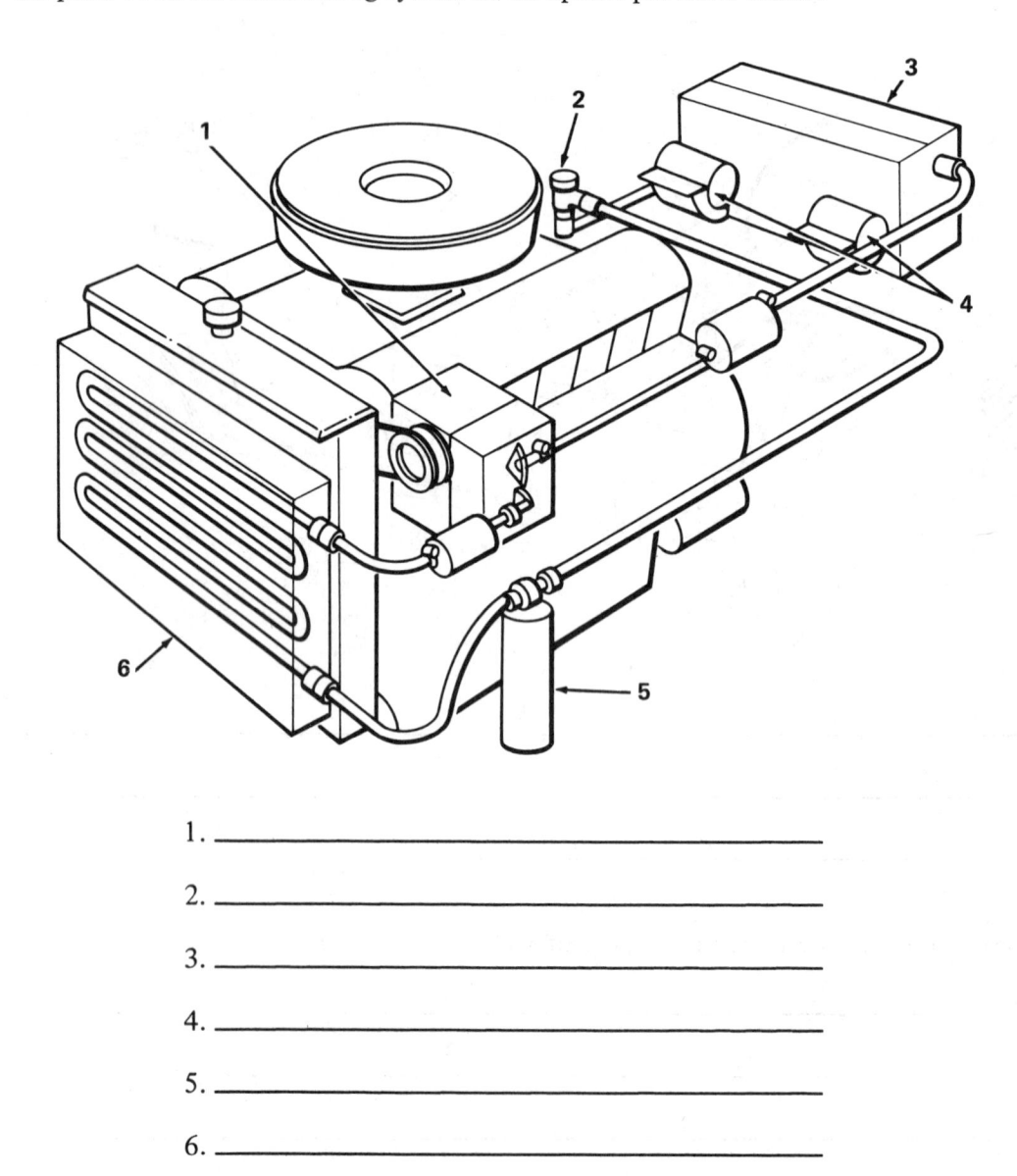

1. _____
2. _____
3. _____
4. _____
5. _____
6. _____

NAME_____ SECTION_____ DATE_____ SCORE_____

Review of New Terms

For each definition in Column 2, select the term in Column 1 that best matches its meaning. Write the identifying *letter* of the term in the Answer column.

Column 1	Column 2	Answer
A. Blower	1. The principles on which air conditioning systems operate.	1. _____
B. Compressor	2. A finned heat exchanger used to cool the air by evaporation.	2. _____
C. Condenser		
D. Evaporator	3. A system designed to warm the air inside the automobile.	3. _____
E. Expansion valve	4. A belt-driven pump used to circulate and increase the pressure of refrigerant.	4. _____
F. Heater core		
G. Heating system	5. A reservoir used to store and dry refrigerant.	5. _____
H. Receiver/drier	6. A fan driven by an electric motor to circulate air.	6. _____
I. Refrigerant		
J. Refrigeration cycle	7. A substance that carries away heat.	7. _____
	8. A heat exchanger used to warm air in the heater system.	8. _____
	9. A valve used to control the flow of refrigerant to the evaporator.	9. _____
	10. A device used to condense the high-pressure, high-temperature refrigerant vapor.	10. _____

263

Chapter 51 EMISSION CONTROL SYSTEMS
ASSIGNMENT SHEET 43

Positive Crankcase Ventilation System

Before you begin: Read Chapter 51 in *Auto Mechanics*. Draw arrows on the figure below to indicate vapor flow through a positive crankcase ventilation system.

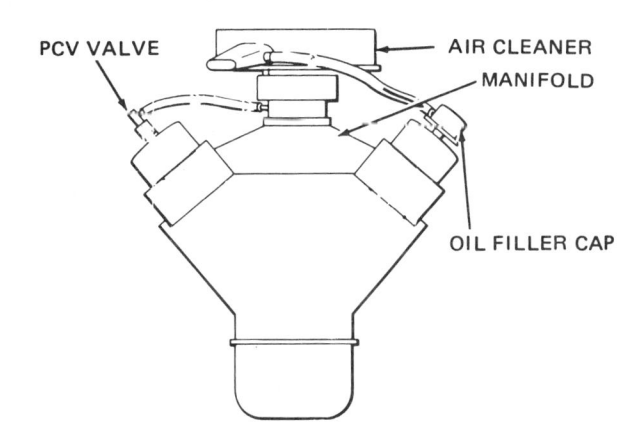

Identify the parts of a positive crankcase ventilation system in the spaces provided below.

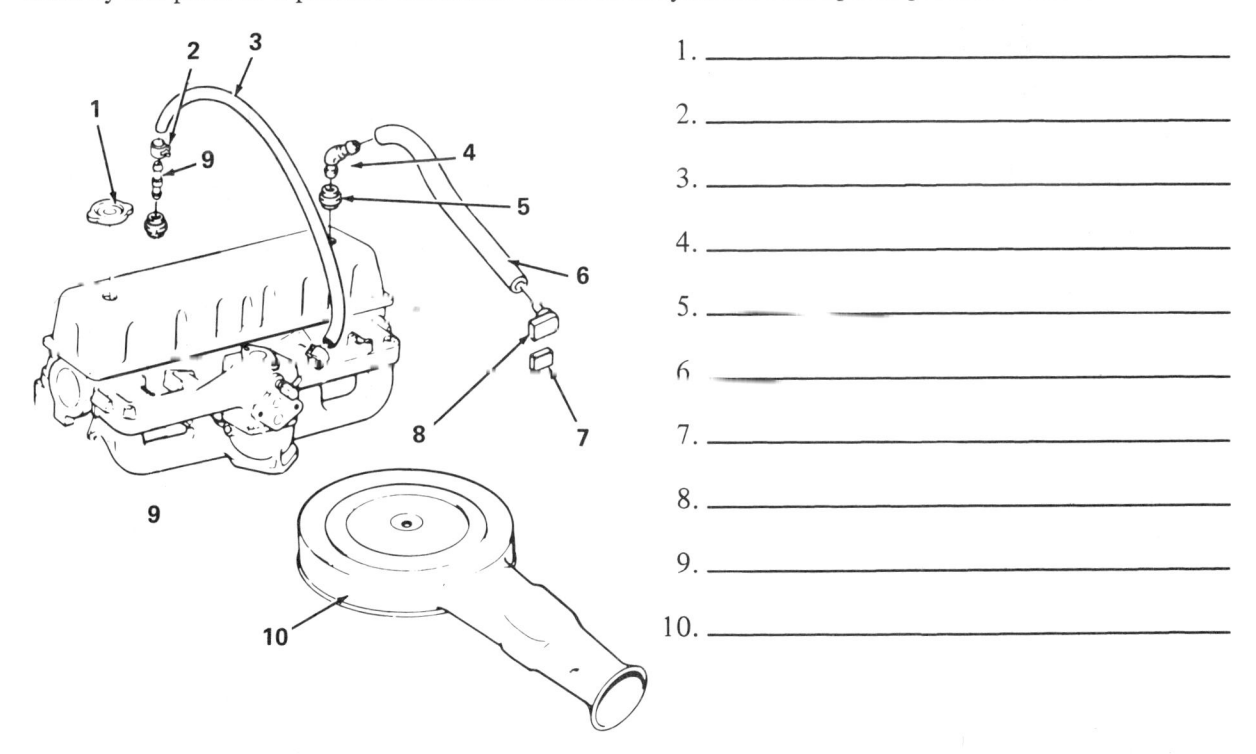

1. _____
2. _____
3. _____
4. _____
5. _____
6. _____
7. _____
8. _____
9. _____
10. _____

265

PCV Valve Operation

In the spaces provided describe the operation and flow when a PCV valve is in each of the positions shown below.

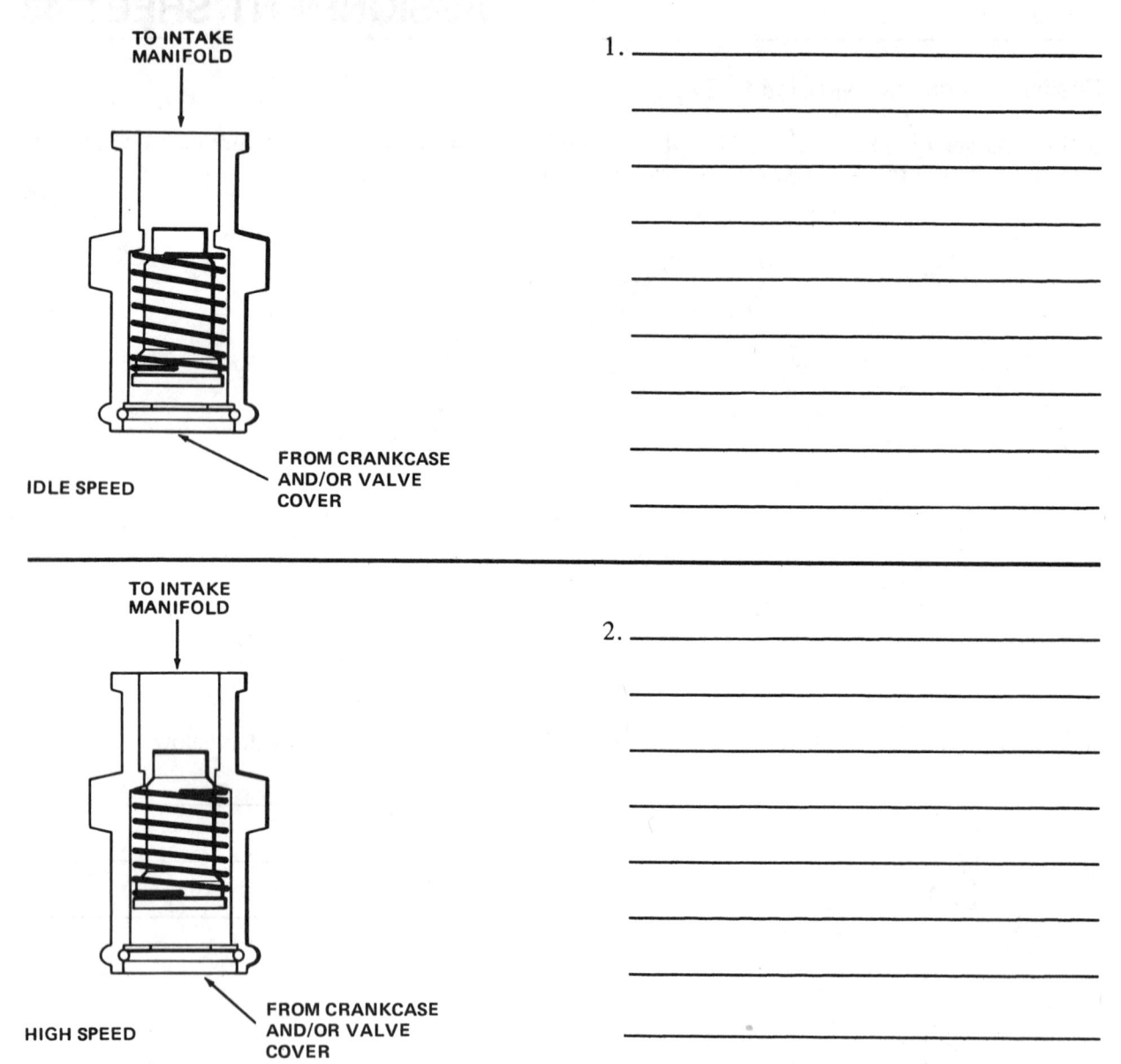

IDLE SPEED

TO INTAKE MANIFOLD

FROM CRANKCASE AND/OR VALVE COVER

1. _____

HIGH SPEED

TO INTAKE MANIFOLD

FROM CRANKCASE AND/OR VALVE COVER

2. _____

NAME _____ SECTION _____ DATE _____ SCORE _____

Chapter 51 EMISSION CONTROL SYSTEMS
ASSIGNMENT SHEET 44

Evaporative Control System

Identify the parts of the evaporative control system in the spaces provided.

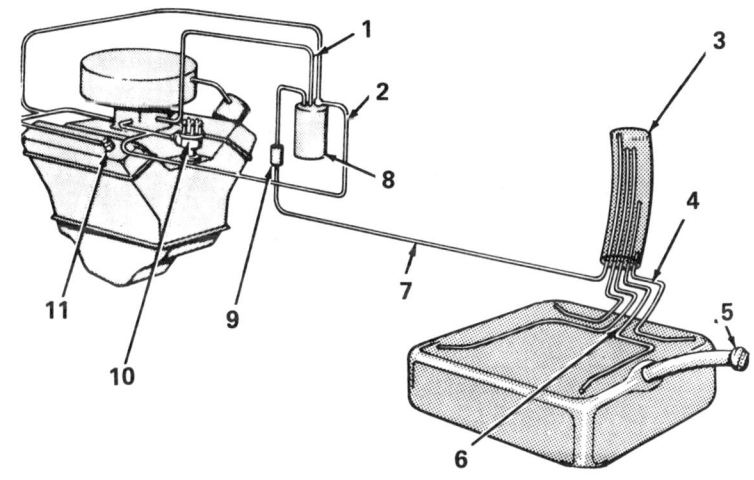

1. _____

2. _____

3. _____

4. _____

5. _____

6. _____

7. _____

8. _____

9. _____

10. _____

11. _____

Identify the components of the EGR system in the spaces provided below.

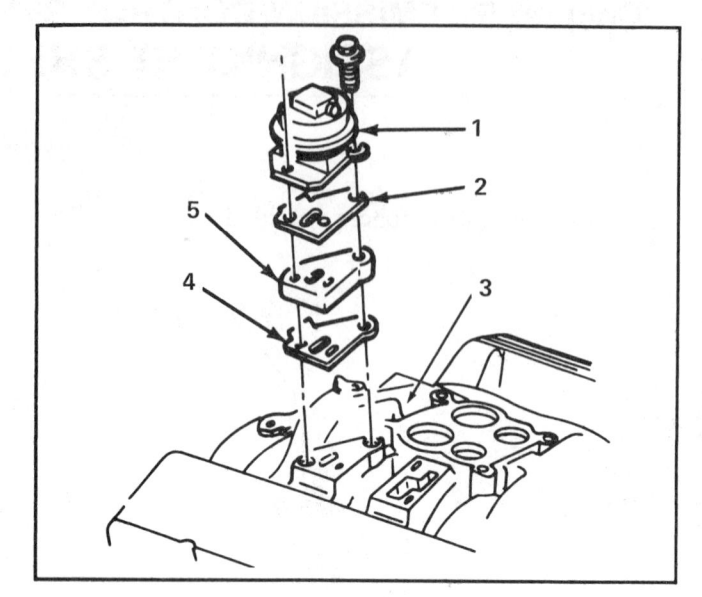

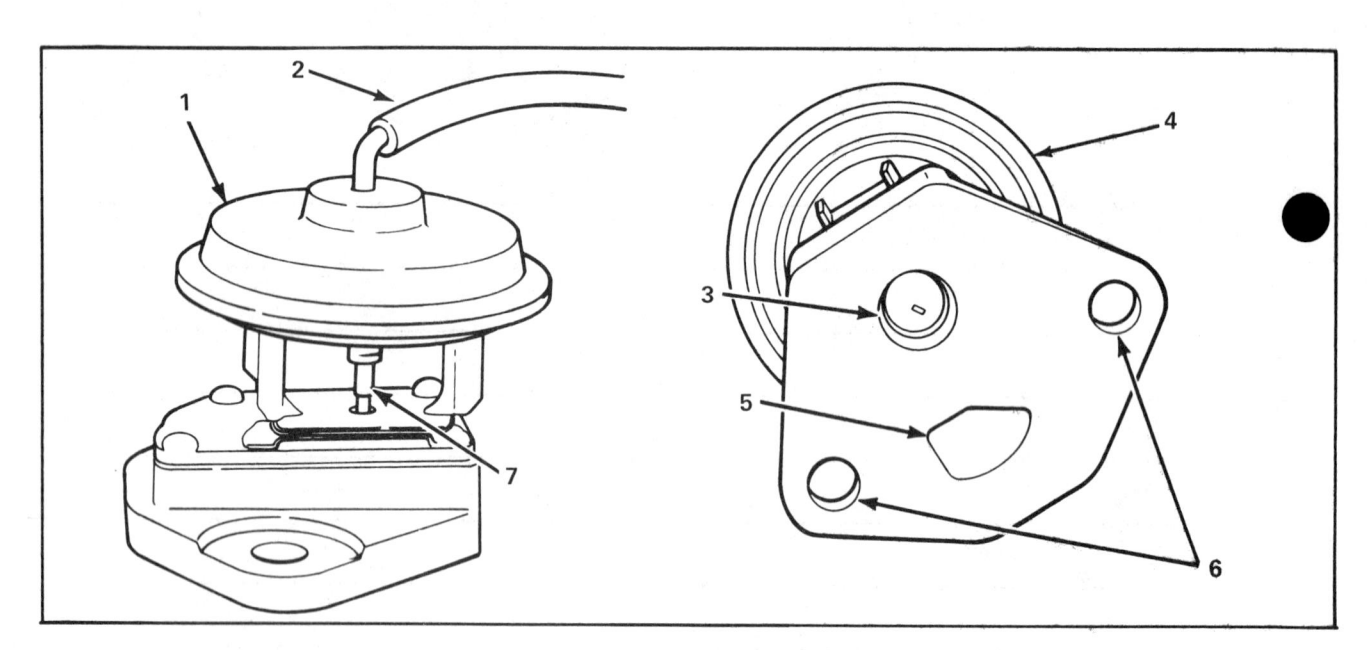

1. _____
2. _____
3. _____
4. _____
5. _____

1. _____   5. _____
2. _____   6. _____
3. _____   7. _____
4. _____

NAME _____ SECTION _____ DATE _____ SCORE _____

Chapter 51 EMISSION CONTROL SYSTEMS
ASSIGNMENT SHEET 45

Air Injection System

Before you begin: Read Chapter 51 in *Auto Mechanics*. Identify the parts of the air injection system in the spaces provided below.

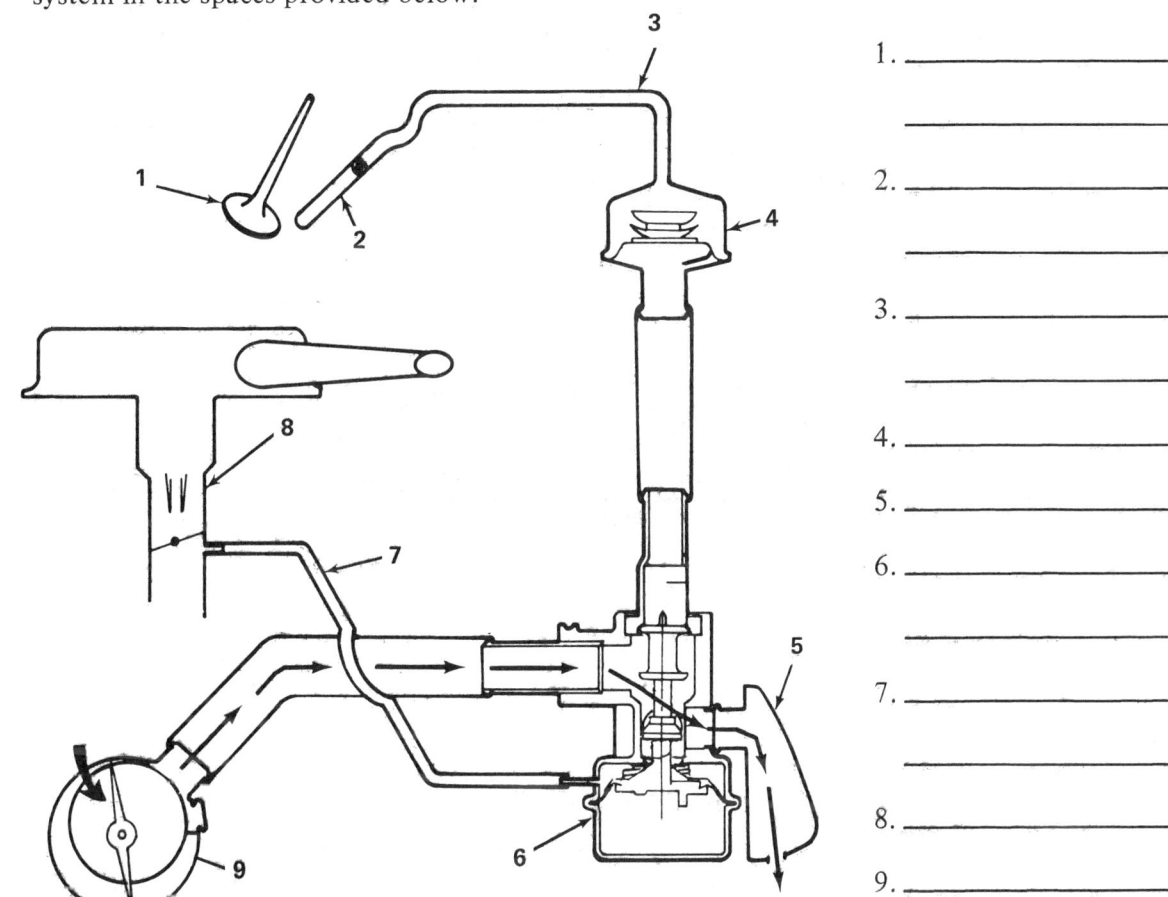

1. _____

2. _____

3. _____

4. _____

5. _____

6. _____

7. _____

8. _____

9. _____

269

Catalytic Converter

Identify the parts of the catalytic converter in the spaces provided below.

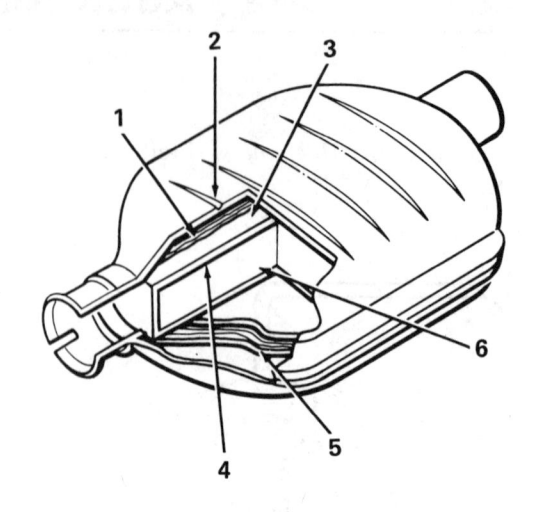

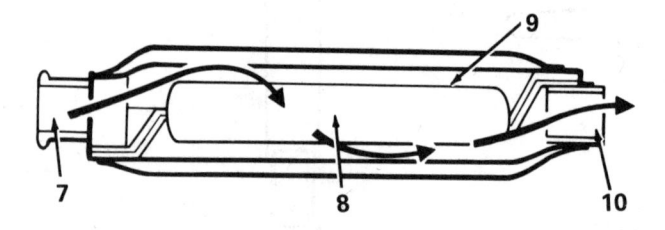

1. _____

2. _____

3. _____
   _____

4. _____

5. _____

6. _____

7. _____

8. _____
   _____

9. _____
   _____

10. _____

NAME _____ SECTION _____ DATE _____ SCORE _____

Review of New Terms

For each definition in Column 2, select the term in Column 1 that best matches its meaning. Write the identifying *letter* of the term in the Answer column.

Column 1	Column 2	Answer
A. Air injection	1. Emissions that result from blow-by in the crankcase.	1. _____
B. Canister vapor storage	2. Pollutants caused by high temperatures in the combustion chamber.	2. _____
C. Catalytic exhaust system	3. Emissions that result from the combustion in the engine's cylinders.	3. _____
D. Controlled timing	4. A system used to burn exhaust emissions in the exhaust manifold.	4. _____
E. Crankcase emissions	5. A system that pushes air into the exhaust to burn emissions.	5. _____
F. Crankcase vapor storage	6. A system that uses a catalyst to change pollution from the exhaust system to harmless compounds.	6. _____
G. Exhaust emissions	7. An evaporative storage system in which vapors are stored in the crankcase.	7. _____
H. Oxides of nitrogen	8. A system that matches the timing to the emission requirements of the engine.	8. _____
I. PCV valve	9. A system in which gasoline vapors are stored in a canister full of charcoal.	9. _____
J. Thermal reactor	10. A positive crankcase valve used to control the flow of blow-by gases.	10. _____
K. Computerized engine control	11. A system that routes heated air to the carburetor during startup and cold operation.	11. _____
L. Exhaust gas recirculation system (EGR)	12. A system that senses the engine air-fuel ratio and corrects it to the ideal air-fuel ratio.	12. _____
M. Feedback system	13. A system which controls the engine ignition, fuel and emission systems with a computer and sets of sensors and actuators.	13. _____
N. Heated inlet air system	14. A system used to reduce oxides of nitrogen (NO_x).	14. _____

NAME _____ SECTION _____ DATE _____ SCORE _____

Chapter 52 EMISSION SYSTEM SERVICE
ASSIGNMENT SHEET 46

Emission Label Interpretation

Before you begin: Read Chapter 52 in *Auto Mechanics.* Study the emission label below and answer the questions in the spaces provided.

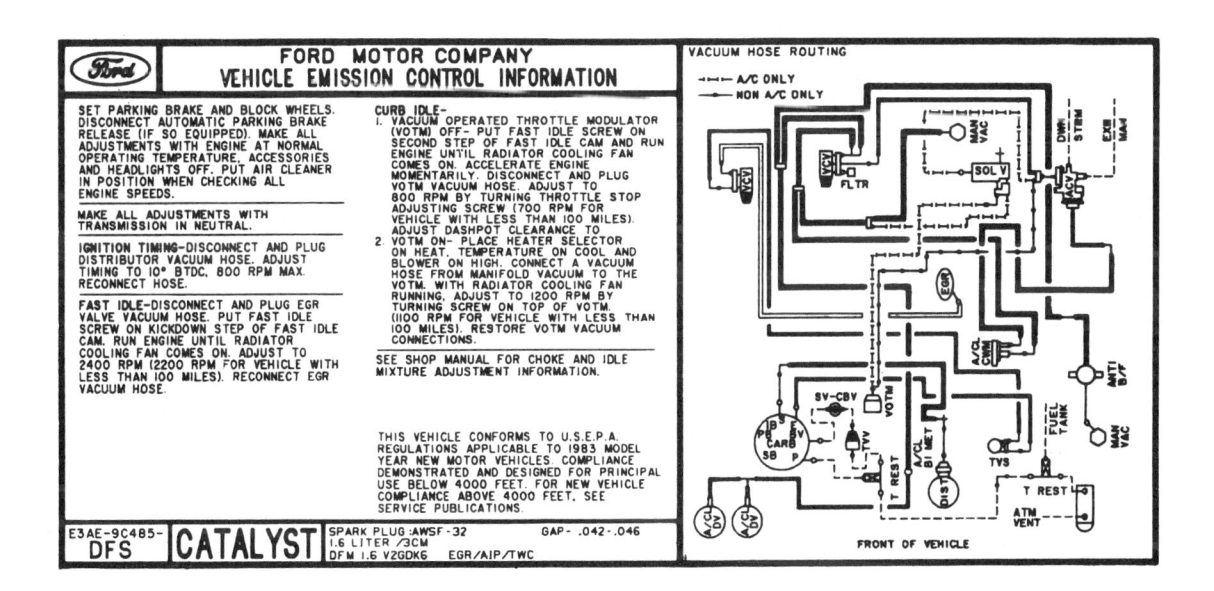

1. What is the purpose of the diagram shown at the right of the label?

2. What does the word catalyst mean at the bottom of the label?

3. Should idle adjustments be made with headlights on or off?

4. Should idle adjustments be made with air cleaner on or off?

5. Should ignition timing be done with the distributor vacuum hose in place or disconnected?

6. What should the ignition timing be adjusted to? _____

7. What should you do to the EGR vacuum hose when adjusting fast idle?
   _____

8. What is the recommended idle speed for a car with under 100 miles?
   _____

9. What is the recommended idle speed for a car with over 100 miles?
   _____

10. Should the fast idle be adjusted with the cooling fan on or off?
    _____

NAME _____ SECTION _____ DATE _____ SCORE _____

Chapter 52 EMISSION SYSTEM SERVICE
ASSIGNMENT SHEET 47

Reading an Exhaust Analyzer

Before you begin: Read Chapter 52 in *Auto Mechanics*. Observe each of the meter readings below and answer the questions in the spaces provided.

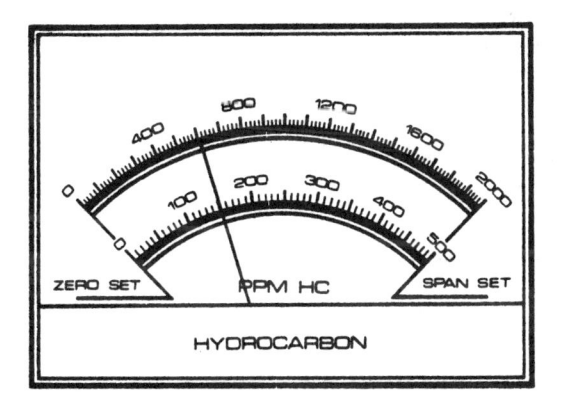

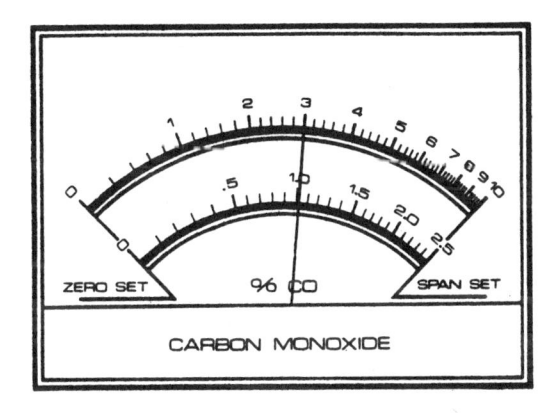

1. What is the hydrocarbon reading on the meter? _____

2. Where can you find specifications for hydrocarbon levels?
   _____

   List three causes of high hydrocarbon levels:

3. _____

4. _____

5. _____

275

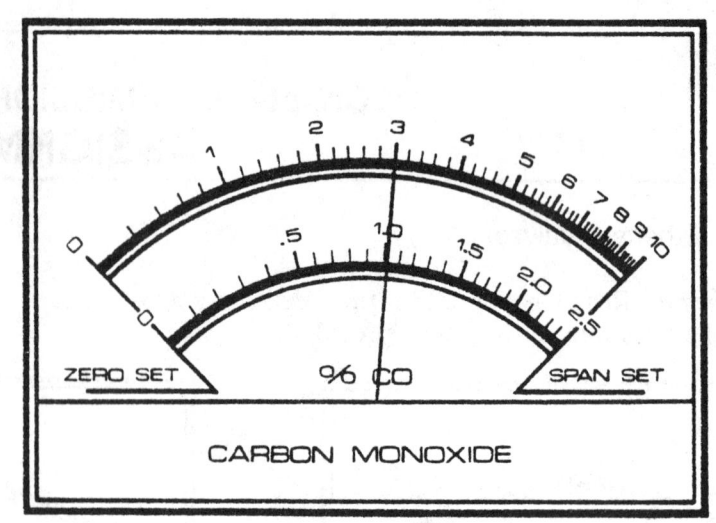

6. What is the carbon monoxide reading shown on the meter?
   _____

7. Where can you find specifications on carbon monoxide levels?
   _____

   List three causes of high carbon monoxide levels:

8. _____

9. _____

10. _____

NAME _____ SECTION _____ DATE _____ SCORE _____

Chapter 53 ELECTRONIC FUEL INJECTION SYSTEMS
ASSIGNMENT SHEET 48

Before you begin: Read Chapter 53 in *Auto Mechanics*. Identify the parts of an electronic fuel injection system by writing the names in the spaces provided below.

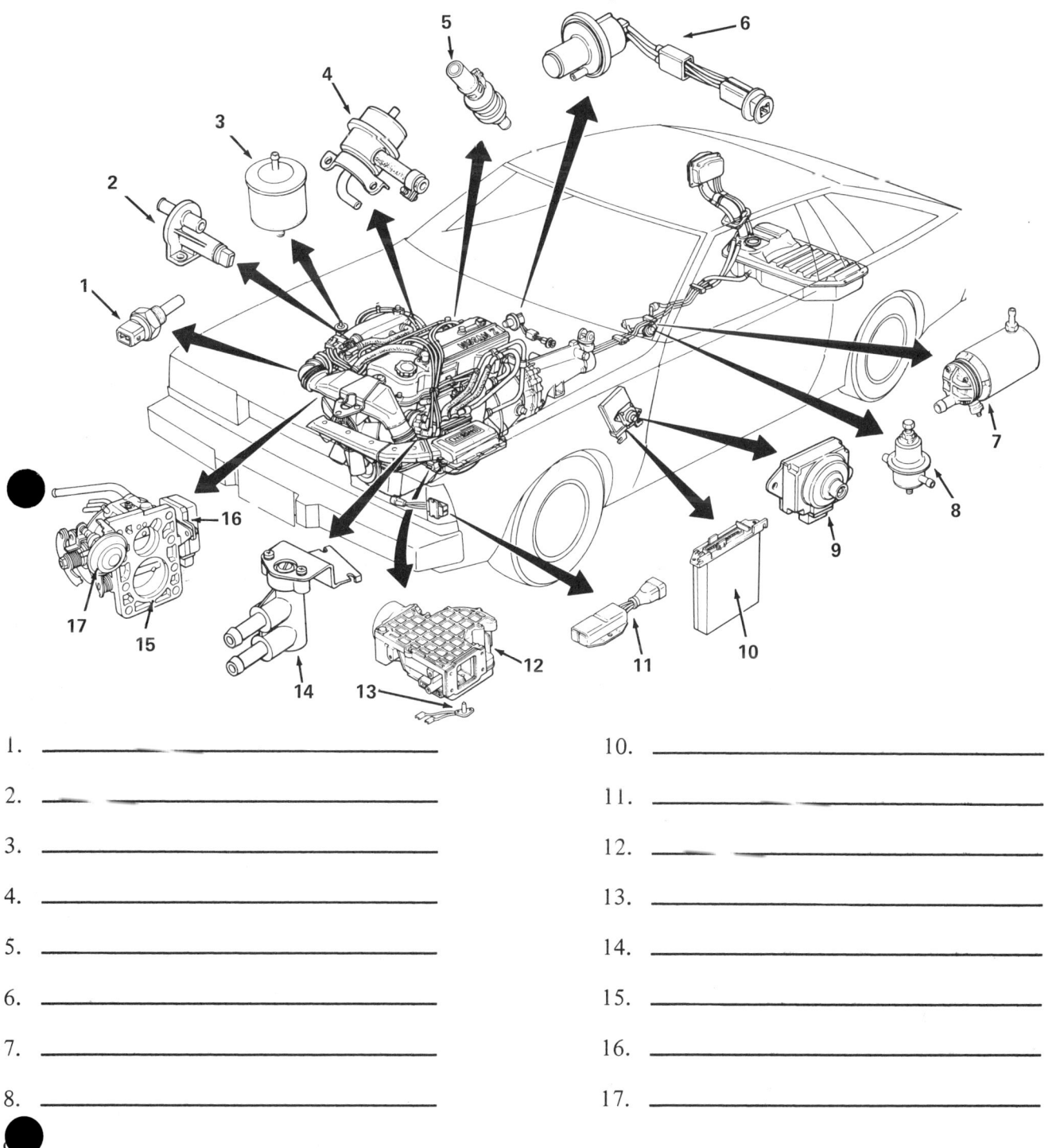

1. _____
2. _____
3. _____
4. _____
5. _____
6. _____
7. _____
8. _____
9. _____
10. _____
11. _____
12. _____
13. _____
14. _____
15. _____
16. _____
17. _____

277

NAME _____ SECTION _____ DATE _____ SCORE _____

Chapter 53 ELECTRONIC FUEL INJECTION SYSTEMS
ASSIGNMENT SHEET 49

Before you begin: Read Chapter 53 in *Auto Mechanics*. Identify the parts of the fuel injector by writing the names in the spaces provided below.

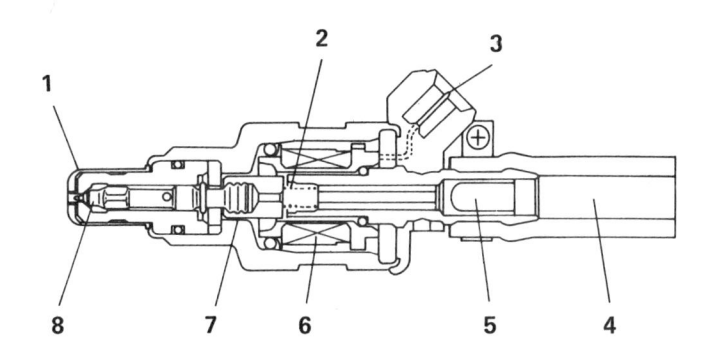

1. _____

2. _____

3. _____

4. _____

5. _____

6. _____

7. _____

8. _____

NAME _____ SECTION _____ DATE _____ SCORE _____

Chapter 53 ELECTRONIC FUEL INJECTION SYSTEMS
ASSIGNMENT SHEET 50

Before you begin: Read Chapter 53 in *Auto Mechanics.* Identify the parts of the airflow meter by writing the names in the spaces provided below.

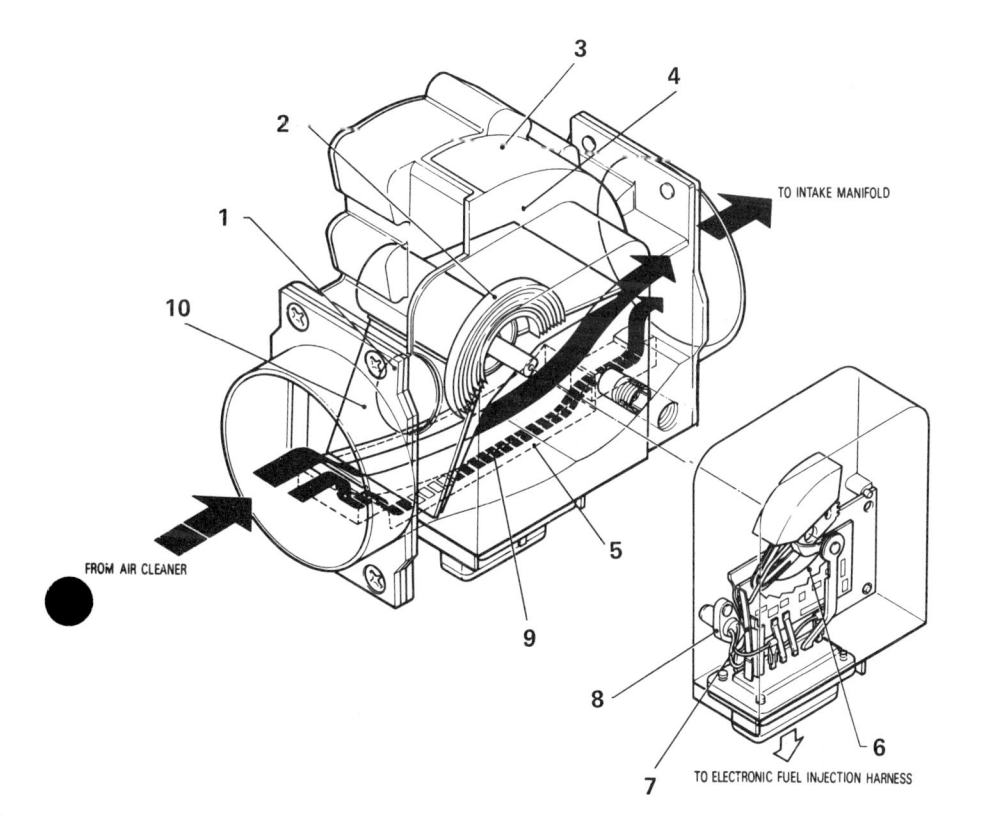

1. _____
2. _____
3. _____
4. _____
5. _____
6. _____
7. _____
8. _____
9. _____
10. _____

281

NAME _____ SECTION _____ DATE _____ SCORE _____

Chapter 53 ELECTRONIC FUEL INJECTION SYSTEMS
ASSIGNMENT SHEET 51

Before you begin: Read Chapter 53 in *Auto Mechanics*. Identify the parts of the continuous flow EFI by writing the names in the spaces provided below.

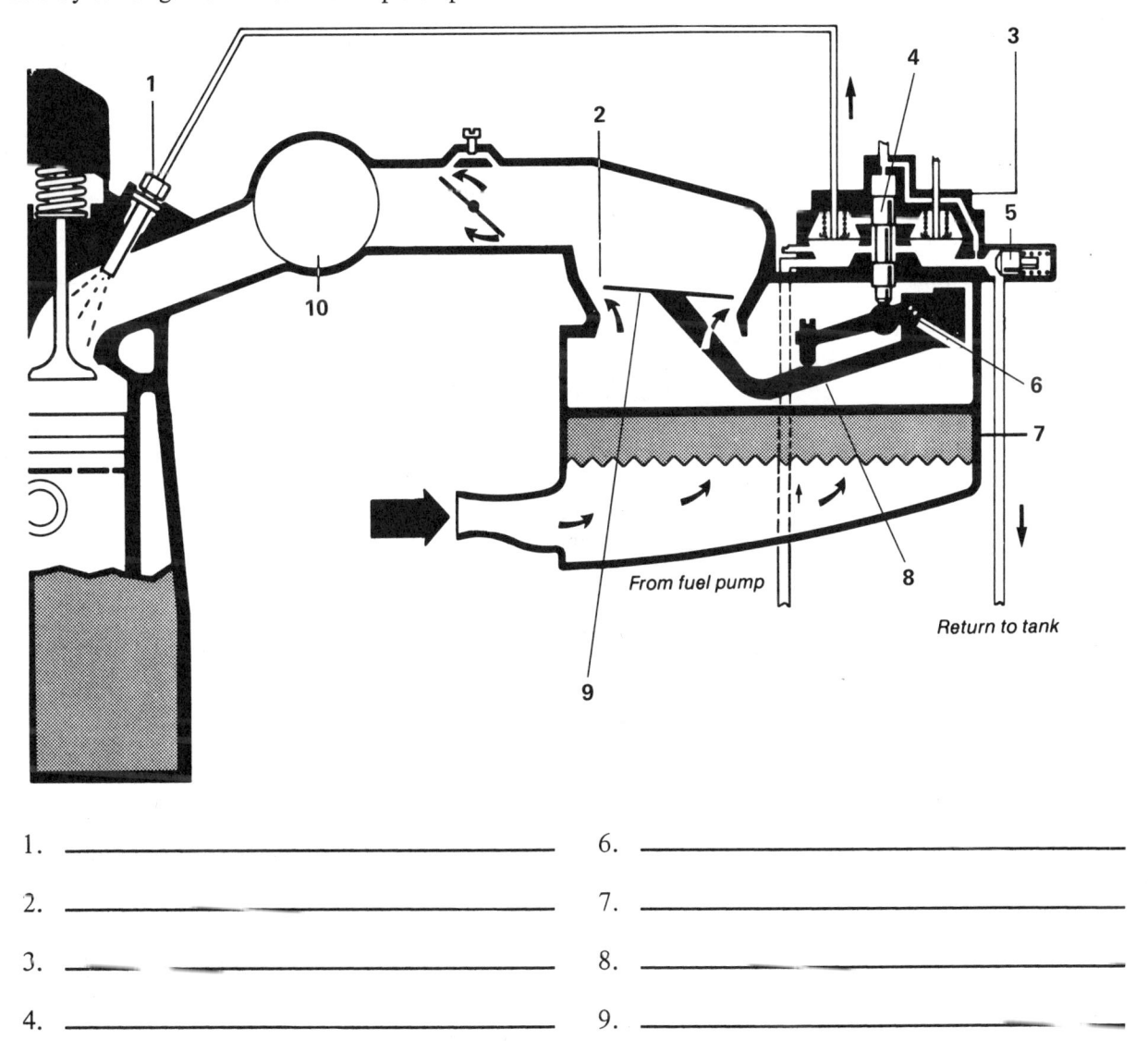

1. _____   6. _____
2. _____   7. _____
3. _____   8. _____
4. _____   9. _____
5. _____   10. _____

NAME _____ SECTION _____ DATE _____ SCORE _____

Review of New Terms

For each definition in Column 2, select the term in Column 1 that best matches its meaning. Write the identifying letter of the term in the Answer column.

Column 1	*Column 2*	Answer
A. Electronic fuel injection	1. An electronic fuel injection system that measures the air entering the engine and regulates the amount of fuel injected into the engine based upon that measurement.	1. _____
B. Airflow controlled electronic fuel injection	2. An electronic fuel injection system that uses a mechanical fuel distributor to regulate the amount of fuel entering the engine.	2. _____
C. Continuous flow electronic fuel injection	3. A fuel injection system that uses electronically controlled injection nozzles to distribute fuel to the engine's cylinders.	3. _____
D. Injector nozzle	4. An electrically controlled device used to spray fuel into the intake manifold in an EFI system.	4. _____
E. Throttle body electronic fuel injection	5. An electronic fuel injection system that uses fuel injection nozzles mounted in a throttle body assembly instead of individually mounted injectors.	5. _____

NAME _____ SECTION _____ DATE _____ SCORE _____

Chapter 54 COMPUTERIZED ENGINE CONTROL SYSTEMS
ASSIGNMENT SHEET 52

Before you begin: Read Chapter 54 in *Auto Mechanics.* Identify the parts of the oxygen sensor by writing the names in the spaces provided below.

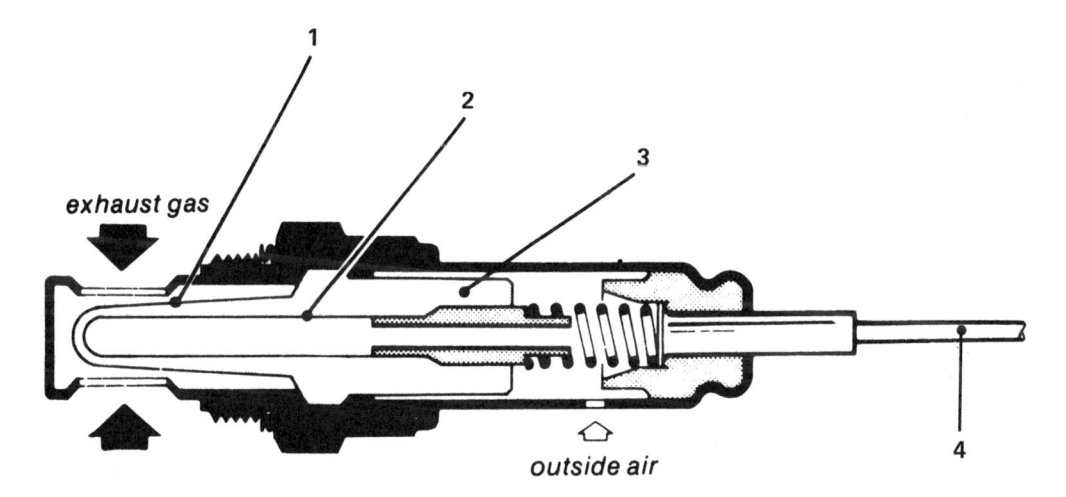

1. _____   3. _____

2. _____   4. _____

NAME _____ SECTION _____ DATE _____ SCORE _____

Chapter 54 COMPUTERIZED ENGINE CONTROL SYSTEMS
ASSIGNMENT SHEET 53

Before you begin: Read Chapter 54 in *Auto Mechanics*. Identify the parts of a carburetor with a mixture control solenoid by writing the names in the spaces provided.

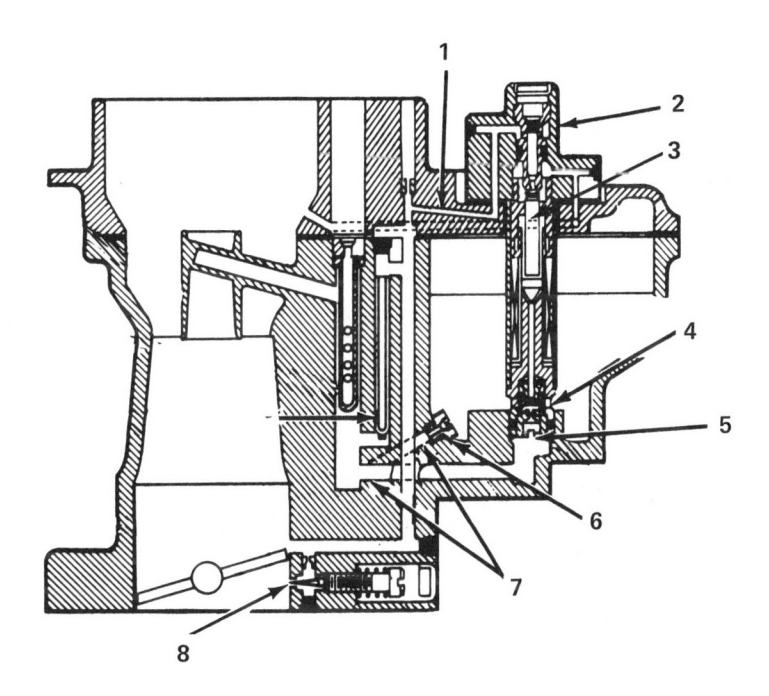

1. _____   5. _____

2. _____   6. _____

3. _____   7. _____

4. _____   8. _____

NAME _____ SECTION _____ DATE _____ SCORE _____

Chapter 54 COMPUTERIZED ENGINE CONTROL SYSTEMS
ASSIGNMENT SHEET 54

Before you begin: Read Chapter 54 in *Auto Mechanics*. Identify the parts of an electronic engine control system by writing the names in the spaces provided below.

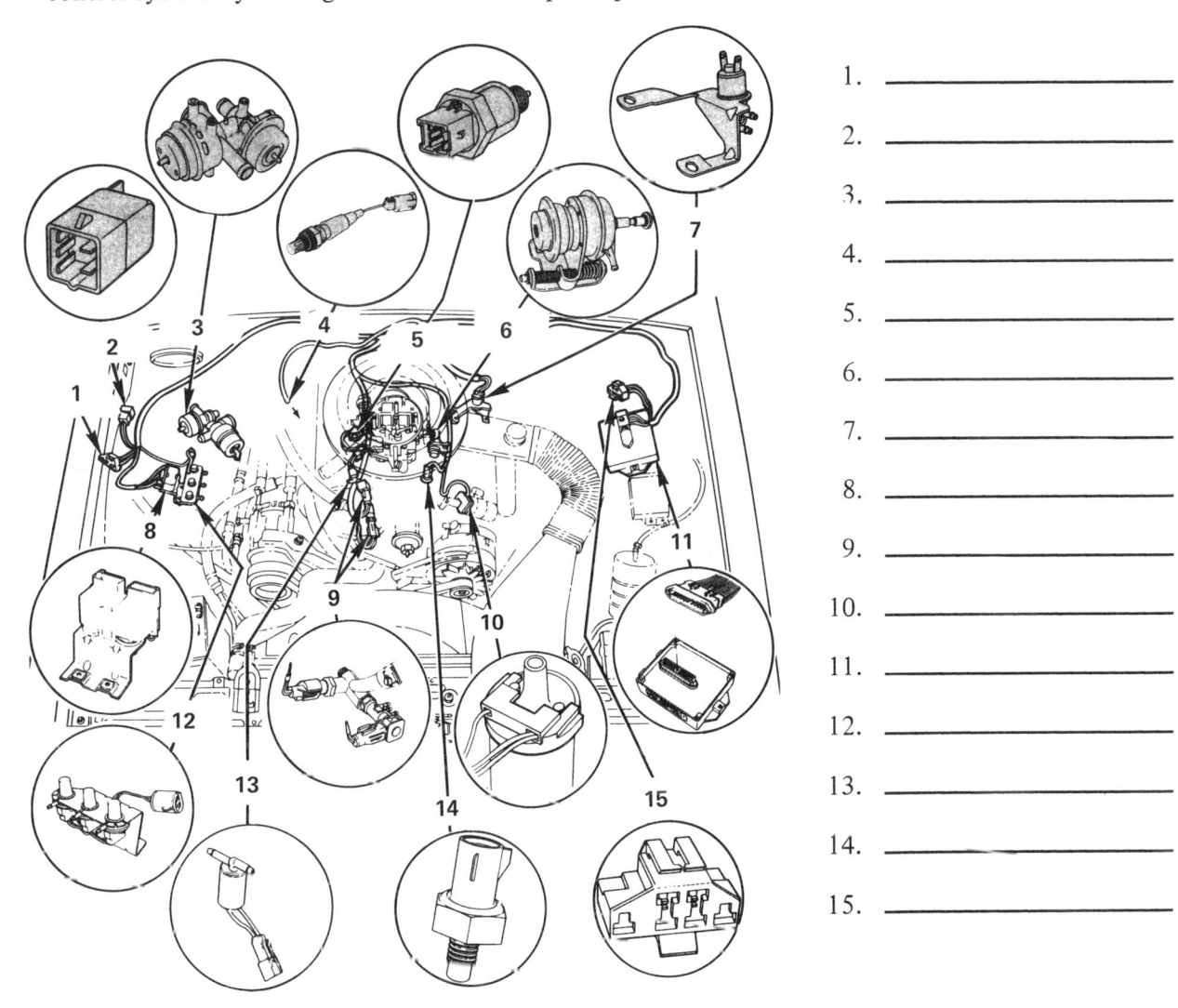

1. _____
2. _____
3. _____
4. _____
5. _____
6. _____
7. _____
8. _____
9. _____
10. _____
11. _____
12. _____
13. _____
14. _____
15. _____

NAME _____ SECTION _____ DATE _____ SCORE _____

Review of New Terms

For each definition in Column 2, select the term in Column 1 that best matches its meaning. Write the identifying letter in the Answer column.

Column 1	*Column 2*	*Answer*
A. Actuators	1. A series of numbers of flashes on a tester or dash light used to determine if there is a fault in a computerized system.	1. _____
B. Codes		
C. Computer	2. A fuel system that monitors the oxygen in the exhaust gas and uses a computer to adjust the air fuel mixture accordingly.	2. _____
D. Feedback fuel system		
E. Sensor	3. A component of the engine control system that monitors some engine function and sends a signal to the computer.	3. _____
F. Column 2		
	4. A microprocessor unit that monitors engine functions and makes adjustments according to its programmable memory.	4. _____
	5. Engine control components that get command from the computer and adjust some engine function.	5. _____

NAME _____ SECTION _____ DATE _____ SCORE _____

Chapter 55 THE FUTURE OF THE AUTOMOBILE
ASSIGNMENT SHEET 55

Stratified Charge Engine

Before you begin: Read Chapter 52 in *Auto Mechanics*. Identify the parts of the stratified charge engine in the spaces provided below.

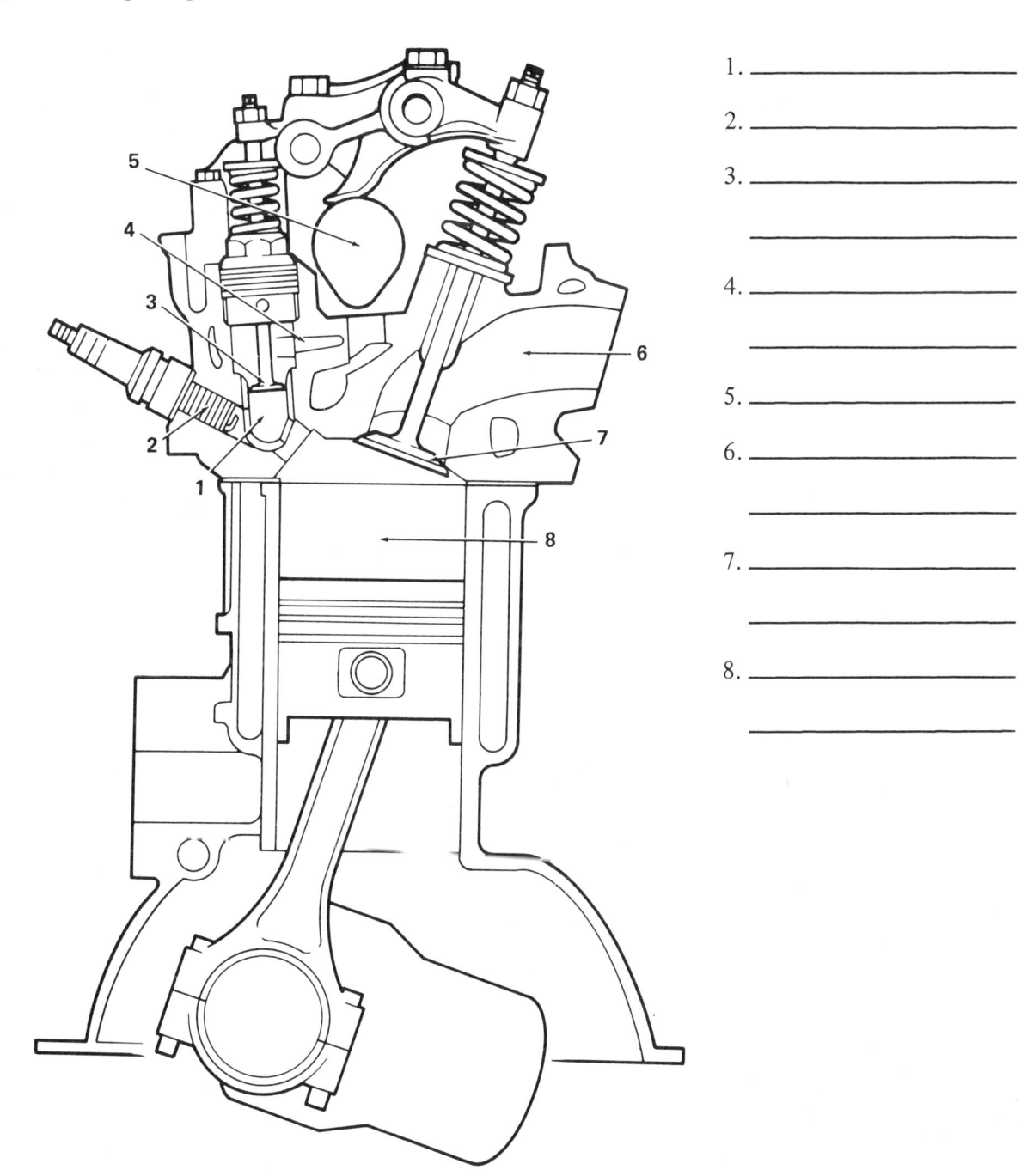

1. _____
2. _____
3. _____
4. _____
5. _____
6. _____
7. _____
8. _____

291

In the spaces provided to the right of each figure, describe the action that takes place in each of the strokes of the stratified charge engine.

1. _____

2. _____

3. _____

4. _____

5. _____

6. _____

NAME _____ SECTION _____ DATE _____ SCORE _____

Chapter 55 THE FUTURE OF THE AUTOMOBILE
ASSIGNMENT SHEET 56

Turbine Engine

Before you begin: Read Chapter 52 in *Auto Mechanics*. Identify the parts of the gas turbine engine in the spaces provided below.

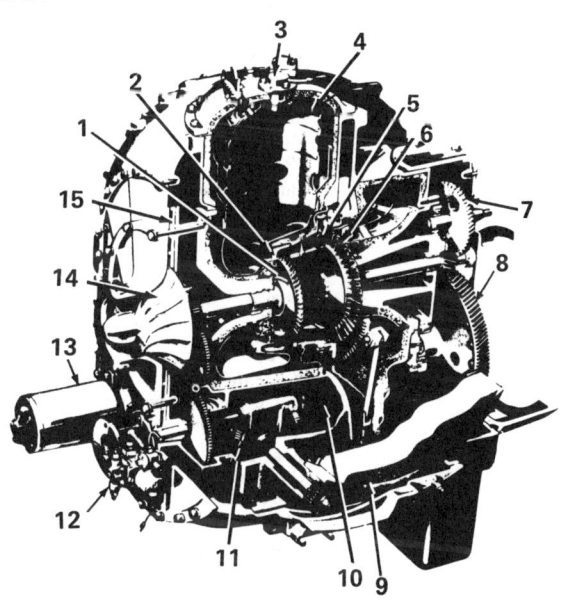

1. _____
   _____

2. _____
   _____

3. _____
   _____

4. _____

5. _____
   _____

6. _____
   _____

7. _____
   _____

8. _____

9. _____

10. _____

11. _____
    _____

12. _____

13. _____

14. _____
    _____

15. _____
    _____

ENGLISH-METRIC CONVERSION

	If You Know	You Can Get	If You Multiply By*
LENGTH	Inches	Millimetres (mm)	25.4
	Millimetres	Inches	0.04
	Inches	Centimetres (cm)	2.54
	Centimetres	Inches	0.4
	Inches	Metres (m)	0.0254
	Metres	Inches	39.37
	Feet	Centimetres	30.5
	Centimetres	Feet	4.8
	Feet	Metres	0.305
	Metres	Feet	3.28
	Miles	Kilometres (km)	1.61
	Kilometre	Miles	0.62
AREA	Inches²	Millimetres² (mm²)	645.2
	Millimetres²	Inches²	0.0016
	Inches²	Centimetres² (cm²)	6.45
	Centimetres²	Inches²	0.16
	Foot²	Metres² (m²)	0.093
	Metres²	Foot²	10.76
CAPACITY-VOLUME	Ounces	Millilitres (ml)	30
	Millilitres	Ounces	0.034
	Pints	Litres (l)	0.47
	Litres	Pints	2.1
	Quarts	Litres	0.95
	Litres	Quarts	1.06
	Gallons	Litres	3.8
	Litres	Gallons	0.26
	Cubic Inches	Litres	0.0164
	Litres	Cubic Inches	61.03
	Cubic Inches	Cubic Centimetres (cc)	16.39
	Cubic Centimetres	Cubic Inches	0.061
WEIGHT (MASS)	Ounces	Grams	28.4
	Grams	Ounces	0.035
	Pounds	Kilograms	0.45
	Kilograms	Pounds	2.2
FORCE	Ounce	Newtons (N)	0.278
	Newtons	Ounces	35.98
	Pound	Newtons	4.448
	Newtons	Pound	0.225
	Newtons	Kilograms (kg)	0.102
	Kilograms	Newtons	9.807
ACCELERATION	Inch/Sec²	Metre/Sec²	.0254
	Metre/Sec²	Inch/Sec²	39.37
	Foot/Sec²	Metre/Sec² (m/s²)	0.3048
	Metre/Sec²	Foot/Sec²	3.280
TORQUE	Pound-Inch (Inch Pound)	Newton-Metres (N-M)	0.113
	Newton-Metres	Pound-Inch	8.857
	Pound-Foot (Foot-Pound)	Newton-Metres	1.356
	Newton-Metres	Pound-Foot	.737
PRESSURE	Pound/sq. in. (PSI)	Kilopascals (kPa)	6.895
	Kilopascals	Pound/sq. in.	0.145
	Inches of Mercury (Hg)	Kilopascals	3.377
	Kilopascals	Inches of Mercury (Hg)	0.296
FUEL PERFORMANCE	Miles/gal	Kilometres/litre (km/l)	0.425
	Kilometres/litre	Miles/gal	2.352
VELOCITY	Miles/hour	Kilometres/hr (km/h)	1.609
	Kilometres/hour	Miles/hour	0.621
TEMPERATURE	Fahrenheit Degrees	Celsius Degrees	5/9 (F°-32)
	Celsius Degrees	Fahrenheit Degrees	9/5 (C°+32) = F

*Approximate Conversion Factors to be used where precision calculations are *not* necessary